Chapter and Verse

Chapter and Verse

New Order, Joy Division and Me

Bernard Sumner

Thomas Dunne Books   St. Martin's Press   ≋   New York

THOMAS DUNNE BOOKS.
An imprint of St. Martin's Press.

CHAPTER AND VERSE. Copyright © 2014 by Bernard Sumner. All rights reserved. Printed
in the United States of America. For information, address St. Martin's Press, 175 Fifth
Avenue, New York, N.Y. 10010.

www.thomasdunnebooks.com
www.stmartins.com

"Run" by Bernard Sumner, Peter Hook, Stephen Paul David Morris,
Gillian Lesley Gilbert and John Denver, Vitalturn Co. Ltd (NS) and Warner/Chappell
Music Publishing Ltd (PRS). All rights on behalf of Vitalturn
Co. Ltd administered by Warner/Chappell Music Ltd.

Library of Congress Cataloging-in-Publication Data

Sumner, Bernard.
    Chapter and verse : New Order, Joy Division and me / Bernard Sumner. — First
U.S. edition.
    p. cm.
    Includes index.
    ISBN 978-1-250-07772-1 (hardcover)
    ISBN 978-1-4668-8988-0 (e-book)
1. Sumner, Bernard. 2. Rock musicians—England—Biography. 3. New Order
(Musical group). 4. Joy Division (Musical group). I. Title.
    ML420.S9526A3 2015
    782.42166092—dc23
    [B]

                                                                    2015025027

Our books may be purchased in bulk for promotional, educational, or
business use. Please contact your local bookseller or the Macmillan
Corporate and Premium Sales Department at (800) 221-7945, extension 5442, or by
e-mail at MacmillanSpecialMarkets@macmillan.com.

First published in Great Britain by Bantam Press, an imprint of Transworld Publishers,
a Random House Group company

First U.S. Edition: November 2015

10 9 8 7 6 5 4 3 2 1

My family
The band
Loyal friends, collaborators
and all those who have passed away
Ian, Martin, Rob, Tony

Acknowledgements

Charlie Connelly
Doug Young
Kevin Conroy Scott
Lizzy Kremer
Alison Barrow
Jack Delaney
Rebecca Boulton and Andy Robinson

Contents

Time

Time is a curious thing. When you have it before you, it's something you take for granted and it moves slowly. Then, as you get older, it accelerates. When I look back, it seems such a long distance travelled, so long ago, so dream-like.

January 1956 on a cold grey northern winter's day I was born in a Manchester hospital called Crumpsall. I can only imagine what Manchester was like in the fifties: black and white, grainy, weird-looking cars and black vans with austere headlamps and radiator grilles, fog, the Midland Hotel, the Central Library, the River Irwell, the bad food, the rain. So I moved to Salford, five miles away.

I lived at 11 Alfred Street, Lower Broughton, Salford 7, red front door, a terraced house in the middle of a community of mostly decent working-class people. My family consisted of my mother, Laura, my grandmother, Laura, and my grandfather, John, and they were all called Sumner.

Of course, I don't remember much about those so-called

formative years, but please see the embarrassing photographs. My earliest memory is of sitting on a brown couch playing with a red and cream plastic guitar that said 'Teen Time' on it.

So that's how it started.

Preface

As I write this, I'm preparing to travel to South America with New Order for gigs in Chile, Argentina, Uruguay and Brazil. We've never particularly promoted ourselves in those countries — in fact, we've never particularly promoted ourselves anywhere outside the UK to any great extent — yet we'll be playing to packed houses in cities about as far in every sense from our Manchester origins as you could possibly imagine.

Joy Division and New Order are international phenomena. Our music has permeated the globe and I'm not sure how or why this has happened: neither group could be described as a conventional pop band churning out hits and earning lots of Top Forty radio airplay. Yet for some reason we've built up a vast and loyal global following that shows no sign of diminishing any time soon, even in the most unlikely settings: only recently, I was at home watching news footage from the Middle East of people running for shelter from a missile attack when a teenage girl ran past the camera wearing an *Unknown Pleasures* T-shirt.

The longevity of the music is something that consistently astounds me. Joy Division started in 1977, and here we are, more than three decades later, as popular as we've ever been, winning over whole new generations and finding new audiences. On our recent tour I asked some fans in their teens how they discovered New Order. Usually their big brother or sister had introduced them to us, or they'd raided their parents' record collections and liked what they heard, which is fantastic to hear.

All this makes these exciting times for New Order. The last few years have proved to be among the busiest and most successful — and in many ways the most enjoyable — in the three-decade history of the band. What began as a couple of charity gigs in 2011 grew into a clutch of festival dates, then, almost before we knew it, we were on a full-blown world tour that lasted several months and covered several continents. Since then it's been more of the same.

The tour re-emphasized for me the very special connection that exists between the fans and the band when it comes to Joy Division and New Order. Everywhere I go I meet a whole range of people, young and old, who approach me with albums to sign and tell me how much our music means to them, how it's been the soundtrack to their lives. Often they ask if they can have a photograph taken: they stand beside me holding out their iPhone to take the picture, and their hand is shaking because they feel so passionate about the music they're struggling to hold the camera still. It's an amazing feeling to think that I've been a part of something that's had that kind of impact on somebody's life, whether they're from the suburbs of Manchester or the suburbs of Lima, Auckland, Tokyo, Berlin or Chicago.

New Order fans are fiercely loyal. They don't just *like* New Order, they feel a profound connection between the band, the music and themselves. It goes way beyond simply liking a catchy tune, it's something deeply personal: it's not just a case of playing our music while they're washing the pots or catching us occasionally on the radio — these are people whose lives have been changed, who've found some kind of solace or inspiration in what we've done.

The main factor in this is of course the music itself: people find something in it that resonates with their own lives on a very profound level, and I've always found it humbling to hear people talking about what our music means to them.

That, however, has always been rather a one-way conversation. Until now.

I am by nature a very private person and have always preferred to let the music speak for me. Over the years, I've given countless interviews about the bands I've been in and the music I've made, but never before have I linked any of it to my personal life. My life in music has been shaped entirely by the person I am and the things that have happened to me. Our music has never been about, for example, being a virtuoso on a particular instrument, it's entirely the product of our personalities and the sum of all our experiences.

Yet while the private aspects of my life have been vital to my creativity, I've always felt very uncomfortable talking about them. I constructed a barrier between the private and public sides of me at an early stage that I have rarely, if ever, opened.

Since we started touring again, however, I've seen the reactions of people to our shows and heard what our music means to them, and it's made me think. I've realized that I owe people a look behind the scenes of my own story, because I don't think anyone can have a true understanding of the music without an insight into where it came from. Life shapes you, and what life does to you shapes your art. It's time for me to fill in the blanks: maybe then people might discern why the music we make affects them so deeply.

I feel that I've reached a point in my life where, if I don't tell my story now, perhaps I never will. There are many things in the pages which follow that I've found difficult to talk about, things I haven't spoken about in public before but which I think are vital to a comprehensive understanding of the person I am, the bands I've played with and the music I've helped to create. My silence regarding anything outside the bands and the music has allowed myths to permeate and untruths to become accepted as fact, so I hope that, along the way, I can correct a few misperceptions and lay to rest as many of those myths as possible.

For one thing, the truth is a far, far better story.

Chapter One

Streetlights

Los Angeles produced the Beach Boys. Dusseldorf produced Kraftwerk. New York produced Chic. Manchester produced Joy Division.

The Beach Boys' harmonies were full of warmth and sunshine, Kraftwerk's groundbreaking electronic pop was suffused with Germany's post-war economic and technological resurgence while Chic's music thrummed with the joyous hedonism of late seventies New York.

Joy Division sounded like Manchester: cold, sparse and, at times, bleak.

There's a moment from my youth that I think illustrates perfectly where the music of Joy Division came from. It's not even an incident as such, more a snapshot, a mental photograph that I've never forgotten.

I was about sixteen. It was a cold, depressing winter night and I was hanging around with some friends on a street in the Ordsall district of Salford doing nothing in particular, too old and restless to sit around at home, too young to go out drinking. I'm fairly sure Peter Hook was there, and so was another friend called Gresty, but the cold had killed the conversation. There was a thick fog draped over Salford that night, the kind of freezing, cloying fog whose chill penetrates right to the bone. Our breath came in clouds, our shoulders were hunched and our hands thrust deep in our pockets. But what I remember most is looking up the street and seeing how the orange sodium streetlights had all been given dirty halos by the fog. Making it feel like you had the flu. The lights would have been dingy enough at the best of times, but the fog, grimy with the dirt and grit of industry, had reduced them to a string of murky globules running the length of the street.

The silence was broken by the roar of an engine and a screech of tyres. A car came racing around the corner, the headlights dazzling us for a moment, and in it I could hear a girl screaming her head off. I couldn't see her, I couldn't see anyone in the car, there was just this raw, terrified screaming as it shot off up the road and disappeared into the fog. Silence descended again and I just thought to myself, There's got to be more than this.

When there's no stimulus to be found on the outside, you have no option but to look inside yourself for inspiration, and when I did it set off a creativity that had always been inside me. It mixed with my environment and life experiences to make something tangible, something that expressed me. For some people it's channelled on to a canvas, for others it emerges on to the page, or maybe in sport. In my case, and those of the people with whom I created the sound of Joy Division, it emerged in music. The sound we made was the sound of that night – cold, bleak, industrial – and it came from within.

Manchester was cold and bleak on the day I was born, Wednesday 4 January 1956, in what is now the North Manchester General

Hospital in Crumpsall. It was barely a decade after the end of the Second World War and the conflict still loomed large over the country, from the bomb sites that remained in every city and the legacy of post-war austerity — meat rationing had only ended eighteen months before I was born — to the all-too-vivid memories of the generations before mine. The spectre of war had not vanished entirely: the Suez Crisis was brewing and Cold War tensions were higher than ever following the formation of the Warsaw Pact the previous year.

It wasn't all negative, though. There were signs that some things were changing. Even though I have to admit that I'm no big fan of the fifties, Bill Haley's 'Rock Around The Clock', one of the most influential records of the century, was top of the charts on the day I was born, and six days later Elvis would go into the RCA studios in Nashville to record 'Heartbreak Hotel'.

I may have arrived on the cusp of an enormous cultural shift, but mine wasn't the usual kind of birth. My mother, Laura Sumner, had cerebral palsy. She was born absolutely fine but after about three days she started having convulsions that left her with a condition that would confine her to a wheelchair her entire life. She would never walk, would always have great difficulty controlling her movements, and the condition would also affect her speech.

I never knew my father. He'd disappeared from the scene before I was born and I still have no idea who he is. Perhaps strangely, it's never bothered me; I certainly don't believe it's really affected me. I think he's dead now; I've just got that feeling. But even if he was alive I wouldn't have any interest in meeting him. I don't think you miss what you've never had.

Alfred Street was a small cobbled street of Victorian terraced houses not far from Strangeways Prison and close to the River Irwell. Lower

Broughton was a typical Salfordian working-class area (the street that inspired Tony Warren to create *Coronation Street* wasn't far away), governed by the needs of industry: Alfred Street and its neighbours provided the labour force for a range of local factories and mills and, within a few minutes' walk, there was a potted version of the entire industrialized north-west: an iron works, copper works, cloth-finishing works, paint factory, chemical works, cotton mill, saw mill and brass foundry. The song 'Dirty Old Town', with its powerful evocation of love in a northern industrial landscape, was written about Lower Broughton. Living close to Strangeways Prison offered additional sobering insight into the underbelly of life: I remember as a boy once asking my grandfather who the line of men in the weird uniforms digging the road were and he told me they were prisoners on a chain gang detail.

Number eleven was my grandparents' house and, when I was born, my mother was still living with them because she needed so much care. Our house was typical of both the area and the time in most respects: downstairs there was a kitchen, main living room, a parlour that was used for special occasions (although in our house my mother slept there, because she wasn't able to get up the stairs), and an outdoor toilet. We didn't have a bathroom. Upstairs, my bedroom was above the living room, my grandparents' above the parlour. Also upstairs was a small storage room that really gave me the spooks as a child: my granddad had been an air-raid warden during the war and it was packed with gas masks, sandbags, blackout curtains and all sorts of other wartime detritus. I don't know if it was because I'd heard tales of the war and the terrible things that happened, but there was always something frightening about that room. I avoided it.

My grandfather John Sumner, a very knowledgeable and interesting man, was like a father to me. He was Salford born and raised and worked as an engineer at the Vickers factory in Trafford

Park. He'd lost his own father when he was ten: my great-grandfather had gone off to the First World War with the Manchester Regiment and been killed at the second Battle of Passchendaele in 1917. My grandmother, Laura, was a very warm, very caring person who came from an old Salford family, the Platts. Her mother, like my mother, was also called Laura: it was a tradition in my family for girls to be named after their mothers, so my grandmother was 'Little Laura' and my great-grandmother was always known as 'Big Laura'.

My granddad had a routine that he'd perform twice a day, once in the morning before leaving for work and once when he returned home in the evening. He'd come through the front door and walk straight through the house exclaiming, 'Ah, fresh air! I need fresh air!', go out into the backyard and take a succession of long, slow, deep breaths. The trouble was, at the end of our street, spewing out noxious fumes was the Wheathill Chemical Works. It was horrible; some days you'd even be told not to go out that day, as they were burning something there. I can almost conjure up the acrid smell today, yet my grandfather would happily breathe it in while extolling the health benefits of inhaling fresh air.

My great-grandmother, Big Laura, lived right opposite the chemical works. She'd had, I think, eight or nine daughters before having a son. Once he'd arrived, she felt she could call it a day. I remember going to visit her when I was very young and seeing my great-grandfather too, a lovely bloke who worked as a wheeltapper on the railways. I remember him being a very warm, kind person, but one day I was told he'd 'gone on a long train journey'. I have very strong memories of him, so he clearly made a big impression on me, yet I recently discovered that I was only about two years old when he died.

After he'd died, my gran used to go and visit my great-grandmother every day, taking her a jug of Guinness from the pub, which she'd sit by the fire and drink — for the iron, she said. It must have worked because, despite living for most of her life opposite a chemical factory that was spewing out all sorts of fumes, she lived to be nearly ninety. Eventually, her house was pulled down and she was moved to the top floor of a fourteen-storey block of flats. I remember visiting her there, looking out at the view from the balcony and thinking, Wow, this is fantastic, you can see for *miles*. All the cars on the streets below looked like Dinky toys and I could see the hills and the countryside beyond the city: to me as a boy it was magical, but of course for an old woman like my great-grandmother, way up there on the fourteenth floor, a long way from anything, it turned out to be more like a prison.

My Auntie Amy stayed on to look after my great-grandmother. All her siblings had married and she effectively gave up her own life in order to help her. It seems that when she grew too old to marry it dawned on her what she'd missed. In dedicating herself to her mother's welfare, her own life had passed her by, and that realization caused a breakdown that left her in Prestwich mental hospital for the next thirty-two years. Occasionally, Auntie Amy would slip out from the hospital unnoticed and head for our house. When she appeared at the door my mum would send me upstairs, telling me to shut my bedroom door and push the bed behind it. I was to stay there until she told me it was safe to come out. I'd hear Auntie Amy saying that a man was coming round with an axe to kill us all, how she'd come to warn us that we were all going to die. My mum would keep her talking until the police arrived and she'd be taken back to Prestwich. It was heartbreaking. All my other aunties were kind, warm and bubbly, and that's the kind of woman Auntie Amy should have been too.

I had lots of friends on Alfred Street, like Raymond Quinn, David Wroe and Barrie Benson, not to mention more members of my family who lived there as well. I didn't have any brothers or sisters, but my Auntie Doreen lived next door with my cousins David and

Stephen and across the road was my Auntie Ruth, who had a daughter, inevitably also called Ruth. My Auntie Ada and Auntie Irene lived on the same street too, with their children, so I had a very sociable childhood. We spent most of our time on the streets. We were always kicking a ball around, hanging out on the corner getting into trouble and wondering what was going on in the other parts of town. What was out there?

While it was a pretty normal working-class Mancunian up-bringing in many ways, the thing that set our family apart was my mother's condition. As well as the obvious physical problems she faced, she was also a very angry person. Whether this was because she was frustrated at her disability, maybe even suffered from depression — something that was rarely diagnosed in those days — I don't know for sure, but whatever the cause, her anger was usually focused on me, to the point at times of something close to cruelty.

With my grandparents being such warm, kind people, I was drawn more to them emotionally than I was to my mother, and this may have contributed to her anger. I had lots of friends locally and was no better or worse behaved than anyone else, but I seemed to be on the receiving end of more, and more severe, punishments than anyone I knew.

I was rarely allowed to go out: when the other kids went to the park or the cinema I wouldn't be allowed to go with them. For some reason, even though ours was a close community with plenty of kids my own age who had plenty of people watching out for them, my mother wanted me pretty much where she could see me. I was allowed out into our street and the immediate vicinity, but there were very strict boundaries as to how far I could go. Kids love to roam, and the children round our way were no exception, but while others would go into Manchester or over to Heaton Park, I'd have to stay put, left on a street corner watching the others disappear into the distance in a laughing, noisy rabble.

I hardly ever went against my mother's wishes through sheer fear of what would happen if I did, but one day I did dare to cross the boundaries she'd set for me. I didn't go very far, just a couple of streets away with a gang of kids, but somebody spotted me and word got back to my mother, who went absolutely ballistic as soon as I walked through the door. I was made to swallow cold, sour tea, leaves and all, until every last drop had gone and then told to stand and face the wall while she told me at length and in no uncertain terms what an awful child I was, something I was made to repeat back to her. I stood there, hands behind my back, nose almost touching the wallpaper, the revolting bitter taste of cold tea still in my mouth and tears running down my face, trying to work out just why she thought I was so terrible. Granted, on this occasion, I had gone against her wishes, probably due to peer pressure more than anything else, but the level of invective being aimed at me as I stood there sobbing against the wall seemed to be about much more than me sneaking quietly out of the front door when nobody was looking. This kind of thing would happen fairly often.

I was far too young to understand at the time of course, but in hindsight I wonder if she was angry at me because my father had disappeared from her life. My mother's circumstances were unusual enough, given her disability, but she was also an unmarried mother, something fairly uncommon in the fifties and sixties. How and why their relationship ended I don't know: my father was never mentioned. Maybe this was one source of her anger at me, that I was the living, breathing legacy of that relationship: I was a permanent reminder of him — maybe I even looked like him. Who knows, perhaps I was kept in because he'd gone out one day and never come back.

When, in the years since, I've tried to work out why she treated me the way she did, it's occurred to me that the horrific Moors Murders might also have had something to do with it. They were going on around that time, so there would have been stories of Manchester kids disappearing. In any case, there were long periods during my childhood where I was kept on an incredibly tight rein. It reared up again when I was older, around sixteen, when my mother didn't want me going to parties and staying out late. When I was allowed to go I'd have to be home by ten o'clock while my mates would be out till midnight.

Yet, for all I've thought about it, I still don't really know why she treated me that way and I probably never will. To an extent, I kind of understand the way she was with me. She felt trapped by her disability: she was effectively a prisoner in her own body. In that situation, it's perhaps understandable that any wrongdoing by me, perceived or actual, was blown up. Life in the working-class districts of Manchester was tough in those days at the best of times, but my mother was a single parent in a wheelchair and I can only guess at what that did to her state of mind. I remember seeing her trying to walk up the stairs: an image that in itself probably best illustrates my mother's battle with what life had given her. She railed against her condition, doing everything she could to make things more bearable. She tried various homeopathic remedies and we'd regularly have all sorts of quacks calling at the house, but for all her efforts her life remained very difficult and she must have felt extremely frustrated. I suppose she had to take it out on someone. Unfortunately, that person happened to be me.

She wasn't cruel all the time; there were definitely happier times and occasions: I remember we had some wonderful, magical Christmases, for example. But the moment I did something wrong, sometimes even the most trivial thing, she almost seemed to relish the prospect of punishing me for it. It didn't fuck me up or anything, but my childhood was played out over a constant undercurrent of fear of my mother.

In 1961 she married a man called James Dickin, who also suffered from cerebral palsy and wore callipers on his legs. She got him to hit me pretty hard a couple of times. I'm sure it was common back then for fathers to hit their sons and I don't really hold it against him, but it didn't make me any less scared of her. The knowledge that, even though she couldn't hit me, there was someone in the house who could made sure the fear was always there, even if most of the punishments were psychological rather than physical.

There was one particular occasion when after some misdemeanour or other my mother had sent Jimmy looking for me. I ran upstairs and hid in my bedroom, where there was a tiny cupboard for the gas meter. Being very little at the time, I just about managed to squeeze in and shut the door. I could see through a gap that Jimmy was looking for me and vividly remember the cold fear in my stomach as he scanned the room, searching under the bed, everywhere. I could hear my mother's voice from downstairs, saying, 'Are you sure he's up there? Are you sure he's not gone out?' I can't even remember what happened in the end, whether Jimmy found me or I eventually came out of my own accord to face the music, but the terror of what lay in store for me was so vivid it's stayed with me to this day.

To an extent I understand the way she was with me. I think it was probably borne more out of deep frustration than malice: I guess she felt trapped by her disability, as indeed she was. It was no easier for her than it would be for you or me. My mother wanted better, she *deserved* better, and was angry at the cards life had dealt her. Her situation, and I don't mean just in terms of her disability, would have depressed anyone and defeated many less strong-willed people. She wasn't angry all the time, only when she felt down — I think she may have suffered from depression — and I understand that. After all, anyone in a situation like hers would need a release of some kind and I think for that reason any perceived or actual wrongdoing by me was greatly amplified. I held it against her for many years until I had a period in my life where I suffered from depression and suddenly had an idea of how she must have felt. Life is hard for some people and much harder for others, and when I began to confront and cope with my depression it opened a door for me just a fraction on what she must have felt like. I forgave her completely.

I was always very conscious of how different she was from other mothers, and I didn't like being marked out from the other kids by having a disabled mother. When you're a child, you don't want to draw attention to yourself, especially with something that could be perceived as a weakness. I wasn't very fair to my mother: I wouldn't even push her down the street in her wheelchair, and it must have bothered her — her own son effectively too ashamed to be seen with her. Lower Broughton was a tough area, and if there was something different about you, something they could get you for, some perceived weakness, you'd be singled out as the weak animal in the herd, and once you were separated from the herd you'd be fighting all the time. Of course, I'd always been taunted — 'Your mum's a spaz', all that stuff — I just didn't want to draw any more attention to it. These days, I'm ashamed I behaved the way I did. Despite my difficult relationship with my mother, I look back at Alfred Street and the times I spent there with a great deal of fondness. I had a tough time at home but, outside the front door, life was very convivial. In summer, on hot days, we kids would be wandering around in our underpants, someone would produce a hosepipe and we'd play in the spray — it was like being on holiday on our own doorsteps. The old people would place chairs outside their houses and sit there in the sun talking to each other. It was such a wonderfully gregarious way of living, the old ladies chatting across the street to each other, looking on happily at the kids running around screaming and shouting, all through the day and right up until midnight.

That community spirit was a great thing: you knew the names of everyone in the street, all their foibles — you knew it all. I don't know if they still have that kind of spirit in the few remaining streets like that in Manchester. I wonder if it still happens.

It wasn't all cosy, though: like everywhere else, there were bad families in the area, the ones who'd have the old folk sucking in their cheeks and raising their eyebrows at the latest gossip. There were certain houses you had to be careful of as you walked past — I'll call them the Whites, the Greens and the Pinks, though those aren't their real names, but they were the ones to avoid if you could. They were huge families with loads of kids, with a near-endless supply of brothers and cousins who were really hard, so much so that you'd frequently plan your route so you wouldn't have to go past their houses.

The Pinks in particular were incredible. Half the family was always in prison: I think they had nine kids, and there were always about four in the nick at any given time. I remember walking along the road late one night and hearing a strange hissing noise. I looked over at the Pinks', and there's one of them standing in the living room at the open sash window pissing out into the street. I once saw the Pinks roll out of their front door like a huge human football, a whole bunch of them all screaming and laying into each other. A young couple moved next door to them, which was a bad move. Apparently, there was some kind of altercation in a pub involving this new guy, and he'd glassed one of them, and shortly afterwards I saw one of the Pinks going at him in the street with an iron bar. He hit him so hard the iron bar ended up bent around his chest.

Mrs Pink had a boyfriend. When I was a bit older, we used to hang around the street corner opposite the Pinks' house and, one night, the lights were on and the curtains open and we could see inside. They had sliding doors that divided the parlour from the living room and, as we watched, the doors slid open and there was Mrs Pink in stockings, suspenders and bra, with another woman dressed the same way. Our eyes were on stalks. Then we saw the boyfriend get up out of the armchair, go to the drinks cabinet, pour himself a drink and all three of them disappeared into the back. They were mad, the Pinks, and they didn't give a fuck about anything.

They didn't bother us much because my cousin Tommy, who lived opposite, was pretty hard himself. Tommy once had a fight with the oldest Pink in which an earlobe got bitten off, and we didn't get any trouble from them after that. I was chased by two older lads once. They were about eighteen or nineteen, and I was only about nine, and they caught up with me and knocked me to the ground. Just as they were about to lay into me I realized they were two of the Pinks, and at the same moment they realized who I was. 'Oh,' one of them said, 'didn't know it was you. All right, leave him.' Thanks, Tommy.

I still occasionally see my aunties and cousins from the street — Irene, Doreen, Steve, David, Lynn, Ruth and Tommy — but not frequently enough, I'm afraid.

Bonfire Night was always a highlight of the year for me. There was a bomb site behind my great-grandmother's house, the legacy of the night a house in the next street had taken a direct hit. People were killed; one of my aunties had been buried in the rubble but was pulled out alive. Although I'd been frightened of my grandfather's store room full of items left over from the war, the bomb site was pretty much the equivalent of our local park, and I loved it. They'd even set up a fairground every so often. In the early seventies it was turned into a proper adventure playground, but for the thirty-odd years after the war it was just a derelict expanse of rubble and scrubland ripe for acting out the fantasies of small boys.

Bonfire Night was the biggest night at the bomb site, and in the weeks leading up to it we used to go round all the houses asking people for any spare wood, then use it to build a huge bonfire with a special den at the top for a watchtower. We needed a watchtower because kids from the neighbouring areas would always come and try to rob our firewood for their own bonfires. A guard would be posted in the lookout and if any gangs with designs on our stack showed up, he'd summon the gang and there'd be a pitched battle, bricks and rocks flying in all directions. It sounds dangerous, but it was all really good fun. I loved it.

I have to admit we did a bit of stealing, too, things like lead from roofs – and, well, I'm not very proud of that. There was a dodgy scrap metal merchant known locally as No Names No Questions, and all the kids used to pinch things and sell them to him because, as his nickname implied, he wasn't too fussed as to provenance. We'd always be on the lookout for things and when the council started pulling the houses down nearby it opened up a whole new market to us fledgling entrepreneurs. I remember exploring one particular abandoned house and finding an old upright piano in the parlour. This is a terrible thing for a musician to admit, but I took a pair of mole grips and some wire cutters and set about this old piano, spending hours cutting out all the strings – nearly blinding myself several times from whiplash – to take to No Names. When we got to his yard, however, he took one look at our booty and sniffed, 'Sorry, lads, it's only copper plate. I can't give you anything for copper plate.'

At this time I was hanging around with a lad called Barrie Benson who was – and is – a mate of mine. His grandmother lived next door but one to me in Alfred Street and Barrie lived over the back in Victor Street. He was pretty much the cock of the walk in the area but he seemed to like me and for the most part we got on. On one occasion we had our eye on a huge reel of copper telephone wire about an inch thick outside a local electrical contractors. It would, we decided, be worth a fortune. Eventually, the opportunity presented itself and Barrie and I managed to manoeuvre it into a sack and balance it on the saddle of my bike. We were wheeling it through Peel Park feeling pretty pleased with ourselves, when someone must have spotted us and called the police. As we came over the bridge, a police car screamed to a halt on the other side, sirens going and lights flashing. Thinking quickly, we dumped the bag, I got on the back of the bike and Barrie on the front and we cycled off before they could catch us. Once we were sure the coast was clear we went back to find that the police had just dropped the wire over a fence, so we loaded it back on to the bike and set off again. Keen we may have been, but experts in scrap metal we definitely were not: the dealer didn't want this wire either, so we took it away and burnt it one Bonfire Night. As well as the main bonfire, we had little fires in which we'd bake potatoes to eat while admiring the fireworks and the magnificent blaze we'd spent the previous weeks defending from marauders. That night we cooked our spuds in this burning copperplated wire, melted plastic and toxic waste dripping on to our dinner. To this day, I suffer a lot from indigestion. So does Barrie, come to think of it.

Another curious trade developed when the council began demolishing houses: people kept discovering old swords hidden behind the fireplaces, apparently left over from the Crimean War. The soldiers, the story went, would return from the fighting and hide their swords and other weapons up the chimney, presumably to keep them out of harm's way. As well as the demolitions, there was a fashion in the sixties for people to knock out original tiled Victorian fireplaces and put in horrible electric fires with glowing plastic coal. When people ripped out the fireplaces they'd often find these swords, sabres, daggers — all sorts of things — hidden away during the wars of the nineteenth century. The kids would collect them, creating a thriving local black market in vintage weaponry. I remember being in the wrong place at the wrong time once and being chased by a gang of kids all waving sabres. It was dangerous stuff but, when you're a kid, you feel as if you're immortal. Some of the things we got up to and the scrapes we got into were frightening when I look back now, but it was just so much fun we didn't notice any danger.

I think the only truly dangerous thing that happened to me as a kid was going to the dentist. I must have been very young, because I think it was the first time I'd ever been, and it turned out I needed no less than seven fillings. My grandfather used to bring home a bar of chocolate every night — to have chocolate suddenly freely available after the end of rationing must have been amazing for that generation, so my grandfather would buy a lot of it — and I'd help him demolish it, along with, it seemed, most of my tooth enamel. I didn't really know what a filling was, so I had no apprehension about what lay in store and went in quite happily. I was almost looking forward to it. They gave me gas and knocked me out and the next thing I remember is waking up with the dentist and his assistant holding me upside down with my head in a big sink, slapping me hard in the face and running cold water over me. When I looked down I could see blood washing down the plughole. I started shouting, demanding to know what was going on, and they said that I'd started screaming and they couldn't get me to stop. Something must have gone dreadfully wrong, because they both looked pale and very panicked. Once I'd recovered a little bit, the dentist drove me home — I remember he had an E-type Jaguar — but for the next few days I was very poorly, with blood constantly seeping from my mouth. I think they must have given me too much gas or got the mixture wrong, and they'd nearly lost me.

By this time I was a pupil at St Clement's Primary School, which was only a short walk from where we lived but still far enough for me to be late most days. I'm one of those people who just seems to be late for everything. I remember one of my teachers telling me, 'Bernard Sumner, you'll be late for your own funeral.' I didn't do particularly well in my school career and I think the way I was taught at primary level is largely responsible for that. I wasn't good at maths, for example, and the way of educating you if you weren't very good at a subject back then was to make you stand on a chair and bombard you with questions or demands to recite your nine times table or somesuch. When you didn't get it right the teachers would deliberately make a fool of you in front of the class. As academic motivation goes, it was a pretty bizarre philosophy. Primary school was a pretty horrible experience, one that set about destroying from a very early age any self-confidence I might have had. It was education through fear, but it didn't toughen me up, it didn't make me learn, it just made me more and more anxious and created a self-perpetuating downward spiral from which I'd never really recover. At least, not during my school years.

There are only two things I can say for my time at St Clement's: I learned to read, and I loved anything to do with art, especially clay modelling. The school had its own kiln and I was never happier than when I was making things. We had a teacher called Mr Strapps who taught us how to work with clay but, instead of a potter's wheel, he used a record player. It was sculpture at 45rpm — unconventional, certainly, but it worked for me.

The downside was that Mr Strapps was an absolutely terrifying man. His name alone sounds like something out of Dickens and he could certainly have stepped straight out of the pages of *Hard Times*. He taught the eldest year at primary school, so you grew up with this dread of the inevitability of Mr Strapps becoming your class tutor. He caned me once: it was raining at playtime and we were all kept inside and I knocked over a bottle of milk. Even though it was clearly an accident, he called me straight to the front of the class-room and thrashed me on the hand as hard as he could with his cane.

My abiding memory of Mr Strapps isn't being caned, however. It's something far crueller.

It was another rainy breaktime, so we were all inside trying to amuse ourselves as best we could. I'd picked out a book of poetry from the school library and was sitting there quietly reading when I sensed Mr Strapps walk up behind me. He looked over my shoulder and when he saw what I was reading, he said, almost in a growl, oozing contempt, 'What are you doing reading that?' I looked up from the book and said, 'What do you mean, Mr Strapps?' He put his hands behind his back, bent down so his mouth was next to my ear and sneered, 'Listen, where you come from, you're just going to end up working in a factory, so there's no point in reading anything like that. Just put it back. Now.'

I'd been brought up by my mother and grandparents to respect authority. He's Mr Strapps, I thought, he's my teacher, so he must know what he's talking about. So I did put the book back and I did stop reading. What a terrible thing for anyone to say to a kid, let alone a teacher.

Despite the efforts of Mr Strapps, remarkably, I did manage to pass my Eleven Plus. I'd been promised a new bike by my grandfather as an incentive, but I think the main reason I passed was fear, and not of Mr Strapps for once. There were two school options beyond the Eleven Plus: if you passed you went to Salford Grammar School and if you failed you were sent to Lower Broughton Modern. One of my cousins had warned me how hard it was at Lower Broughton: if you went there, he told me, you got the shit beaten out of you every week for the entire first year without fail. In reality, it was probably no worse than my primary school, where we had our share of kids from hard families, but my jaw dropped and I was determined not to end up at Lower Broughton Modern. So I studied like mad and went into the exams praying that I'd pass. I missed one part of the exams because I had measles, and when I'd recovered I had to go in on my own, sit in a freezing cold classroom while all my mates were out playing and do the exam I'd missed. There were a few fretful weeks waiting for the results, but when the headmaster read out the names of those who'd passed and mine was among them I felt a fantastic mixture of relief and genuine happiness. Passing my Eleven Plus felt like a real achievement, because I'd had no confidence in myself; it had been destroyed by the teachers. The moment my name was read out that day, however, I did get a real boost. I'd also, of course, earned myself a new bike, and I spent the long summer evenings bombing around the streets among the lengthening shadows and looking forward to starting at Salford Grammar. I knew things were about to change. I had absolutely no idea just how much.

Chapter Two

Youth

'Come and sit down, Bernard. There's something we need to tell you.'

My mouth went dry. What had I done this time?

I had an inkling something was going on. For a few weeks, there'd been times when I'd go into the living room and the conversation would stop dead, or I'd be up in my bedroom and I'd hear a murmur from downstairs, my grandparents, my mother and Jimmy talking in low voices. I'd wracked my brains, but I couldn't for the life of me think what I'd done. It was obviously something serious, as there'd never been a build-up like this before. I sat down, picked nervously at the seam of the seat cushion and looked from my mother to Jimmy and back again, a familiar creeping fear chilling my stomach. My mother paused for a moment.

'We're moving out of here, Bernard,' she said. 'You, me and Jimmy. We're moving to our own flat in Greengate.'

It took a moment for me to process. My first feeling was a wave of relief that I didn't seem to be in trouble, but that was soon replaced by an overwhelming sense of confusion. I'd prepared myself for punishment, but this, this was something completely unexpected and I didn't know how to react.

'It's a nice place,' she continued, 'in one of the new blocks. It's got a bathroom and everything. It's not too far away, so we can come back here and visit any time.'

I just looked at her, not knowing what to think, let alone say.

'Also . . .' She paused and looked at Jimmy. 'Also, Jimmy's going to be your father now. We've made it formal. Jimmy's adopting you. From now on, your name isn't Bernard Sumner, it's Bernard Dickin.'

I still didn't know what to say but in any case it was clear that the matter wasn't up for discussion. They left me alone in the room and I replayed what my mother had said in my head, trying to make sense of it. Moving to a flat — well, that was quite exciting. I remembered how much I'd loved the view from my great-grandmother's place, and we weren't moving too far from Alfred Street. That part sounded like an adventure. The announcement that Jimmy would be my dad and that I'd have to take his surname — well, that was a different proposition altogether and much harder to take in. I'd always been a Sumner, from the day I was born. It was my mother's name; it was the name I shared with the grandparents I loved and whose house I'd grown up in. It was my family name, part of me; it was effectively the most tangible expression of my identity I had. Yet now, without any kind of consultation, I was no longer a Sumner, I was a Dickin. As for Jimmy being my father, I'd coped perfectly well without one of those for eleven years and, suddenly, here I was having one more or less thrust upon me. I thought of my grandfather, the man who had always been the closest to a father I'd ever had: not only was his role in my life being usurped, so was his name.

I was determined that it wasn't going to happen; the more I

thought about it, the more I resented having been presented with this *fait accompli*. I didn't blame Jimmy, it wasn't his fault. My relationship with him was all right, but he'd come into my life too late to take up any kind of paternal role. As a person he was OK, if very quiet, and the two things I remember most about him are that he had an incredibly strong right hand and he was very good at chess. He had an extremely hard life, too: despite being quite badly disabled himself, he had a job as a cleaner in a cotton mill, which must have been pretty rotten. I respected Jimmy, but I didn't feel emotionally attached to him — there was no bond, we didn't even really speak to each other that much.

To his credit, Jimmy did a really good job of looking after my mother, but I remember them having blazing rows when they were first married, real shouting matches. My mother was the same with Jimmy as she was with me, insofar as she didn't like him going out. If he ever came home late from work they'd have these huge arguments. I'd be in my room with my fingers in my ears trying to block it out, but I could still hear this yelling and shouting coming up through the floor and I found it very distressing. Things calmed down a bit when we moved to the flat. Maybe having their own space helped; I think that was probably the idea behind the move.

Once the excitement at the prospect of moving had died down I realized just what a wrench it was leaving Alfred Street. Of course I understand why my mother decided we should have our own place: for all her health issues, she was a married woman in her midthirties still living with her parents, but I had to quickly get used to it being just the three of us — me, Jimmy and my mother — and it was a huge adjustment to make for a small boy who'd known nothing else but living in a house with his grandparents.

At first I thought our new home was fantastic; it was the best thing that had ever happened to me. We lived quite low down in the tower, so I didn't have the same breathtaking view my great-grandmother had, but we had a proper bathroom with a bath, which we'd never had at Alfred Street. We also had a boiler, so we even had an airing cupboard for drying clothes. I soon learned that when you turned up the heating you could go and sit in the airing cupboard. It was like being in a sauna.

From my bedroom window I could see a little spindly tree and a patch of grass in front of the tower block. I used to look at it and think how great it was, how lucky I was to live there: we had a tree and a lawn, an airing cupboard and a bathroom with a bath. It blew me away at first. But of course, after a while, reality set in and I realized that what it had in amenities, it was lacking in so many other ways. There was no community there, the tower blocks just isolated people, especially the old folk who'd lived such social lives before. There was nowhere to put a chair out and sit in the sun chatting to the neighbours, no street for the kids to play in, no hosepipe for those summer fountains. The towers were probably a great idea on the architects' drawing boards and at the town planners' meetings, but they didn't meet the needs of the people who lived there. They were an economical solution but at too great a social cost. And of course the architects and town planners didn't live in the tower blocks.

Around the time we moved into the flat the family began to experience some more serious health issues. My grandfather developed a brain tumour and had to have a major operation to remove it in the Jewish hospital that used to be close to Strangeways Prison. I don't know why he was in a Jewish hospital — he wasn't Jewish — but although we were very concerned for a while, thankfully the operation was successful. Unfortunately, it turned out to be just the start.

Soon after my grandfather had come out of hospital my

grandmother had to go in for what should have been a routine operation for glaucoma. It was a straightforward process; hospitals performed them all the time, and still do. On this occasion, though, something went disastrously wrong and my grandmother was left completely blind. She didn't see anything again as long as she lived. As well as being a genuine tragedy, my grandmother's blindness had knock-on effects throughout the family. She had always done a lot to help my mother and, although we'd moved out and now had Jimmy, my grandmother had still helped but could no longer do so. It also meant that my grandfather — not long recovered from his brain tumour — was now the only able-bodied person in the family. My grandmother had worked as a cleaner, but obviously had to give her job up when she lost her sight, which made things even more difficult back at Alfred Street. It was an awful time, but I think to a certain extent the family kept the full implications of what happened to my grandmother from me. I don't remember it being discussed when I was around. I do vividly recall her becoming upset talking about it, though, about how this stupid doctor had cost her her sight. I suppose, these days, you could sue for medical negligence, but back then you pretty much just had to put up with it. We were a poor working-class family, so what could we have done?

My new school should have provided a welcome respite from everything that was happening at home, but things weren't great there either. The school may have been different, but the story remained the same: I struggled academically as much at Salford Grammar as I had at St Clement's. Maths was still my particular weakness, and I think in the first year maths exam I only got something like 5 or 6 per cent. The self-confidence I'd developed through passing my Eleven Plus was soon in shreds again. Despite my clear lack of aptitude for maths, the staff still tried to force it into me. It was pointless. I was much better at art than any other subject — I was top of the class, in fact – but instead of nurturing that, all the focus was on how bad my maths was. People are good at different things, and I think education should reflect that. School should give you a basic grounding in the subjects you're not so strong in, but surely the role of education is to find out what you're good at and embrace that, encourage it. After all, you wouldn't take a kid who's a weedy, skinny academic wearing thick glasses and drum it into him that he's got to be a super athlete and captain of the rugby team. That would be utterly ridiculous. Surely by that logic, taking someone who is artistic and clearly talented in that area and forcing them to become brilliant at algebra is equally futile?

Not being a high-flyer, I was one of the kids who'd sit at the back of the class at school. At Salford Grammar, just like any school, there were the good boys and there were the bad boys. The good boys sat at the front and the bad boys would gather along the back row. I was always in the back row, not because I was stupid or a bad kid, but because I found the curriculum and the way it was taught incredibly dull. I just wasn't stimulated. Even history didn't do anything for me, and I *love* history now. I'm convinced it's to do with the nature of the syllabus: I wasn't interested in the Corn Laws or the Spinning Jenny, none of us were, but these were the things we had to learn. For all the years I spent in history classes, the only thing I remember was the time a spider suddenly dangled down from the end of the teacher's nose while he held forth on nineteenth-century bread prices or something. That's it. That's all I took away from the subject at school, yet today I devour books about history.

Science wasn't much better either, but then our science teacher, who died years ago, was very strict, and very peculiar. We were warned about him in advance; people would say, 'God help you, he's a nutter.' He was certainly very eccentric, to say the least: in our very first lesson he instructed us that we had to spell everything the American way — they used fewer letters, so we'd save on ink.

He drove a little three-wheeler car that we could see parked from our classroom. One day near the end of the school year we were in the science teacher's class when, through the window, we saw some of the sixth formers, who were leaving school and so were demob happy, go over to his car, lean in through the window, release the handbrake and start pushing the car out of its space. It was parked at the top of a slope and, before long, these lads had set it rolling down the hill right outside our classroom. The science teacher was completely oblivious, because he had his back to the window, but we had a grandstand view of his three-wheeler trundling past the window, bouncing down the slope and crashing into a wall. It was pretty hilarious from where we were sitting, but we were so terrified of him that not one of us laughed. We were all biting the inside of our cheeks, staring hard at our textbooks, whatever it took not to react to the unfortunate demise of his little car.

Frightened as we were of him, however, none of us could have predicted the extraordinary way in which he ended his teaching career at Salford Grammar. We were in maths one day when all of a sudden there was the sound of breaking glass coming from outside. We all ran over just in time to see chairs being thrown through the windows of the science teacher's classroom and landing on the tarmac below. Our first thought was that he must have been in a particularly bad mood that day and caught someone laughing or something, but the truth was far worse.

First, he'd taken all the handles off the Bunsen burners so they were stuck open with no way of regulating the gas supply. Then he'd separated the Jewish kids in the class from the rest, sent the others out, locked the classroom door, gone into his little room and turned the gas on. What we were seeing and hearing were these poor kids throwing chairs through the windows so they could breathe. It was absolutely horrendous. Surprisingly, we never saw him again after that. I presume he was carried away in a straitjacket. The odd Holocaust incident aside, my time at Salford Grammar was similar in many ways to my time at St Clement's. It was bigger than St Clement's, so I found more like-minded kids and we drifted towards each other and became a group of no-good layabouts at the back of the class. One of these boys at the back was a lad called Peter Hook and I suppose, looking back, we must have met for the first time in the back row of a classroom at Salford Grammar. There was a group of us: Hooky, Terry Mason and Dave Pearce, who was a lovely guy whose father was a policeman (I believe Dave himself went on to become a police marksman). When we could get away with it, we'd while away boring lessons talking about girls and music, and when we couldn't we'd just sit there bored, watching the clock and waiting for the lesson to finish. We were a bit like kids in *The Inbetweeners* in many ways: hopeless lost cases, but having a good time being hopeless lost cases. I remember one of my mates being very popular one day because he'd brought in a porn mag. They were very hard to get hold of in those days.

Another member of the back-row crowd was a mischievous lad called Gresty who had a particular classroom trick that ran very successfully for a long time. He kept a big spanner in his briefcase which, when the teacher wasn't looking, he'd drop on the floor with an enormous clang, then he'd pick it up and shove it back in his bag before the teacher could see where the noise had come from. It took considerable skill and sleight of hand and was very impressive to witness. Of course, every show runs its course and Gresty eventually realized he needed some new material. One day we all filed into our maths lesson and slouched off towards the back row, but when we got there we saw that Gresty had parked himself at the front. We all looked at each other in horror. What on earth was he doing? Our maths teacher was called Johnny Barker, and he was another one we were very scared of. I think he'd been through the war and seen a few things. He hated the way we carried our books in satchels, for example, and he'd go off into a rant and say, 'You're ruining those books in those satchels, my mate went through the war so you could have those books.' From there, he'd lose himself and spend the rest of the class telling us how we didn't know how lucky we were, how his mate had had this terrible time in the war making sure we could have books, and there we were, ruining them by putting them in satchels. It was a bit strange, but fine by us, as it was less time spent on maths.

One feature of Mr Barker's class was that he'd tell everyone to take out their homework then go from pupil to pupil checking it, starting with the lads at the front. We rarely did our homework — at least not our own: we'd occasionally copy someone's in the toilets before the class — so what we'd try to do was distract him. The best way of achieving this was to get him talking about something he felt strongly about, and we soon narrowed this down to the war and cricket. One of us would put on our most innocent voice and ask something like, 'Sir, what was it like in the war? Were Spitfires really as good as they were cracked up to be?' or 'Who's the best team Lancashire ever had, sir?' More often than not, he'd look out of the window and launch into a monologue about the versatility of the Spitfire or some great Lancashire county championship-winning side from the thirties, and the clock would tick by until the bell went and we'd get away with not doing our homework. Again. We really had it sussed.

But on this particular day Gresty had sat at the front, and none of us could work out what was going on: he was sure to be asked for his homework sitting right up there. Mr Barker, like Mr Upton, wouldn't tolerate any misbehaviour in his class: there was no talking, no laughing; even smirking could land you in detention. Gresty knew this. We all knew it. The class started and Mr Barker was walking up and down talking about sines and co-sines or whatever. He walked past Gresty, who then sat back in his seat and put his hands behind his head in order that we could see that not only did he have his briefcase on his lap, but that it was rising and falling, apparently of its own accord. He'd summoned an erection and was using it to repeatedly levitate his briefcase. This was his new trick. It was a good one. And we couldn't laugh.

Phallic gymnastics aside, the grammar school is largely responsible for some of my earliest musical influences — not from music lessons, but from the kids I hung out with. Also, we had one super-cool geography teacher, a young guy with long hair whose name I wish I could remember. He said to us, 'Look, I know some of you might find geography boring. I understand that. But do me a favour, if that's the case, just don't cause any trouble in my class. If you don't cause any trouble, there's a room over there with my record player in it and you can go in there at break time and play records.' He was great, a really cool guy, all the kids respected him. He was always asking what you were listening to, so we started bringing music in. He helped to foster a culture of music at the school away from the curriculum. I think the school was doing *Joseph and the Amazing Technicolor Dreamcoat* around that time, and it was just awful. We wanted nothing to do with it. We wanted to hear Jimi Hendrix, the Stones and The Kinks, not some kid murdering bloody 'Any Dream Will Do'. We looked at things like *Joseph* and thought it was shit. If I remember rightly, most kids just sat through the music classes pretending to sing but with a porn mag tucked inside their music books.

I'd not grown up in any kind of musical atmosphere until that point. My grandparents had a gramophone, and they'd put on an old 78 now and again, but that didn't do much for me. I'd heard The Kinks on the radio when I was very young and really liked them. I think it was when we were away on holiday and I'd hear transistor radios on beaches in Torquay or wherever we'd gone, a tinny rendition of 'You Really Got Me', 'Lola', or The Beatles or the Stones, and I remember thinking I really liked them. Then I'd hear on the news about their depraved behaviour – the drug busts and what have you. I distinctly remember hearing on the radio that a famous singer's house had been raided and he'd been found in bed with not one but two girls. I was, of course, horrified. It didn't put me off music, though.

At St Clement's, the headmaster, Mr Alkister, would come in every morning with a record player and play us a different piece of classical music. He'd say, 'Right, this is called "A Night on Bare Mountain" and it's by a Russian composer called Mussorgsky,' drop the needle, and we'd all sit there listening. I didn't really understand it, but I often wonder whether it left some sort of subconscious imprint. However, I think classical music was too refined, too mature for a young Salford street kid's mind at that stage. I'm not saying it was bad, it wasn't that I didn't like it, but I wanted to hear something thuggish like the Stones. You'd listen to the Stones and that would lead you on to something else, and eventually you'd be led back to classical music. But, at that age, I think we were too young to appreciate it.

North Salford Youth Club was a big musical influence too. Youth clubs back then were pretty good and the people were cool. Obviously, the main attraction was the opportunity to meet girls and hang out, and they had a disco that played Tamla Motown, soul and ska downstairs for all the skinheads, suedeheads and scooter boys, of which I was one. I owned a scooter when I turned sixteen, a GP225 Lambretta, which was a really cool scooter, as it happens, and I was wearing a crombie, the red silk handkerchief with a diamond stuck in it, two-tone trousers, all that gear. From the disco you'd drift to the upstairs part where the people with long hair gathered to play Led Zeppelin, Santana, the Stones and maybe Black Sabbath. They had a record player up there with stereo speakers, and we were all, 'Fucking hell, this is amazing! The sound starts over there and moves across to the other speaker!' You could take in your own albums and everyone would sit around listening: a group of like-minded people listening to similar music. I learnt a lot about music up there. As scooter boys, we were supposed to be listening to soul, but we liked rock music as well. We'd spend half the night downstairs in the disco and then move upstairs to be exposed to completely different styles of music.

When I was about fifteen I remember hearing 'Ride a White Swan' by T Rex on the radio and going straight out to buy it. I loved that track — the guitar sound, the tune, everything. I brought it home and put it on the record player I'd got for Christmas, and it sounded amazing. It finished after about three minutes and I thought right, what do I do now? OK, play the B side. I played the B side and didn't really like it, so I kept on putting 'Ride a White Swan' on. After a while I thought, I can't be doing with this, playing the same record over and over again, and went out to find the album of the music that had really opened my ears for the first time.

It might surprise you to learn this, but the first piece of music to really knock me sideways, the one that I can say probably more than most set me on the path that my life has taken, wasn't one I heard downstairs at the youth club disco or upstairs with the rock fans. It didn't come via one of those school break time sessions with the geography teacher's record player and it didn't come from the radio. Of all places, it came from the cinema.

I'd never seen anything like *The Good, the Bad and the Ugly* before and, what's more, I'd never *heard* anything like it before. I'd been visually orientated from an early age and I loved the way the film looked: it was shot in a really peculiar way, with massive close-ups. I loved how it was ambiguous as to who the bad guy was, because *everyone* was bad, there was no good guy – up to that point it had been all corny John Wayne cowboy films, black hats and white hats, and then all of a sudden along came Sergio Leone to make these subversive films that broke all the rules. They were grittier than anything that had come before; you could see the sweat and the dust, almost feel the burning sun. The dialogue was pretty sparse, and great swathes of the film were made up of long silences.

Leone's westerns were also strangely funny, they had this weird, dark humour about them, but what really blew me away was Ennio Morricone's soundtrack. That simple whistle theme, the twangy guitar sound, the coyote howl of the vocal parts, the echo effects, the great spaces between the notes that made the music fit the bare, harsh location of the film perfectly, it was just so incredibly evocative, and I loved it. I came out of the cinema and immediately went hunting for the soundtrack album. Of course, there was no Internet then, so it took me a while to find it, but when I did – in HMV in Manchester, I think – I'd play it again and again. I also bought the soundtracks to *A Fistful of Dollars* and *A Few Dollars More*, one LP with one film on each side, and I couldn't stop listening to this incredible music. It was as if a switch had been flipped somewhere inside me from being not that interested in music to being massively interested in it.

It turned out that Hooky was just as interested in music as I was, and we'd usually be at one another's houses playing records (we used to be at Gresty's house quite a lot too, because his dad worked at Cadbury's and could lay his hands on vast quantities of Flake cakes). We started going to the youth club together most of the time, me riding my scooter, with Hooky on the back. I remember one time, we thought we'd try and impress the girls standing around outside the youth club waiting to get in. Hooky climbed on the back, as usual, I revved the engine and the intention was to roar off up the grassy knoll outside the club like Salford's own version of Peter Fonda and Dennis Hopper in *Easy Rider*, but the back wheel just started spinning around, the scooter shot from beneath us and we both ended up in a heap in this great big muddy puddle. Right in front of all these girls. Ouch.

I'm ashamed to admit a couple of us used to go to Manchester and do a bit of shoplifting now and then, mostly out of boredom. Jeans, mainly. Loads of kids did it. We couldn't afford Levi's or Wrangler's but wanted to look cool when we went to the youth club. So, occasionally, we nicked them. That was about as far as the shoplifting went: it was the challenge as much as any real criminal intent. It didn't last, though — there was a pen-nicking competition once, and I got caught with one by a bloke who said that if I didn't put it back he was taking me to the management. After that, I never nicked anything ever again. For one thing, my mother would have murdered me. The potential consequences just weren't worth it.

Girls and clothes aside, by my mid-teens it was all about music. It was like a box had been opened and out of the box came this very strong light, and that light was music. We became fanatical about it, Hooky and I. I don't know if it was because we found everything else boring at school or it happened to be a particular period in time when there was a lot of good music around, but it fascinated us to the point of obsession.

One big event while I was still at school was when Jimi Hendrix died in 1970. I liked guitar music, but I couldn't find much of a tune in Jimi's stuff. I sat next to this lad who was generally quiet, kept himself to himself, and I said, 'You like Jimi Hendrix, don't you? He's just died, hasn't he?' 'Yeah, yeah I do,' he replied. I said, 'I've tried to get into his stuff, but I can't find the tune in it — what's it all about?' He turned round, looked me in the eye and said, quite calmly, 'I just like it. All right?' I thought this was a strange reaction, and it made me even more curious. Polydor released an EP when Hendrix died with 'Voodoo Chile', 'All Along the Watchtower' and 'Hey Joe' on it. I put it on the record player and listened to it, and the first couple of times I thought it was just a noise. I couldn't work out what people saw in it. But then, *pow!* Suddenly, I heard it. It took me a while, but thank you, whoever you were who wouldn't give me an explanation that day at Salford Grammar, because you made me keep at it until it just clicked.

I used to like early Fleetwood Mac too, particularly Peter Green's songwriting and guitar playing. Not so much the bluesy stuff, though. It always confused me how British bands would bang on and on about the blues. I didn't like the tracks they released that sounded like the blues, I liked the ones that sounded like they were a band from England – the songs they wrote when they weren't trying to be a blues band from America. I remember having a Rolling Stones album with an octagonal cover, *Through the Past, Darkly*, it was called, and it had all the hits, 'Jumping Jack Flash', 'Street Fighting Man': I loved that stuff. '2000 Light Years From Home' in particular was a great track, because it didn't sound like a blues band, it just sounded like The Rolling Stones. Obviously, there are and were some great original American blues artists out there, but the stuff I liked wasn't the blues, it was when a band had ingested the blues and something completely different was coming out; they'd filtered it through their own experiences and environments. That's what worked best for me, and still does.

Certainly the music I've made has been the product of the experiences I've had. And, as I moved into my late teens, those experiences were coming thick and fast.

Chapter Three

Complex

Even after we'd moved to the flat across the river in Greengate, I was still spending most of my time back at Alfred Street. It was like a magnet to me; I'd always be over there visiting my grandparents and hanging out with my friends. I certainly wouldn't say I had a miserable childhood; it was a difficult childhood in many ways, certainly compared to some people's, but it definitely wasn't miserable.

I loved growing up in Salford. I really felt part of the community there, felt that I belonged. I had a lot of fun too, some fantastic times. My horizons didn't extend far beyond a few local streets, and I knew every inch of them. Sometimes we'd get out on the scooters to the Pennines, the moors, Blackpool, wagging school and just taking off. When I first saw the countryside, it was like a different world. Our world was red brick, dirt and dust. But on our scooters we'd drive out even in the middle of winter, through the Pennines in snow and fog on these little scooters with twelve-inch wheels, no crash helmets or anything. It was completely insane. But, again, there was a strange kind of youthful innocence about it all. If you were walking at night you had to have your wits about you and be a bit streetwise, you had to think about where you were going and who with, because you wouldn't want to walk into the wrong mob at the wrong time, or you'd get leathered. There were a few psychos about, people with sharpened umbrellas, hammers and, on the odd occasion, swords and that kind of thing, but you'd just try and avoid the loons.

Salford was my world. You'd make the most of what you had, the best of what you'd got. You wouldn't know there was anything better. I didn't know what else was out there and, in many respects, it didn't matter: I had the magnetic pull of my family, so there was never any question of leaving, and it was such an intense period of my life that I have vivid recurring dreams about those days even today, what, forty-odd years later. These were some of the happiest times of my life and the reasons for that are family, community, friends, a sense of place and a wonderful lack of responsibility.

But, as I was about to find out, nothing lasts for ever. I remember coming home from school one day and finding a national newspaper on the table, one of the London ones, open at a page dominated by a big article about 'Britain's biggest slum'. I picked it up and started reading. The thrust of the piece was how Britain was home to the largest and worst slum in Europe, an eyesore, a place of which the nation should be ashamed, and as I read on I saw that this terrible place, this blight on Britain, was Salford. I thought, Hang on a minute, that's where I live. I don't live in a slum. I felt really insulted, not to mention confused, because, as far as I was concerned, this was a good place to live. They obviously measured things in a different way down south.

Before long, the council began getting rid of parts of this alleged eyesore and plans were put into action to take people out of the old Victorian streets and rehouse them in new tower blocks. From their point of view, it was cheaper to put everyone in a tower block than to renovate the old Victorian terraces, put central heating and proper bathrooms into the houses, which they could easily have done, as most of the houses had a third bedroom. They decided to just pull everything down and shove everyone into these human beehives. The architects thought only in terms of concrete and La Corbusier, not community. Why would they?

If that wasn't unsettling enough, it was around this time that more things began to go wrong in the health department at home. One day, my granddad had what the doctors said was a stroke; something that affected him mentally as well as physically. Looking back now, maybe it was something to do with his brain tumour, but where, before, he'd been a kind, thoughtful man, suddenly he was angry, roaring and shouting all the time.

And of course my grandmother was blind. She was upstairs in the house; my grandfather now slept downstairs. It was a terrible situation, because my grandfather had gone out of his mind and now my grandmother had him to cope with as well as her blindness.

It was heartbreaking, and there was nothing I could do. I remember being at the house in Alfred Street, looking around and thinking, This is the place where I grew up, where I've spent my happiest days, and suddenly everything is going so *wrong*. The council was moving people out of the street whether they wanted to leave or not, and boarding up the houses as they went, gradually turning it into a ghost street, with desolation and abandonment creeping along it house by house. The community was being scattered across the region, to the likes of Swinton and Little Hulton, places that had just been names to us before. It was being torn apart with no consultation, nothing: no one had any say; no one had any choice. Where once the street was full of the noise of kids playing and the hubbub of neighbourly conversation, now it was quiet save for the hammering of the council workmen boarding up the windows and doors of the empty houses. Before long, there were just three houses on the street still occupied; the rest were all dark, soulless and home only to ghosts and memories. In one of these last three houses to still have a light burning in the window were my grandmother, completely blind, and my grandfather, out of his mind. To this day I have a recurring dream where I see the street all boarded up and my grandmother in the house in despair, tears running down her face. Even now in this dream I feel completely helpless. I was only young at the time and I didn't know how to help. My grandparents had effectively brought me up and shown me nothing but love and kindness my whole life, and here I was unable to do anything to stop this tide of change and misery that was swamping them. I watched this wonderful, vibrant community that I'd thought would last for ever reduced to nothing, the people knitted together by that binding sense of community thrown to the winds.

I'd really believed that everyone would live there for ever; that there'd always be Bonfire Nights and the Pinks getting into scrapes, the old women in their chairs soaking up the sunshine and my granddad filling his lungs twice a day in the backyard. All of it had been wiped out in a sudden flurry of class-based cleansing, one that I suppose was well intentioned but was actually entirely disconnected from reality.

Eventually, my grandfather was moved into hospital, which was a blessing, but he lived only another six months. This left my grandmother living with one of her sisters in this desolate street, no more than two other houses on the street still occupied. Finally, they moved my grandmother to a sheltered housing place in Swinton, which she hated. She didn't want to move out of the house where she'd lived for nigh on fifty years; a house that in her mind's eye was still the same domestic haven it had been when she still had her sight.

I remember going to visit her in the old house in Alfred Street towards the end, and there were mice and she didn't know because she couldn't see them. We'd never had mice; she'd always kept everything scrupulously clean. It was just horrific, an image that summed up what had become of the community as a whole. Once the last residents had left, all the history, people, families, homes, pride, dignity – everything – had gone and been left to the mice.

I was barely eighteen years old, and everything I'd ever known had been destroyed.

Witnessing this had a big psychological impact on me; it made me a bit hard emotionally. That was the only way I could deal with it: to harden my heart. I imagine it's a bit like being a doctor – they have to be quite hard in a way, because they see awful things and have to break a lot of bad news to people. It's either that or you just completely crumble. That was the choice I faced as I watched the disintegration of our world.

Everything had gone; even the school was eventually pulled down. It was almost as if someone was actively trying to erase my memories. All the parts you could touch, feel, even smell, they were all gone and would never come back. My transition from childhood hadn't exactly been gentle: I was wrenched from it and dragged into adulthood before I was ready, and I didn't like it. Suddenly everything had become really fucking serious and I'd had to grow up fast. I don't think it's a coincidence that this is when I got even more into music, because what happened around that time has really influenced the music I've made. I think you can hear the death of a community and the death of my adolescence in my contribution to the music of Joy Division.

Chapter Four

Scumbags

I left school in 1972 with an O level in English and a grade A O level in art. I wanted to go on and do something with art, because it was what I loved doing most of all. I was mad about music of course, yet hadn't really thought about making my own at this stage. As well as the record player, my mother had also bought me an electric guitar — I don't know why I'd asked for it, but I'd always loved the sound of the guitar, so the logical thing was to get one — and I'd made a few token attempts to play it. To be honest, I just found it all a bit aimless: I didn't know where to go with it. So it was left it in the corner of the room, where it became coated in dust. That was dead end number one.

So, fresh out of school at sixteen, art was the direction in which I wanted to go. The careers officer at Salford Grammar was hopeless. I went to see him and told him I'd really like to do something involving art, and he thought for a moment before announcing there were two jobs for me. One was working in a hairdresser's; the other was cutting the white borders from around photographs. And that was dead end number two.

It looked as though working at anything creative was out of the question, and I was under pressure from my mother to find a job in order to start bringing some money into the household. I had applied to Bolton College of Art when I left school, as it had a good reputation, and I was absolutely delighted when I was offered a place. However, when I told my mother, she didn't seem exactly enthusiastic about it and, the next thing I knew, an uncle from Jimmy's side of the family I didn't know very well had come round to the flat to have a little chat with me. He sat me down and explained that the family couldn't afford for me to go to art college, I should forget about it and concentrate on getting a steady job. I understood the situation, because we clearly didn't have much money, but I was pretty upset. Maybe Mr Strapps had been right after all. And thus I arrived at dead end number three.

My mother knew a local councillor, who secured me a job interview at Salford town hall, as a result of which I joined the ranks of the gainfully employed. I didn't know what I'd be doing, but at least it was a job, and there weren't exactly a surfeit of those in the mid-seventies. I worked in the treasury department, where my role was to send out rates bills, folding the bill, putting it in an envelope, taking a roller and some water and sticking the envelope down. Over and over again, thousands of times a week. Our office was in the town hall itself, and it had an enquiries window where members of the public would come and moan about their bills. Nobody liked dealing with their queries, so I had to do it. Another part of my job was to take the city treasurer his coffee in the morning. He'd have a pot of hot coffee and a pot of hot milk and I'd have to take it in and pour it for him.

A lot of the people working in our office had been doing the same job for forty years and were bored out of their heads. It was a slow death really. There was one guy who always fell asleep at his desk after lunch. One day, some bright spark put the clock forward to five thirty, and we all started making a load of noise and pretending to put our coats on like we were packing up for the day.. The commotion woke the guy up with a start and he shot off out of the door and went home.

I'd not been working there very long when a weird guy turned up at the window wearing these old-fashioned Victorian-style clothes, head to toe in black and pissed out of his brains. Everyone who sat near the window hid. There was one guy in the office who was actually all right; he looked just like Terry-Thomas, waxed RAF moustache and all. He had a bit of spirit about him, despite the tedium of the job. He called me over and whispered, 'You'll have to deal with him, he's the city coroner. He comes in with a list of the bodies he's dealt with and we pay him his cash and he spends it all on booze.' He was half propped up at the window, this coroner, effing and blinding and saying, 'Look here, I cut eight bodies up this week, I've come for my money. If I don't get it, you'll be the next one.' Everyone was shit scared of this guy, so they pushed me to the window. I gave him his money then told him to fuck off. After the door had closed behind him. Well, I was only sixteen and a half.

I can't remember his name, the Terry-Thomas guy, but he was a really nice man. He had a Volkswagen camper van, one of those cool ones, and the odd lunchtime about five of us would pile into it and go swimming at Broughton Baths. He was the only guy in the place with a bit of life in him, he was funny — in fact, I'm sure it was him who'd turned the clock forward that day.

I had a very weird dream about him after I'd left that job. In it I'd gone back to the office and was looking through the enquiries window at him. He had his back to me and I was knocking on the window and calling his name, but he didn't turn round. I kept shouting until eventually he turned to face me, and all the veins and sinews of his face were on the outside. It looked terrible, really horrific. I woke up thinking what a horrible dream it was. A little bit later I was in a nightclub in Manchester and I bumped into a couple of guys that still worked there, and they told me he'd died in a crash in his Volkswagen camper. It was awful news to hear at the best of times, and it gave me a strange feeling in the light of that dream.

It was a really odd place to work — a cul-de-sac of life, in a sense. These were people who'd stepped off the highway of their lives to be content in this quiet, unhurried dead end of existence, counting the years down until retirement. There was one guy who worked in town planning (so was probably one of those responsible for pulling down my grandmother's house). Every now and again he'd come up to me all furtive and say, 'I've got a letter, can you post it through the franking machine for me?' When I'd done it, he'd go, 'Good lad, here's a sweet for you,' and I'd get a sweet for doing it. Local government corruption, eh?

I was called into the deputy city treasurer's office once. He was actually all right too: he sat me down and said, 'Bernard, you're new to this job, aren't you? How long have you been here?' I replied that it was four or five months, whatever it was. He paused for a moment, looked me up and down, nodded at the wall and said, 'Look at that painting. Do you know what it is?'

'No,' I replied.

'It's *Whistler's Mother*,' he said, then paused and looked at his feet for a while, as if he didn't relish what he was about to say to me.

'It . . . it's just the clothes you wear,' he said. I had a Fair Isle jumper on — they were kind of cool in those days — and a budgie shirt under it.

'How can I put this?' he said. 'You wouldn't go to a funeral dressed as you are now, would you?' I replied that, no, I wouldn't go to a funeral dressed as I was. In a slightly pained tone of voice he said, 'Well, why do you come to work dressed like that?'

The funeral analogy was quite apposite for that office, and I wonder if it was a comparison he'd made deliberately, as if to say, Look, I know what it's like, but we're all just trying to get on with it here while causing as few ripples as possible. The relevance of the painting, I still wonder about to this day.

It was a curious place — a bit like working in the clerk's office in *A Christmas Carol*, especially when the coroner came round in his strange Victorian clothes with his breath smelling of embalming fluid. I knew I had to get out, and I think the final straw came when they sent me to college to study local and central government. It was like being at school all over again: we'd learn about things like *Hansard* and how all the bureaucracy worked, and I wasn't in the slightest bit interested. Predictably, I did really badly in the exam. Here we go again, I thought, and that was the cue for me to get out. I stuck it out for a year in all and must have done a quarter of a million of those envelopes in that time, none of which was ever good news for the people receiving them.

I wrote to loads of advertising agencies in Manchester, because they were the only places with any scope for anything to do with art back then. I went for a few interviews and was offered two jobs at the same time. Both were for less money than I was on at the town hall, but that didn't really matter: I just wanted to do something I could put a bit of heart into. I told one company I could start immediately and the other I could start a couple of weeks later, at which point I'd throw a sickie at the first one and decide which job I preferred. So I went to the first one, and it was just fucking horrible, doing those terrible adverts you see in newspapers — '10% off NOW!' inside a big star — and I thought, This isn't art, it's just toss. I stuck it for about a week.

The second place was called Greendow Commercials, and they did TV adverts, including the *TV Times* commercials. There was a connection with Granada Television too; most of the people working there had been graphic artists at Granada but had gone freelance and then moved here. They had a film editing suite, a rostrum camera and a sound dubbing suite, so just about everything was done in-house. I was employed as a runner and my boss was a guy called Simon Bosanquet, the nephew of Reginald Bosanquet, the newsreader. He was all right – he'd made a pop video for Bryan Ferry, 'A Hard Rain's A-Gonna Fall', of which he was very proud. All the people were great there; I really liked it. They were all creative types, and there was a much better atmosphere than at the job I'd endured at the town hall. I think I'd only really got this one because I had the scooter (I was a runner, so I had to drop films off to people around Manchester), but I certainly wasn't complaining. They were really into music there; you could play music all day on a record player. A lot of people – not all of them – would moan when I put mine on, saying, 'How can you listen to that shit?', but they were all older than me.

I hadn't been there very long when we received the bad news that the place was shutting down. We were called in to see the boss, a guy called Gerry Dow, and he said they were sorry but for one reason or another the place was going bust. However, they were planning on starting up something new soon and would be in touch. The two deputy bosses were called Brian Cosgrove and Mark Hall, and they were really good to me. I was on about ten pounds a week at the time, and they very kindly kept me on at eight quid a week to go up to their house and do odd jobs – helping out in the garden, that kind of thing – until they got the new company going.

Despite Greendow closing, Thames Television in London were keen to keep using part of the old department, so Mark and Brian were going to set up a new company in Chorlton. Sure enough, about six to eight months after the demise of Greendow, they set up Cosgrove Hall Animation, and I became a filler on kids' cartoons like *Jamie and the Magic Torch*, painting the colours on to the cells after they'd been drawn by the animators. It was definitely a step up from being a runner, but not having an art qualification higher than my O level did hold me back a bit. Everyone at Cosgrove Hall had been to art college except me, so I was always going to be behind in the pecking order. I liked the job, but it was very repetitive and, aware I couldn't really progress any further, I grew bored. I signed up for art classes at night school and, as usual, I turned up late for the first one. I opened the door and rushed in, and there in the middle of the room was a completely naked middle-aged woman, surrounded by people with easels. Everyone looked at me; I looked at everyone, I looked at the model; she looked at me and my jaw dropped. I hadn't expected that at all. Either way, it didn't really help me with graphic art and animation, which is what I needed to learn. I asked Cosgrove Hall if I could go on day release to college, but they said they couldn't really stretch to that.

So I started getting a bit restless, despite the fact I loved the people, especially an animator called Graham Garside. There was also a grumpy guy called Keith. You'd say good morning to him and he'd just look at you and not reply. He said to me one day, 'Look at you, dead skinny. One day you'll wake up, get out of bed and you'll have a gut, you mark my words.' It was such a horrible thing to say it actually made me laugh, but, well, he was right: that's exactly what happened. We made the tea for him, and he liked it really strong so we'd get a rotten old pair of socks, hoick a couple of old teabags out of the bin, put them in the socks, say, 'Do you want a brew, Keith?', squeeze this sock juice into a cup and give it to him.

Outside work, my time — and money — was mainly spent on

music and my scooter. There wasn't really much to do in Salford back then; it was a pretty closed community and you didn't leave very often. Occasionally, we'd venture a bit further: a load of scooter boys would go on a trip to Blackpool or Southport, for instance. Once, when I was about seventeen, a little group of us went all the way down to Brighton. I ended up being caught by the police, because I didn't have a tax disc. My grandfather, God bless his soul, had lent me £175 to buy my Lambretta, which was a lot of money in those days, and I was really proud of it (and proud of the fact that I paid my grandfather back out of my wages). He'd also given me £10 to buy a tax disc for it, but I didn't, I bought an album instead, *Argus* by Wishbone Ash, who I'd never heard of before but bought on the off-chance. I took it home and found I didn't like it at all, but when I took it back to the shop they wouldn't return my money. So I'd spent my road-tax money on an album I didn't like and, to add insult to injury I was stopped by the police on my scooter with L plates on and a girl on the back. And no road tax, of course, which meant I didn't have any insurance either. I got the book thrown at me for that one. I think I had a helmet on, but that was the only thing about the entire scenario that was legal and the police weren't very understanding.

A couple of years later, Peter Hook got a scooter and we started hanging around with other scooter boys. We'd race around Salford precinct, a concrete monstrosity of a shopping centre, and would often end up being pulled over by the police. They'd stop you on the flimsiest of premises and then try to extract information from you about local criminals — 'We'll let you off if you tell us about so-and-so' — but, even if we knew anything, we never grassed.

It was around this time that we started going to gigs. This came about mainly through Terry Mason, another friend from the back row of the grammar school who would go on to play several roles in the Joy Division and New Order stories and distinguish himself by not being particularly good at any of them. Terry was a misfit like us. He was all right, Terry, quite a harmless character, not particularly brilliant at any one thing, so we tried him in various roles to keep him involved and in the hope we could find something he *was* reasonably good at. We tried him as a drummer in the very early days of Joy Division. His mum bought him a drum kit, but it was about the worst drum kit on the planet – the legs were as thin as knitting needles and the kit would walk away from him as he was playing, leaving him on his stool reaching out after it. He looked more like a water-skier than a drummer. It didn't help that he was a terrible drummer, even for a punk band. He had no sense of rhythm and would just make a terrible racket.

Terry looked like a cross between the Gestapo officer from *Raiders of the Lost Ark* and Alan Carr, the comedian. I thought he was a funny guy – though his jokes were pretty disgusting, you couldn't help but laugh. Back in those early days, though, he was pretty well up on gigs, mainly because he used to read the music press, and we didn't. He'd spot gigs coming up that he thought we should go to and, usually, he was pretty spot on.

Sometimes the venues would turn out to be student places and we wouldn't get in because you had to have a student card, and often they wouldn't let us into gigs because we looked like skinheads even though we were suedeheads really. The Students' Union on Oxford Street would never let us in because we didn't look like hippies. It became frustrating, because all the bands back then only played at the universities and colleges. They obviously thought we were scum and, well, we were.

One place we could get into was the Free Trade Hall, and one of the first gigs I remember is seeing Lou Reed there in 1974. I was a big fan; I loved his solo stuff. I got into *Transformer*, his live album, *Rock and Roll Animal*, and *Berlin* before I'd even heard the Velvet Underground. I think this was the *Sally Can't Dance* tour, and I was really looking forward to seeing him live. The band came on and started playing 'Sweet Jane' and I was thinking about how great it was going to be when Lou himself finally came on. Then this short-arse guy with blond hair started singing, and I thought, that can't be Lou Reed, can it? But it was.

He was off his chump — *really* off his chump; he kept smashing microphones one after the other — but it was a fantastic concert, and the audience was really up for it. I guess in a way this was my first punk gig, but I didn't know it. They finished the set with a storming 'Goodnight Ladies' and trooped off. Everyone expected them to come out for an encore, but the stage remained resolutely empty and the crowd began to grow restless. I was near this guy who looked like a Rod Stewart clone and he lobbed this beer bottle from about five hundred yards, with phenomenal accuracy, straight through the skin of the bass drum. And that was it. Pandemonium. People swarming on to the stage, getting into fights with the roadies and security, everything. Lou Reed never came back to Manchester after that, all because of one bloke with a dodgy haircut and incredible aim.

Hooky liked Deep Purple. I wasn't so sure, but we ended up with tickets to see them, and off we went. I remember having a bad tooth abscess at the time but I was talked into going. It's never a good idea going to see a band with a tooth abscess, but it's even worse when it's a band you're not that keen on. There was one song where the singer was screaming higher and higher as the song went on — 'Child In Time', I think it was — and my tooth was throbbing away as if his voice was actually pulling at the nerve. It was agony. There were quite a few knobheads in the audience as well, and the whole experience was doing my head in.

At one point the keyboard player was immersed in an

interminable prog-rock solo about twenty minutes long, my tooth was agony, and I was thinking, This is really fucking shit, it's too loud and my tooth's killing me. I was feeling properly sorry for myself when, in the middle of this endless solo, the keyboardist started playing 'I Do Like To Be Beside The Seaside', as if it was some kind of witty aside. I thought, Ok, he's having a bit of a joke, that's quite funny then another ten minutes went past and he went into the theme from *Coronation Street*. At that point I thought, 'He's fucking taking the piss out of us, the soft southern — I bet he's from London!' That was the last straw. I walked out. We ended up playing with Deep Purple in France a few years ago. They'd cut their solos right down.

Santana at the Hardrock Hall in Stretford was another memorable gig. It was November 1972 and I'd never been to see a big American group like that before. I loved the sound of Carlos Santana's guitar and I really liked the way he played, so it was a gig I was pretty excited about. But at that stage he'd just entered his jazzy, metaphysical phase — his album *Caravanserai* had just come out — and he came on and said, 'I'd like to begin with a few moments' meditation,' Meditation. In Stretford, south Manchester. He put his hands together, bowed his head and just stood there in silence. Naturally, this didn't really go down too well with a crowd of Mancunian music fans who'd already enjoyed a few pints. 'Fucking get on with it' was about the politest comment that broke the meditative silence.

The Buxton Festival, out in the Derbyshire hills, was another one that stood out. Me, Hooky and a couple of scooter boys headed over there, only to find the field packed with Hells Angels. We thought we were in trouble, a bunch of short-haired lads at what was basically a long hair event, but we didn't get any hassle.

Family were on when we arrived, and I was really impressed with them because they looked as though they were completely off their faces. I thought, That's fucking great, they just don't give a shit. Wishbone Ash were on the bill too, the architects of my tax-disc downfall. They ended up as headliners, when Curved Air refused to go on because it was too cold. The *Argus* album I hadn't liked had really taken off for Wishbone Ash, so I thought I'd give them another go — but I still thought it was a load of twaddle.

The main thing I remember about that night is a spectacular meteor shower. Out there in the hills, there was no light pollution, so we probably had the best view in the country. There was a huge canopy of stars above our heads with specks of light flinging themselves across the sky and disappearing. They played the *Doctor Who* theme through the PA, which made the whole thing pretty wacky. I was awestruck; I sat there looking up, my mouth hanging open, absolutely enchanted. It probably sounds a bit naive now, but I'd never been to a festival before, let alone seen a meteor shower. I thought it was amazing.

For all the celestial fireworks, ill-conceived mass meditation workshops and dead-eye bottle throwing, however, there was to be one gig that has come to be remembered above all the others. A gig that has, for better or worse, been analysed, mythologized and proselytized probably more than any other concert in the history of music. It was a gig that many identify as one that changed everything.

And I was there.

Chapter Five

Rebellion

One day early in the summer of 1976 Terry Mason showed us a copy of the *New Musical Express* and started gushing about this new band he'd been reading about called the Sex Pistols. 'They keep getting in fights and being canned off,' he said. 'They sound great, just the kind of thing we'd like.' He'd found out they were playing at the Lesser Free Trade Hall in Manchester on 4 June so off we went, me, Hooky, Terry and a couple of others. There weren't many people there at all – I've heard people say the crowd was about forty – but it's become such a milestone of Manchester musical heritage that if everyone who's claimed they were there had actually been, they'd fill Old Trafford.

It was still early days for the Pistols; they were just about to properly break, and certainly in Manchester nobody really knew who they were. They sounded worth seeing, though, so we wandered up and paid our fifty pences to Malcolm McLaren, who was on the door, on the till and on the make, and went in, not really sure what to expect.

It's an occasion that's gone down in history, as much for the people who were in the audience as the gig itself: Mark E. Smith was there, so was Morrissey, so were Tony Wilson and Paul Morley, and the gig had been arranged by Pete Shelley and Howard Devoto of the Buzzcocks. I wasn't really bothered about who else was there: once the band came on and started playing I was too blown away to worry about who was in the crowd. From the moment they swaggered on to the stage, picked up their instruments and launched into 'Did You No Wrong', I knew that this was something different. It was their attitude that hit me; there was a real spite in their performance, sheer aggression combined with an indifference to the audience that occasionally bordered on outright contempt. It was like nothing I'd ever seen before; it was along the lines of Lou Reed's anarchic performance at the Free Trade Hall, but about as far from Santana's call to meditation as you could possibly imagine. This was something special.

For the first time at a live performance I found I could truly identify with and relate to the people on the stage. We'd had the same kind of 'fuck authority' attitude ourselves since we were at school, this underlying resentment at being told what to do all the bloody time and how to behave. At school it was the teachers, and when we left school it was the need to fit into a preordained role in a society that I didn't feel a part of. At every turn there seemed to be older people telling us what to do and being quick to remind us how shit we were. Then the Sex Pistols came along and made us feel *we* were right. Not only that, they showed us that we'd been right all along. Punk was something giving us a voice for the first time, and that voice was screaming at the top of its lungs there right in front of me. It justified our outlook and at the same time made us feel we *were* worth something after all.

That night has developed a mythology of its own over the last thirty-odd years. Rock 'n' roll had begun as something raw and simple, but by the mid-seventies it had become largely about people showing off. Before the Pistols and the other punk bands came along, music seemed like a private members club that belonged increasingly to virtuosos. A great deal — but not all — of the music around at that time was overblown, self-indulgent, bloated nonsense. Prog rock was the main culprit, and it seemed to have stifled music, smothering it beneath a thick layer of concepts, capes and navel-gazing noodling that was far too pleased with itself for its own good.

I'd been a very young kid in the sixties, listening to the Stones and The Beatles, The Animals, The Kinks, etc. etc., bands who played great songs and had great guitar sounds. The whole was always greater than the individual for those bands, but by the mid-seventies a lot of music had taken a turn for the pompous. There was a cult of cleverness: you had bands like Emerson, Lake and Palmer and Yes, with their interminable concept albums, which were the antithesis of everything I liked about music.

Punk and the Pistols blew a sneering path right through the middle of all that puffed-up musical pomposity. They arrived at exactly the right time, with exactly the right attitude. As we stood in that sticky-floored room at the top of the Free Trade Hall watching a group of lads who seemed a bit like us but belting out this wall of sheer attitude, it confirmed that we were not alone, that there were others out there who felt the way we did. I suppose I must have had an inkling that this wasn't going to be just another gig, because I took along a cassette player and recorded it (when I took it home and played it back, though, it was completely distorted — it could have been my rubbish tape recorder, or maybe the Pistols just sounded like that . . .) but, either way, something resonated with us. Whether it was a completely new revelation or whether it had just nourished something already planted is hard to say. But there was something in the air that summer, and we'd caught a whiff of its heady, sweaty aroma.

Sometimes I think people make a bit more of the significance of that night than was probably the case. The way I look at it is this: there was at that time a movement called punk that struck a chord with a lot of people, just like later there was a movement called acid house that would do likewise. We'd go to punk concerts because that was what was happening, the same as we'd later go to acid-house nights. It was a great experience, there's no doubt about that, and the Pistols obviously went on to be really influential. The fact there were certain people in the audience that night who went on to do certain things makes it a good story, but has a wider context been grafted on to it in later years by people who weren't even there? To me, it wasn't exactly a shaft-of-sunlight-from-the-heavens moment, as some have made out, but it was certainly inspirational, and there is a subtle difference.

I think the mythology that's grown up around that gig needs a certain amount of focus. Punk was an interesting, exciting new movement of which a few people in Manchester were aware through the music press and certain people attended that concert as a result. I'd seen the Buzzcocks before I saw the Sex Pistols — they had some great songs and they were also an influence on us and should certainly not go unmentioned just because that Pistols gig has become such a cultural touchstone.

I believe some people can pick up on a kind of zeitgeist, and that zeitgeist is the catalyst for the release of their creativity or expression. I don't think it's a conscious thing; it's not learnt behaviour but something else, something instinctive. There are different ways in which a person can acquire knowledge: going to school, listening to the teachers and writing down everything they say, learning by rote being the traditional way. But there is another way, and it evolves through observing the world and making up your own mind based on what you experience; absorbing the things that are right for you and interpreting them, filtering them through your own perception and learning how and when to trust your instincts. That's how I discovered and explored music and how I developed my influences in order to create it myself.

Punk had become the main focus of our cultural lives during that summer of 1976. We liked the anti-authoritarian aspect of it, but one thing people often forget about punk is that one of its primary messages was not to take yourself too seriously. Yes, rail against the system, but remember to have a laugh while you're doing it. You're young, you should be enjoying yourself despite all the shit you have to put up with. There was a fantastic energy in the music, like nothing I'd ever heard. At that age, in your teens and your early twenties, you're brimming with energy and need an outlet for it. Punk gigs were perfect; you could just go crazy: it was as much like going to a party as being at a gig. It was similar to acid house in that way, only without the drugs. Well, maybe different drugs.

From a childhood that had featured very little in the way of music, I'd had the most tremendous adolescent crash course. It was as if I'd been moving quickly up through the gears musically, and punk saw me changing up to fifth. In the aftermath of the Pistols gig I looked at the abandoned guitar my mother had bought me years earlier in a new light. Now I'd heard punk, suddenly it had a purpose beyond just standing in the corner of my room gathering dust and being handy for hanging clothes on. So one night I closed my bedroom door, sat on the bed, blew off some of the dust, opened the 'how to play a guitar' book I'd bought and set about learning to play.

It wasn't an auspicious start: the first pages of the book gave instructions on how to tune the guitar, but I didn't know which way was up and which was down. I didn't have the most finely honed ear at that stage anyway, so the noises I was making must have sounded pretty horrible. But I kept at it, because music had become the biggest thing in my life. I'd listened to it, I'd bought it, I'd watched people playing it, and now I was determined to make it myself.

After the Pistols gig Hooky had gone into Manchester and bought himself a bass guitar and a book like mine on how to play it. I think it cost him about £35, which was quite a lot back then. The trouble with the books was that they were based on the twelve-bar progression, which forms the basis of nearly all blues and rock 'n' roll. All the examples of songs in the book dated from the fifties, real hoary old standards in which we had no interest. I didn't like the blues much anyhow, and I didn't like rock 'n' roll: what I wanted to learn about was punk and, funnily enough, there was no book out there that could teach me that.

Despite this, I kept plugging away, learning chords late into the night until my red-raw fingertips hardened and the beginners' pains in my hands finally began to subside. It didn't take me long to realize that once you have the basic major and minor chords under your belt you've pretty much got 90 per cent of everything: the rest is all about your imagination, and you definitely can't buy books on that. Once you've got those basic building blocks, you can go on to make something out of them. You don't need to know how to play 'Rock Around The Clock' or 'Heartbreak Hotel' to make your own music; just get a few chords together, make up a few scales of your own, and away you go. If it sounds good to you, that's all that counts.

Music began to take up most of our spare time. Where Hooky and I had gone to my grandmother's and messed around with hypnotism, and taken the piss out of each other and sat around talking about scooters and spark plugs, in the summer of 1976 we started trying to make music together. Our own music. It became a regular Sunday-night thing at the house in Alfred Street. My gran had a gramophone on which she'd play her old 78s, but when I looked at it I didn't just see an old gramophone, I saw the closest thing we had to a guitar amp and set about turning it into one. I removed the stylus and soldered a couple of jack plugs into its place, Hooky plugged his bass into one, I plugged my guitar into the other and we had a sound. It wasn't the greatest PA we'd ever play through, it certainly wasn't the greatest sound we'd ever have, but there was a definite semblance of something coming out of the speaker. It wasn't very loud, but it had valves and it *glowed*!

We weren't virtuosos by any stretch of the imagination, but because we were creating our own music almost as we learned how to play, it was an ideal way to develop our own methodology and sound. We had no preconceptions about chord progressions or scales, so we were able to just try things out until we'd hit on something that sounded good to us. I'd be saying, 'Oh that sounds great with that chord, what about if you hold that note a bit longer but I change the chord?' We were just fumbling around, like a pair of kids finding their way in the first year at primary school, not really sure what we were doing, but we'd get there in the end through trial and error. We kept this up for a good while, spending every weekend working away until we realized we'd reached the next logical step in forming a band: we started to think about finding a singer.

Initially, we thought about whether we knew someone already who might be a candidate. The list would have been pretty short. I can't remember exactly who was on it, but a few months ago I bumped into an old friend from those times called David Wroe, and he told me, 'I was going to be your singer at the start but my mum wouldn't let me.' I'm sure a few names were bandied about, but there were no serious contenders from within our circle. Essentially, we wanted someone who was into the same scene and liked the sort of music that we liked; who seemed like a good person, wasn't an arsehole, was someone we could get on with.

In the end we wrote out an advert and stuck it in the window of the old Virgin Records shop on Lever Street in Manchester, the obvious place, because that's where everyone went to buy their punk records. Virgin had also become one of the main meeting places in the city for people who were in bands, starting bands or thinking of starting bands, so was an active hub for would-be musicians. We had a phone in the flat in Greengate, so I put my number on the ad, stuck it in the window, went home and waited for it to ring.

I had a few calls, mostly from complete basket cases. I remember going to see one guy who'd sounded vaguely promising on the phone who lived over in Didsbury. I took Terry with me, we knocked on the door and this hippie answered, hair practically down to his waist. He was wearing massive flares and had a top on that looked like it was made from a cushion cover with holes cut out for his arms and head. I took one look at him and thought he just wasn't for us. He did little to dispel this first impression by putting a couple of cushions down and inviting us to sit on the floor. Terry and I were already giving each other sideways looks when he said he'd dig out some of his poetry and sing it to us. Poetry? This didn't sound much like what we had in mind. Next thing we knew the guy had smoothed out these crumpled sheets of paper on the floor, reached behind the sofa, pulled out a balalaika and started strumming away, singing this soppy poetry at us. What made it even more awkward was that he was staring right into our eyes from barely three feet away, all the while singing this plaintive, winsome nonsense. I didn't dare catch Terry's eye, but I could hear him sniggering. I was doing everything I could not to burst out laughing, then Terry let out this little snort and that was it, we both just fell about. Eventually, we said, 'Look, sorry mate, we just came here to tell you the job's been filled, but thanks anyway.' And with that we bolted for the door and legged it back to Salford, doubled up with laughter.

That seemed to set the tone for the next couple of weeks. I'd get all these crank phone calls – 'Are you a punk, then? Are you? You're a punk, are you? Well *fuck off* then' – and the ones that weren't just abusive were from weirdos. It had got to the stage where I was almost dreading the sound of the phone.

One night the phone rang at about eight o'clock. I sighed, went into my mother's bedroom and lifted the receiver. 'Yeah, hello,' I said flatly. A voice at the other end said, 'I'm phoning about the singer's job in the Virgin window.' I rolled my eyes and asked who he was. He said his name was Ian, and immediately I thought, Hang on, this one doesn't sound mad. This lad sounds all right. I asked what sort of music he was into and he said he was into punk, Iggy and the Stooges, Velvet Underground, all that kind of stuff. It was then that I thought I recognized his voice. I said to him that I thought we might have met; told him that I hung out with a guy called Hooky and a guy called Terry. Did he have a donkey jacket with 'HATE' written on the back? 'Yeah, I do,' he said. 'That's me.' I told him we'd met the previous week at a gig at the Electric Circus: he was one of the two Ians (he had a mate called Iain that he hung around with, and they were known imaginatively as 'the two Ians').

'Yeah,' he said. 'I'm Ian Curtis.'

'Oh right,' I said. 'Well, you've got the job.'

I was so relieved to get a call from someone who wasn't a weirdo or a mad hippie, let alone the fact that this was someone I'd already met. I'd bumped into him before and he wasn't a lunatic – those were the criteria I took into consideration when I took the executive decision to say yes to Ian Curtis.

'Oh, right,' he said. 'Well, what happens now?'

We arranged a rehearsal in a room above a pub in Weaste called the Grey Mare, which was the headquarters of an organization called the Royal Antediluvian Order of Buffaloes. They were a kind of freemasons for the working and middle classes. At one end of the room we used there was a great big chest full of buffalo skins which they wore for their ceremonies. Despite this, it was quite a good room to rehearse in, and it was made even better because it turned out Ian had his own PA system.

At this stage we'd decided to let Terry try being a second guitarist after his failed attempt at being our drummer. I'd bought a Zenith guitar amp, but it was terrible, this horrible transistor thing that had a really thin, clean sound. I was trying to do punk music, but it made us sound more like Mark Knopfler: I kept turning it up, but no matter how hard I drove it, it just seemed to sound cleaner and cleaner and really hurt your ears. (Incomprehensibly, I've just bought another one on eBay. I don't know why. Nostalgia?)

Ian's PA amp was also rubbish: it sounded horrible and distorted, but his speakers were OK. We got him a new amp and Terry used the old one to put his guitar through, but he played deliberately quietly so you wouldn't hear him anyway.

The next thing was to find a drummer to complete the jigsaw: the classic punk line-up of singer, guitar, bass and drums. This turned out to be a process that featured another litany of lunatics, nutters and arseholes, and that's even after we'd tried Terry. Drummers, it turned out, are even worse in that respect than singers, and we ended up auditioning quite a few. Some of them were decent enough drummers but were complete pains in the arse. I remember one guy who seemed to think he was auditioning *us*, to see if we were good enough for him. Another guy was studying to be a PE teacher at some college somewhere, and he seemed quite promising but we didn't feel that he really fitted in. Trouble was, we'd already told him he'd got the gig. Hooky and I drove over to Middleton to see him and, feeling a bit bad about it, on the way we stopped at a shop and bought him a box of chocolates, thinking it might soften the blow. We arrived at his college, walked in and found him fooling around with his mates, flicking wet towels at each other, real student antics.

We called him over, sat him down and told him we had some bad news. We didn't have the guts to tell him we didn't want him, so we made out that the whole band wasn't really working out and we were calling it a day. We apologized for messing him around and solemnly handed over this double-layer box of Milk Tray as a token of our appreciation. He was a little non-plussed to say the least, but it seemed like the right thing to do at the time. We were quite nice people and felt bad about it, especially as we'd never sacked anyone before.

But we were still without a drummer, a situation whose urgency was expedited when our first gig landed in our laps, opening for the Buzzcocks on 29 May 1977 at the Electric Circus. We'd become friends with the Buzzcocks and would ask them for advice. We didn't know anything about amps, guitars or any of the things you needed to know about being in a band. We used to drive around with them in Terry's car sometimes. He had a really, really shit car, a Vauxhall Viva: the seats didn't recline, no central locking, no cup holders . . . One day, the Buzzcocks were in the back, I was in the front and Terry was driving. In the door pocket he kept loads of sheets of sandpaper. It was a 'project car', which he was in the process of doing up, even while he was driving it, and every time he'd stop at traffic lights he'd wind his window down, get a sheet of sandpaper, lean out and start sanding down the bodywork. It was so knackered that at every other set of lights the engine would conk out, and the only way he could get it to start again was to get this rubber tube, suck petrol out of the fuel tank into his mouth, get someone to turn the ignition over, and then he'd blow petrol into the carburettor to get the engine going again. God knows how the Buzzcocks gave us the time of day with stuff like that going on. They did call Terry 'petrol sucker' after that, but Terry already called Pete Shelley 'stale butter breath'. Neither of them knew, of course. They could be pretty weird, too, though, the Buzzcocks. Once, Pete Shelley pulled out his wallet, produced this horrible scaly-looking thing like an old rotten cornflake and showed it to me. I said, 'What on earth's that?' He said, 'I fell over the other day, cut my elbow and this is the scab.' Anyway, Richard Boon, the Buzzcocks' manager, was very supportive of us and had got us this date at the Electric Circus, which we were really excited about. Trouble was, at this stage we had neither a name nor a drummer. As well as providing us with our first gig, the Buzzcocks also tried to help us out with a name. We had a few knocking around that we were discussing: Hooky had come up with The Out of Town Torpedoes and someone else suggested The Slaves of Venus — imagine if either of those had caught on. We had to come up with a name, and quickly. Richard Boon suggested Stiff Kittens, which appealed to us at first because it sounded like a good punk name, but we discussed it and thought about how long a name like that was going to last? Also, if I'm honest, the fact we hadn't thought of it ourselves also contributed to us deciding it wasn't really a viable proposition. The name we did come up with that we could all agree on was Warsaw. We felt that the music we were making had a cold, austere feeling to it, and Warsaw seemed to us to be a cold, austere place (even though none of us had ever been there). So we became Warsaw, a name that was never intended to be much more than a place holder. It would do for the time being.

At that point we weren't looking to go out and make an immediate blazing impact on the world, we just wanted to do our first gig, acquire the experience of playing live and learn what it was like to stand up and play in front of an audience. This was to be our first foot through the door, our first low key step on the path. Anyway, it turned out there was already a band called Warsaw Pakt, so we'd have had to change our name at some point in any case, but for the time being we were Warsaw. As I recall, it was a decision made too late for the gig posters, on which we were Stiff Kittens.

So, we'd sorted ourselves out with a name and shortly before the gig we drafted in a drummer called Tony Tabac. We were ready for our first gig. Well, readyish.

Chapter Six

Awaking

The Electric Circus was in a part of Manchester called Collyhurst. I believe the building started out as a variety club and had been a cinema, but by 1977 it was a well-known punk venue. I think The Clash played there; certainly many of the punk bands coming to Manchester would have played there. It was quite a rough area, and the club was opposite the Collyhurst Flats, from where the kids would stand on the balconies lobbing bottles down at the punks queuing to get in. The punks couldn't really complain because, well, throwing bottles off a balcony was quite a punk thing to do and, anyway, it looked quite good fun. The Electric Circus was a really good venue, though, and there were definitely worse options to host our first tentative foray into live performance.

On the night of 29 May 1977, while the punks outside were dodging bottles falling from the sky, we were inside finishing our soundcheck, sipping our rider beer and counting down the minutes until our first ever gig. It was a set that would sound pretty unrecognizable now, it must be said. I don't think any of the songs we played that night have survived the test of time. In our sessions at the Grey Mare we'd written and rehearsed a bunch of songs, maybe eight or nine, over a period of a couple of weeks that were all very punk, very 'one-two-three-four!'. They were shite really, thinking back, but even then we knew it was all part of a learning process, that the songs we'd write later would be better, have more depth, be better crafted, would sound more like *us* rather than like every other punk band thrashing away at a hundred miles an hour. We were like apprentice bricklayers: with that first set of songs we were building a wall just to see how it was done, in the full knowledge that afterwards we were going to knock down that wall and build a house. The songs we played that night at the Electric Circus were the wall, and the house we'd build after that would become *Unknown Pleasures*.

We were first on, before a band from Newcastle called Penetration. The Buzzcocks would close the night. I think John Cooper Clarke was on the bill as well. On the face of it, things didn't look entirely promising: we were calling ourselves a different name from the one on the poster, had a drummer we barely knew and a set of songs that even we would admit were never destined to be classics. It wasn't the most meticulously structured, smoothly prepared debut in music history.

You might expect, given that it was a landmark moment at the beginning of a long and remarkable story, that I'd have every moment of that first gig etched into my memory, but I've played literally thousands of gigs of all shapes and sizes since, so it's very hard to put myself back in the situation of playing in front of an audience for the first time. Having said that, I do remember a little of what it felt like. When I was a kid back at the house on Alfred Street my grandfather had taught me to swim by putting a stool on the floor and having me lie on it while he showed me the different strokes. I'd be teetering on the stool, arms and legs going like the clappers, thrashing away at the air, while he instructed me on the basics. Eventually, it was time to go to the swimming baths, slip apprehensively into the water and put what I'd learned into practice. That first gig was a little like the moment I first pushed myself away from the side of the pool. Nothing to hold on to, no going back, trusting in myself and what I'd learned to keep my head above water and reach the other side. That's the overriding feeling I've retained from that gig.

As for the specifics, I remember very little, other than I broke a guitar string in the middle of a solo during a song called 'Novelty'. To be honest, I don't really regard that first gig as a big deal. If, during this life, I've climbed a mountain to get to where I am now, then that was just the first glimpse of the mountain, that's all. I had no feeling that this was what I was born to do. It was an important experience, of course: our first lessons in stagecraft, deciding who stands where, how to set up on a stage, how to do a soundcheck, riders, dressing rooms and finding out what it feels like to be on a stage performing before a room full of people. It also answered a few questions that I'd had in my head, questions like, Do I really want to do this? What is being a musician about? What is being in a band about? What does all of it really mean? And it raised some new questions. There was a huge part of music that I didn't like at the time — mainstream pop in the seventies, most daytime radio, shit like that — and suddenly I'd found myself possibly about to become a part of that world, part of that system. Was I going to get sucked into it and become a cog in this machine called the music business? What sort of control would I have? So that first gig wasn't life-changing, but I had found out that yes, I could swim at the deep end. Very badly, admittedly — I was just about keeping my head above the surface and I needed a few more lessons – but I could do it. I wanted to do it and I wanted to do it my own way. I also wanted to be *good* at it.

A couple of reviews came out afterwards. One was good, apparently (I think Paul Morley was there and said he'd liked us, but he'd like us better in six months' time, and he did), but I looked at the other review, which was really bad. It was totally dismissive and singled me out in particular as looking too young to be in a band and claiming I came across like a public schoolboy. I thought, Well, what's wrong with looking young? And I clearly wasn't a public schoolboy: reverse snobbery is one of my pet hates. I was learning early on that it's best never to read reviews, good or bad. (These days, I can't even look at photographs of myself, let alone read reviews or interviews.)

By this time, we'd had to move on from the buffalo skins and the Grey Mare pub and found a new rehearsal space. A new landlord arrived who, strangely enough, decided he didn't need a punk band making a racket in a room above his pub and threw us out. We tried an Irish pub, and the landlord told us we could rehearse there, but when we went in to set up he told us to fuck off. We also tried a church hall, and they too advised us we were better off looking elsewhere, because there was no room at the inn for a bunch of scruffy herberts toting noisy guitars. I think we then moved to another pub down the road from the Grey Mare. Back in the early days, we moved around to quite a few places. Recently, I found a review of the Grey Mare on the Internet. It said it was a dive, 'but probably the best you'll find on Eccles New Rd'. The guy wrote that the last time he'd passed it he had to 'swerve to avoid two drunken old men stumbling out after a fight, dripping blood on to the tram lines'. Online reviews aren't always right, but I think we'll wait for the area to be a little bit 'gentrified' before New Order go looking to move back there for rehearsals.

Anyhow, despite this peripatetic existence, we were learning all the time, and learning fast. In addition, we were finding out how serious we wanted to be about what we were doing and where we wanted to take it. There was no moment of catharsis as such, but we found ourselves being gradually seduced by what we were achieving to the point where it became the most important focus of our lives. We found that we loved coming up with ideas for songs, loved playing our instruments, even in such a naïve way, and loved the social aspect of it all: going to gigs and seeing other bands, watching, listening and learning. After all, when push came to shove, we were all just fans of music at heart: it filled the hole that living in Salford in the seventies had opened in us.

What the Sex Pistols had done was show us that you didn't have to be a virtuoso to write music and lyrics that could affect those who heard them, to create songs that mean something to people. Energy was one of the keys, not how dextrous the lead guitarist was or how many synths the keyboard player could have banked around him. We were underpinned by a 'fuck you' attitude to the sections of society we felt were stopping us: teachers, the police, older people telling us how we should be, what we should be doing with our lives. It's an uncomfortable fact, however, that youth is always right: it's the runner that picks up the baton that needs it, not the one who's giving it away. At this point in British social and cultural history, being a misfit was for once not just an advantage but an opportunity, and there were very few opportunities for a regular working-class kid from Salford with next to no qualifications. And we were having a *ball*.

Music had grown quickly to become a very important, if not the defining, factor in my life. It was a little as if I'd been born blind and then suddenly at the age of about sixteen had my sight restored and been utterly overwhelmed by all the light, colour, contrast and beauty I saw. There had been music in my house when I was growing up, but not much. What little there was was my grandparents' taste. My gran used to sing sometimes. She used to love singing and once told me that in her younger days she'd thought about becoming a professional singer. But she sang old music hall numbers from the thirties that weren't really what a small boy in the sixties wanted to hear. Sometimes the radio would be on and I'd hear music on that, but most of it, with a few exceptions, was rubbish to my ears: all balladeers and crooners on what I think was the BBC Light Programme. (We had a television when I was a little older but it could only receive one channel: ITV. I think my granddad could have got up a ladder and turned the aerial a few degrees so that we could have got the BBC, but for whatever reason he couldn't be arsed. We could hear the sound of BBC television, but there was no picture. I remember that's how I found out about the 1966 Aberfan disaster, where a whole school had been destroyed with the children in it: hearing the sound of the television news but seeing only ghostly distorted pictures and everyone in the house being very quiet at this terrible news.)

From the unlikeliest of starts, then, music had become the driving force in my life. And now the band was finding its feet, learning what to do and — equally importantly — what not to do. We were going to see other bands as much as we could, going to punk clubs and hearing what they were playing and trying really hard to get more gigs. Finally, a couple of months or so after the Electric Circus gig, we settled on our perfect line-up: a huge step forward. Tony Tabac was a good drummer but, for whatever reason, he didn't last and we replaced him with a guy called Steve Brotherdale, who played with another local band called Panik. Again, a decent drummer, but another guy who wasn't quite right for us. For one thing, he used to bring his girlfriend along to all of the gigs, and we didn't really like that; we thought the band should just be about the band. It was like bringing your girlfriend to work.

Thankfully, we found Steve Morris, who'd answered an ad Ian had placed in the window of the Jones Music Store in Macclesfield — a shop which is still there, incidentally — and it was immediately obvious he was the right guy for us. He was a great drummer, for a start, and he just seemed to balance the rest of us perfectly.

Steve is a hard character to define, but I'll give it a go. He doesn't like confrontation at all, to the extent that he'll rarely give you a yes or no answer to a question. Instead of telling you what he thinks, he may, if you're very lucky, tell you what he doesn't think. He's quite eccentric, almost in a John Cleese kind of way. He collects tanks, for example. Not models — real, full-size tanks. I believe he was quite wild when he was at school and he was quite wild in the band but, if he feels like it, I'll leave him to say more about that in his own book. He's a drummer, and drummers are odd people. They like hitting things for a living and Steve hits things very, very well.

Brandon Flowers from The Killers said when he first met us, 'I get everyone, but I just can't read Steve. I don't think he likes me.' Not true, Brandon! Steve is just . . . well . . . Steve, and is actually very funny indeed. When we first met him, it was clear he was very chilled out and had that Macc thing going on, in common with Ian, a tangible Macc mentality that's hard to define. I'm still not quite sure what it is even today, but whatever it was, they had it, and with Hooky and me coming from Salford it was a good combination. Steve was a great drummer, he lived near Ian in Macclesfield, he had his own kit, he had a car and he was a nice bloke. Perfect. He was — and still is — a bit odd, but odd in a really good way. Ian Curtis, Steve Morris, Peter Hook and me. The jigsaw was complete.

This sounded the death knell for Terry as a member of the band, so we had to find something else for him to do. So we made him our manager, a move that produced results that can most politely be described as 'mixed'. For example, at one point during that summer of 1977 we'd made some demos of material we'd written, and Ian asked Terry to make copies and send the tapes off to record companies. Days turned into weeks, and we'd had no response whatsoever. Ian was fuming, saying, 'Those songs were all right, what's going on?' I took Terry to one side and asked him whether he'd actually sent off the tapes. He said he has, and pulled one out of his pocket. He put it on and the quality was atrocious from the start, all hissy and clicky. Then, all of a sudden, a few seconds in, the music was drowned out by the theme from *Coronation Street*. Not only that, next you heard Terry's mum's voice saying, 'Terry, come and get your tea before it goes cold.'

I looked at him. 'Terry,' I said levelly, 'how did you make the copies?'

'Well,' he said, 'I got two tape recorders and put them next to each other with a microphone so I could record one from the other. I thought it would save a bit of money on having proper copies made.' And he'd sent all these tapes off to some of the biggest record companies in the country. He wasn't exactly Brian Epstein.

We were writing so many songs by this stage that the songs on the demo were probably not representative of our output even by the time Terry had got around to posting his iffy tapes. Joy Division songs were always a collaborative thing. I'd come up with the guitar and keyboard parts, Hooky would write his bass line and Steve would contribute his drum part. While Ian didn't write music, he had a terrific ear: he was brilliant at spotting a great riff or a hook for a song, so he'd have that input as well. Normally, I'd arrange this rough collection of parts, saying, 'That's a good bit for the chorus' or 'We can put that bit in the verse.' By then we'd have the basics of a crude but coherent track which we'd record on the world's worst cassette recorder, using the world's worst microphone, then Ian would take the tape away and write the lyrics.

Ian was a wonderful writer; he loved words and had a natural gift for them. He loved writing and had a box file of stuff he'd written, a jumble of paper on which he'd jotted down ideas or phrases to return to later as well as properly polished, honed material. He usually wrote with a bottle of something close at hand. I remember he liked Carlsberg Special Brew, which was horrible stuff, like drinking fizzy cough medicine. He'd either pick out some words he'd already written that fitted the song or he'd write some new ones. It was a straightforward process for Ian, because he was in his element when writing. When I'm writing lyrics it takes a really concerted effort because I don't find it easy. I have to force myself to sit down and find the right words and phrases and make them fit the music. Ian was basically a Mount Etna of words; they would erupt out of him. He would be writing anyway, even if he didn't have a song to work on. If Ian hadn't been in a band, he would have still been writing something, somewhere, somehow.

Of course, we studiously ignored what he was writing about. It all sounded so bloody *personal*.

You might have seen Ian playing guitar on a couple of tracks, most notably 'Love Will Tear Us Apart', but also 'Heart and Soul'. Basically, we made him play the guitar because we wanted him to join in more, to make the process more inclusive, which meant he was playing under duress. His guitar was a Vox Phantom, a curious-looking, angular thing that had its own peculiar sound and lots of switches, the purpose of most of which was a complete mystery to him. He'd bought it because he thought it looked cool. Some of the control knobs even had misspellings on them. It looked mad, this guitar, which was the main reason Ian liked it. (I'd go on to use Ian's guitar later, when we recorded 'Everything's Gone Green' with New Order, because it had this particular thin sound I wanted that you wouldn't find anywhere else.) His playing was pretty rudimentary (on 'Heart and Soul', it's just a D minor chord all the way through) and he was a very reluctant guitarist. Fair play to him, he gave it a go, but obviously words were his gift and his strength.

Ian read a hell of a lot — philosophy, and he really liked William Burroughs; *Junkie* was a favourite of his — but we'd never really sit around and talk about books. We'd never really talk about music either, any of us: we found the more we talked about it, the worse the music we wrote became. We'd sometimes come into rehearsals and play records on a record player, one or more of us raving about Iggy or Bowie's new record, or maybe some older stuff, and possibly suggest that we wrote something like what we were hearing, but it would never turn out quite like what we were hearing. Generally, we avoided talking about music and bands, something which maybe contributed to our developing what was a unique sound.

We'd never play other people's songs either. When Rob Gretton came along as our manager, he effectively barred us from playing cover versions, but we were never really that way inclined anyway. Why take time learning someone else's song when we could be spending that time writing a new one of our own? We once tried learning '7 And 7 Is' by Love, but we got about eight bars into it and gave up. I think when it got to a difficult bit we just decided it was too hard, scratched our heads and went back to our own stuff.

The way we wrote, with the three of us coming up with the music and Ian adding the lyrics, meant we could put a song together pretty fast: we found the process easy, it worked and it was quick. When Ian died, all that would change, it upset that natural balance, but the songs came thick and fast in those early days. We were pretty focused too — when we had a gig coming up, we'd try and write a new song for that gig and see how it went down. There's no better barometer than audience reaction and it was a really good way of honing our set and identifying the songs that worked and the songs that didn't.

We wrote so many songs using that trusted formula that it's hard to look back and separate them. 'Love Will Tear Us Apart' emerged in that way and has proved to be one of the most enduring songs we've ever written, if not *the* most. It remains a key part of our live set and it's won a slew of awards over the years: as recently as 2012, an Irish radio station presented us with a gong for 'the greatest song of all time', and Ian's daughter, Natalie, travelled to Dublin with us to receive it. We wrote the song more than three decades ago, yet something about it continues to resonate with people, and generation after generation seems to discover it anew. I have to confess that we had absolutely no idea that it would take off the way it did; at the time it was just one song among the many we were writing, and it came together so effortlessly. I suppose subsequent events made it an incredibly poignant song, but its combination of the aggression of punk and a heartbreaking love song seems to give it *something* that is eternal.

We'd always begin with the drums, then jam along until something happened and, like virtually all our songs, 'Love Will Tear Us Apart' came about in exactly that way. It was a four-square effort: Hooky wrote the riff, Steve wrote the drums, Ian wrote the vocal and I wrote and arranged the other parts. I distinctly remember Ian spotting the riff while we were jamming, and it was his suggestion to keep it going all the way through the song. Then he took it away and came up with those extraordinary lyrics. The intro may have been unintentionally influenced by the Sex Pistols' 'Anarchy in the UK' — that kind of droney, beaty power — while the riff sounds like a second cousin of an earlier song we'd written called 'Novelty'.

I think 'Love Will Tear Us Apart' is one of the most beautiful love songs ever written. It's not a love song for the sake of it, it's no vacuous paean to pretend heartbreak or anything like that, it's genuine, it's real, it swings back and forth between full-blown power and reflective introspection, because that was exactly what was happening to the person writing the lyrics. 'Love Will Tear Us Apart' is a raw slice of real life that remains caught in time.

We knew it was a good song, but our primary aim had been simply to come up with something that would fit well into the live set, a bit of a rabble rouser to turn the crowd into a churning mass of arms and legs. It is unquestionably a great song, though, with its contrasts, peaks, troughs, and it's quite unusual in that it doesn't conform to a regular structure: it's got no middle eight, for example, but it's a great song to play live, an absolute stormer.

The gigs were picking up, even though it seemed that the only ones we could get were in the red-light districts of various cities across the Pennines, which meant driving along the M62 through blizzards and all sorts of weather. In fact, after a few months of that, Steve and Hooky got knocks on the door from the police, because it was the time of the Yorkshire Ripper and Hooky's van and Steve's car had been clocked on the motorway close to where some of the girls had gone missing. Neither of them was arrested or anything; it never got any further than a few questions, as it was soon clear that they could account for their movements, but of course Ian and I found the whole thing extremely amusing.

Ian had become our unofficial agent, in the sense that he was going out and getting us most of our early gigs. Most were great, but of course there'd be the odd dud, nights you'd spend travelling three hours each way to play to fifteen people in a pub in Huddersfield or somewhere, getting home at God knows what time and having to be up early for work the next day. One gig was in a place called Walkden and turned out to be some kind of talent night at a social club for old biddies. Basically, it was a procession of cheesy cabaret singers in dress shirts and massive bow ties . . . and then us. Following a load of fellas in purple velvet tuxes singing 'My Way' with Ian in his Jim Morrison leather trousers fronting this punk band, you can imagine the reaction. Every time Ian jumped in the air or did anything at all, the whole audience would scream, and I don't think it was lust. We got in the car afterwards, and everyone was moaning at Ian and he was saying, 'Fucking hell, I had no idea it was going to be like that.' We drove straight to the Ranch Club, one of our regular Manchester hangouts, opened the boot, took the gear out and did an impromptu gig there and then. And it was a storming gig, maybe because we were all so pissed off. But even farcical gigs like Walkden were part of the learning process.

As 1977 turned into 1978, we were aware we needed a new and final name for the band. It was a struggle, though: it's harder than you might think to come up with a good name for a band. I'd go into bookshops with Ian, looking at the names of books to try and find some inspiration. Around this time I was reading *House of Dolls* by Karol Cetinsky, a harrowing book about the Nazi concentration camps which someone at work had given me, and I came across a reference to a section where women were housed for the pleasure of Nazi officers on leave. It was known as the *Freudenabteilung*, the Joy Division, and that phrase just leapt out at me immediately as the perfect name for the band. Of course I knew straightaway that this was dodgy ground, but this was the height of punk, a period where it was acceptable to be unacceptable. After weeks of trying, we hadn't come up with anything nearly as good as Joy Division. It wasn't about shock value, not at all — I truly believed it was a great name for a band. Not just any band, either, for our band. For me, it seemed to meet all the criteria we were looking for: our sound, our image, even the way the words looked physically on paper. Ian and I looked at it, thought about it, talked about it and decided we really liked it. We took it to Steve and Hooky, and they both liked it as well, so we were all agreed: we'd call ourselves Joy Division. It might get us into trouble, we were aware of that, but above everything else it was a great name for a band. It certainly didn't mean we were Nazis or had any kind of sympathy with them, because we didn't. We knew we weren't Nazis, so any controversy would pass over our heads. There was a feeling that the name would get up certain people's noses, though, and we did quite like that aspect of it. Now, in my more mature years, I probably wouldn't pick it, because I know it would offend and hurt people, but back then I was very young and, well, selfish. Calling ourselves Joy Division was a bit mischievous, yes, but if we got into trouble for it, fuck it, we'd been getting into trouble all our lives. Punk was about upsetting the status quo and upsetting people. Look at the Sex Pistols' television interview with Bill Grundy: that kind of controversial mischief-making was in the air and we were just one band among many feeling the need to be irreverent.

The next stage in our slow climb was to go into the studio and record our first EP, *An Ideal for Living*. We went to Pennine Studios in Oldham and recorded four tracks: 'Warsaw', 'No Love Lost', 'Leaders of Men' and 'Failures', tracks that were probably the cream of that tentative first crop of songs we'd written, that first wall we'd built. We didn't have much money so had gone for a cheap package option: the recording, mastering and pressing all for one price, and financed it with the money Ian had got for his twenty-first birthday. Unfortunately, the cheapness of the deal meant that the finished product was not exactly what we'd had in mind. The economy option we'd taken meant that the studio didn't exactly knock themselves out making it into something to be proud of and, sure enough, when we heard the record it sounded *terrible*. Where we'd built up quite a strong, powerful live sound, what came out of the speakers when you played *An Ideal for Living* was this thin, weedy, tinny noise, barely recognizable as what we'd actually played during the recording. For all the lack of meticulous care in the recording and mastering, though, where we'd really messed up was in putting it on a seven-inch. Having four songs on a seven-inch record meant that the grooves on the vinyl were bunched too close together, something that would have had a hugely detrimental effect on the sound even if it had been produced to a chart-topping standard in the first place. If we'd opted for a twelve-inch, the sound would have been much, much better — in fact, we did do this at a later date — but I don't think Ian's birthday money would have stretched that far.

In the end, the only aspect of the final product we had a say in was the cover, as it wasn't part of the deal and was something we had to sort out ourselves. I was still working for Cosgrove Hall at the time, and on my lunchbreaks I'd go to Manchester Central Library to research ideas for graphic images for the band. One I'd found was of a Hitler Youth drummer battering a big drum slung around his neck. This really struck me as a powerful image that blended perfectly with our new name, our sound and with the kind of image we had in mind for Joy Division. It was a very controversial choice, obviously, but again I thought, Fuck it. It was rather naïve in hindsight: common sense was overruled by the strength of the image. I traced it with a pencil, inked it on to a piece of paper and the drummer boy became the illustration on the cover of the EP. Which did cause a bit of a stir, it's fair to say.

It was on this sleeve that I called myself Bernard Albrecht, something that has been the subject of more than a little speculation and myth-making over the years. Basically, it was just a bit of fun. I'm not entirely sure why I did it. People in bands in those days were calling themselves all sorts of daft names, so I thought I'd call myself a daft name too. I was half asleep on my mum's settee with the television on and there was a programme about Bertholt Brecht. I half heard it while dozing and it sounded a little bit like Bernard Albrecht, and I just thought, That'll do.

There is a bit of context to it, though, I suppose, as I did have an unusual thing going on with names. I was born Bernard Sumner, and then when I went to grammar school, my surname was changed to Dickin, as Jimmy had legally adopted me. I wasn't happy about it, as I've said, so maybe it was some kind of subconscious reaction to that, putting Albrecht on the EP sleeve. Maybe there was a sense that for the first time in my life I had control over what I could call myself. But if that was one hundred per cent the case, I would probably have called myself Sumner, something I did legally on the birth of my first child, James, in 1983 (my mother didn't speak to me for six months). Essentially, I felt like a Sumner. The older I got the more I felt I should be who I wanted to be but, either way, there was no great intention behind the Albrecht thing, it just seemed like a good idea at the time. Which, in hindsight, it wasn't.

Incidentally, another thing people seem to make a big deal about is my nickname, Barney. It came about when a group of us kids were walking down Elton Street in Salford one day: me, Barrie Benson, Raymond Quinn and, I think, David Wroe. One of us said we should all have nicknames and we all made up stupid ones for each other on the spot. For some reason, mine was Barney, and it stuck for a while. It certainly didn't bother me: I was wholly indifferent to it. Hooky, in particular, would use it, because I think he thought it annoyed me, but it really didn't. My surname did because that's more personal, but the Barney thing? Not at all. Everyone calls me Bernard now anyway. Which is my name, obviously, but to be honest I don't particularly like that, either. I don't know what it is, but I don't really feel like a Bernard.

In any case, *An Ideal for Living*'s cover caused a bit of a stir, and causing a stir was all very well, but it was now nearly a year since we'd played our first gig. We were keeping busy, but what we needed was someone to take us in hand, to help us achieve what we wanted to achieve and stop us from making daft decisions like putting four tracks on a seven-inch record. Fortunately, exactly the right person was just around the corner.

Chapter Seven

The organization

Our first gig as Joy Division was at Pips in Manchester on 25 January 1978 – a gig notable mainly for the fact that a massive fight broke out in the audience – then we continued playing our itinerary of the north's red-light districts and endless dodgy pubs in out-of-the-way places. We were busy, and the gigs were great experience, but we felt we were treading water a little. I felt we needed to step up to the next level, or at least get ourselves noticed by someone who mattered.

In April 1978 we made it on to the bill for a gig at Rafters on Oxford Street in Manchester organized jointly by Stiff Records and Chiswick Records. It was a 'battle of the bands' in all but name, designed to encourage local young musicians and give them a chance to get on stage and play in front of two of the country's most exciting record labels of the time. The names Stiff and Chiswick would bring people in, so you were pretty much guaranteed to play in front of a decent crowd. It was a popular gig: there were something like seventeen bands on the bill, and we were due to go on last. Inevitably, with that amount of bands, the show soon began to overrun and it was clear that by the time we got on most people would have gone home. One of the acts ahead of us was a pseudo-punk band, a send-up put together for the occasion by Paul Morley, photographer Kevin Cummins and Richard Boon. They were treating it as a big laugh when for us it was, potentially, an important night. This was something that certainly wasn't lost on Ian.

Ian was one of the most polite, gentle people you could ever meet, a lovely guy, but if something rubbed him up the wrong way it would fester and flourish, and you'd see him pacing up and down, nurturing this growing rage until, eventually, he'd explode. It didn't happen that often, but when it did it could be pretty spectacular. And that night it was pretty spectacular. He'd already been up to Tony Wilson and called him a cunt for not putting us on his TV show (Tony was actually very impressed by this, I think, because people were usually hanging off him trying to butter him up), but it was Paul, Kevin and Richard who were really in his crosshairs that night. Backstage, Ian walked up to the dressing room they were in, kicked the lock off the door (or kicked the door off its hinges, I can't remember which), marched in and started shouting his head off, jabbing his finger at them and screaming, 'You're not going on next, we're fucking going on next or there'll be fucking trouble. No fucking arguments.'

Unsurprisingly in the face of this onslaught, Paul, Kevin and Richard gave way immediately, so we went on at about half past one in the morning and played a blisteringly aggressive, angry set. In hindsight, I'm grateful to Paul, Kevin and Richard because they'd inadvertently built Ian up into this fizzing ball of rage. It meant that when we finally went on he just fucking went for it, not because he was trying to impress Tony or anyone else but simply because he was so wound up. Whether we played a brilliant gig or not I can't really say, but the fallout afterwards confirmed that we'd certainly made an impression.

The next day I was in a phone box on Spring Gardens in central Manchester when I felt the door open behind me and a tap on my shoulder. I turned round and saw this guy standing there, looking all eager and clearly wanting to speak to me. I said, 'Just a minute, mate,' and carried on with my call. No sooner had I put the receiver down than he was introducing himself as Rob Gretton, saying he'd seen us at Rafters the previous night and thought we were absolutely fucking amazing.

'I want to be your manager,' he said. 'I'm on my way to a job interview now, but I don't want the job, I want to manage Joy Division.'

'Hmm,' I said, a little bit on the back foot after this burst of unsolicited gushing. 'Well, the best thing to do is come to our next rehearsal on Wednesday.'

By this time we were rehearsing at TJ Davidson's, not far from where the Haçienda would be, in central Manchester. It was where we'd go on to film the video for 'Love Will Tear Us Apart', and where some famous photographs were taken, particularly of Ian in his big coat looking miserable. TJ Davidson was a nice guy: he looked a bit like Pedro, the drummer from Frankie Goes to Hollywood, and I think his dad was a jeweller; they were certainly a well-off family. They'd bought this old disused warehouse as a potential investment property, and it was in a bit of a state, all smashed windows, no heating, dead rats in the toilet and freezing cold, but it was a good place to rehearse in the sense that it was better than having no place to rehearse at all.

I'd forgotten all about the meeting with Rob almost as soon as he'd walked off to his job interview, so when we were all playing away and he strolled in, I thought, Oh, fucking hell, it's him, he's turned up. Everyone else looked at him as if to say, 'Who the fuck's this?', so I stopped the song and explained. Poor old Rob was really embarrassed — he thought we'd all be expecting him, and instead he's being looked up and down like he's just gatecrashed a wedding ceremony or something. Despite having this sprung on him, Ian suggested we all went to the pub at the end of the road to talk about it. It seems strange now, but in those days we didn't buy rounds of drinks, we each went to the bar and bought our own. I think it might have been a Salford thing, as Rob told us later that it freaked him out a bit, how we'd all gone to the bar and got ourselves a drink and not bought him one.

We had a chat around the table in the pub, and he immediately sounded both interesting and interested. He told us he was a DJ, that he already managed a local punk band called The Panik and that at Rafters we were easily the best thing he'd ever seen. Not only that, he knew Tony Wilson and said Tony had been impressed too.

We met up again a short while later and talked about more specific plans, and Rob said, 'The first thing is, fucking re-release that EP as a twelve-inch with a different sleeve and, in the meantime, I'll talk to Tony and see if I can get you on the telly. Otherwise, you look really cool the way you are, just keep looking the same and keep doing what you're doing.'

And, with that, Rob Gretton became our manager.

My first impressions of Rob were of someone who really liked us, wanted to help us and clearly knew what he was doing. While he knew how the business worked, he wanted to work as far as possible outside the system. He also saw the potential for the whole thing to be fun, which for us made him fit the bill perfectly. He was one of us right from the start, even though he thought me and Peter were Salford scumbags and that Ian and Steve came from this really weird place called Macclesfield on the peripheries of Manchester some- where, a place he probably couldn't even point to on a map. Rob was from Wythenshawe, so it was a bit rich him looking down on Salford.

Rob was a big Manchester City fan, which he didn't declare at first, so that was a drawback, but he was properly immersed in the city of Manchester. He loved it. He loved music deeply too, although his taste was geared more towards soul – Marvin Gaye, that kind of thing. Right from the start he gave me the impression of being on a mission of some kind. He'd seen something in us and wanted to make us a big part of this Manchester musical odyssey on which he was embarking. Our job was to play good gigs and write good songs, and his job was to point us in the right direction and get us noticed, a job about which we didn't have a clue but at which he excelled instinctively.

While he thought we were a great band, he didn't take any shit from us. I remember, on one of our first trips down to London we stayed in a place that was more like a youth hostel than a hotel. I immediately set about getting up to mischief, trying to get into one of the other rooms or something, and he dived on me in the corridor, wrestled me to the floor and started shouting at me to fucking behave. He was just what we needed really, a strong figure. He instantly tuned into the dynamics of the band and the dynamics of the individuals. You had me as Mr Mischief; Hooky, who seemed to me to be gradually turning into Mr Ego; Ian, who had the tempera- ment of a volcano; and then Steve as Mr Wacky, who sat on the fence between all of us. Rob could read us all perfectly and knew exactly how to handle us as individuals, trying to calm us down when we got too hyperactive and adolescent and chivvy us up when we were down and needed a kick up the arse.

Another advantage of being managed by Rob was that he forged close connections with Tony Wilson and his partners. The initial people who set Factory up were Tony, Alan Erasmus and Peter Saville, and thanks to Rob we were right in there at the start. We'd heard they intended to start a record company, Rob and Tony thought we should sign with them and, eventually, that's what we did. We weren't really consulted about it, other than Rob saying he thought we should go with a local label. There would be other labels with an interest in us, and vice versa: RCA, Martin Rushent's label Genetic and an American-based label which could have been disastrous — more of which anon — but a hometown indie label seemed exactly the right fit for us at that time.

With Rob becoming our manager and his relationship with Tony drawing us all into each other's orbits, it meant that we could concentrate on the music while Rob — and later Tony — looked after the business side of things. Looking back, at least you can say we looked after the music ...

We liked Tony. We'd met him, and he seemed to be really into the music and youth scene of Manchester. Despite this, he got a lot of grief at gigs. I'd seen it myself: you'd be queuing up outside a venue and he'd walk past the queue and go straight in, with his bloody saddlebags and his jacket draped over his shoulders. He'd be getting all sorts of abuse from the punks in the queue: 'Wilson, you twat, get in the fucking queue like everyone else' — but he took it all in his stride.

Tony loved Manchester, too, something he had in common with Rob and which bound them together in their working relationship. They were very proud of the city. Tony loved its history; he'd talk about all the famous people and great things that had happened in Manchester: Alan Turing, how the atom had first been split there. Manchester's scientific heritage was something of which he was particularly proud. Tony and Rob both felt that the city was losing touch with its extraordinary legacy and wanted to do what they could to revive it, to make the city a better place to live. Rob's philosophy was that while you lived in Manchester you should strive to make the city better and so make it a better place for you, too. Be proud, Mancunians, that was his attitude.

To be honest, I don't really feel this as strongly as Rob and Tony did. I don't think any one place is better than another, just different, and I certainly never wanted to become a 'professional Mancunian'. Manchester, as I see it, is a very fine northern British city among other fine northern British cities. To this day, I don't really have a favourite city: they all have their own distinct characters and aren't up for comparison. Manchester's character back then was northern, industrial and Victorian. I've never been a fan of Victorian architecture, so I didn't think it was that beautiful: in those days, it was a decaying city that had seen better times and, as a kid, all those austere buildings kind of gave me the creeps. In Heaton Park you can still see the original façade of Manchester Town Hall, which dates back to Georgian times, a really beautiful thing, but they took it down and replaced it with the harsher Victorian one (though I have to say some of the interiors are quite nice). They did a similar thing in London at Euston train station, a place I frequently travel through, but they replaced a Regency façade with a nasty sixties monstrosity. As the gateway to the north, I have to say it stinks.

Back in the late seventies, Manchester was not the place it is now. I know I'm probably supposed to subscribe to the received wisdom that Manchester back then was a gritty northern city with bags of character and that I'd give anything to go back, but I wouldn't. I absolutely wouldn't. I much prefer Manchester the way it is now. I know it sounds like a contradiction to what I've just said about architecture, but I think the new buildings provide a good visual foil for the remaining Victoriana, most of which is good quality. I guess the key word here is 'good'. There are parts of it I miss: it had a great community spirit, and I've already talked at length about how much I loved that aspect of growing up in Salford. The city is a bit homogenized now — for the most part, the shops are the same as they are everywhere else — but I think it's definitely a more pleasant place to be today than it was back then. It's less threatening at night, for example — to get a late Saturday-night bus back to parts of Salford back then could be a *refreshing* experience, to say the least. You could get stabbed quite easily, and I certainly don't miss that.

As I see it, the things of value in the city have been made better, while great strides have been made in eliminating the bad things. They've put the tram link back in, having removed it in the late sixties, and it's returned an artery to the centre of the city; it's added to the life of it. The decay's all but gone. Not all of it has been replaced with something beautiful, admittedly, but modern Manchester has a renewed vibrancy which I much prefer to how it was in the old days. I think Manchester got a bit lost in the late seventies; there was a stoop-shouldered sense of 'we used to be a big manufacturing hub but we don't make anything any more; there are no jobs in the factories; thank you, Margaret Thatcher'. The place was down on its luck and to a certain extent was wallowing in it, but it's managed to revitalize itself and become a better place.

I miss a few old nooks and crannies in the city, odd places where sometimes you could find yourself in some sort of crumbling Dickensian village that seemed self-contained and cut off from the rest of the world, or you'd find quirky shops or old places selling bits for valve radios, curiosities and anachronisms, places that had been there for seventy years, completely out of date, with mad old men selling knick-knacks from another age. Now that it's all Starbucks and Costa, I do miss that aspect of the old Manchester, coming across the skeleton of an old barge or a disused lock-keeper's cottage slowly decaying into dust. Now, there'll be a gastropub there.

Rob and Tony bonded over their vision for Manchester and its culture, but they also knew what was best for us and acted on it. Hence, one of the first things Rob did was to secure us a spot on Tony's show, *Granada Reports*, which had succeeded his popular *So It Goes*. We made our television debut on 20 September 1978, playing a new song we'd been working on, 'Shadowplay'. It was a little bit terrifying, being up there on live television in the artificial setting of a TV studio, but we played all right. The director overlaid us with these gritty shots of cars on a freeway reversed out so it looked like a negative, which added to the starkness of the song and our performance. It looked really good.

Clearly, having Rob and Tony on board was going to make a difference.

Tony's first line when entering a room was always, 'I can't stay, darlings, I've just come to say you're doing a great job, I've heard the new stuff, it's fabulous, got to dash, goodbye!' He could never stay in one place for very long. It was as if he'd briefly sample what was going on then go away and ponder in private rather than any more direct interaction. He always meant well, he wanted to help the city and the music scene in city. His attitude was to question why everything had to be in London, which we thought was great. Both questioning it and London, to be honest.

As I think the *Granada Reports* performance shows, we were starting to find our feet by this stage. We were getting plenty of gigs, our live set was really tight and we were always coming up with new material. Not only was the number of gigs increasing, we were going down really well at them too. In the early days, when we were criss-crossing the Pennines, sometimes we'd even have to pay to play; we'd do anything just to get that vital experience behind us. Now, playing new venues and meeting people who hadn't heard us before, we were finding we always got a strong reaction from the crowd.

We knew we were on to something. We were building a following through our live performances of a tight set of songs. We were good, and we knew it. It was time to go into the studio and demonstrate *how* good we were.

Chapter Eight

Cold winds blowing

Our first proper experience in a studio had been the *An Ideal for Living* session, the one that ended up sounding terrible because of the slapdash way it was recorded and produced and the disastrous way we'd had it pressed. After that, we felt nothing could be that bad again, so when we next entered a recording studio, in May 1978, we felt a mixture of apprehension and cautious optimism. We were going in to record our first album but, as it turned out, it would be one that would never see the light of day, at least officially.

Ian had got to know a guy called Richard Searling, who was something high up at RCA Records' office in Manchester, and Richard had told Ian about a guy he knew who was interested in signing us to a soul label from America. He'd heard that punk was the new big thing and he wanted to sign a punk band. Richard put us in touch and booked some studio time for us to go in and record.

It turned out that the guy was a complete nightmare. Here was someone not remotely interested in anything we wanted to do, just a time-is-money merchant, a clock-watcher and watch-tapper who was only concerned about how large he could make the figure at the bottom of the balance sheet.

The studio we used was owned by Greendow Commercials, where I worked. They had a graphics and film department where they did a lot of editing and rostrum camera work for Granada, and there was also a sound effects studio which I'd worked in occasionally. At the back of the building they'd installed a recording studio intended mainly for recording commercials and voiceovers, but it was a full studio nonetheless. I managed to negotiate us a cheap rate and we all turned up there one morning excited about recording our first album. When we arrived, there was a guy already in the studio finishing off a voiceover for Littlewoods Lotteries. I can still remember how it went: 'Littlewoods Lotteries, more and more win Littlewoods!', because he needed several goes at it before he got it right, and we had to wait for him to finish. This didn't bode well for making a classic album, but this was about as good as the session would get.

The guy from the record label arrived and announced he wanted us to record the album in one day and he'd mix it the next. As soon as we set up the gear my guitar amp started buzzing and the guy went mad at me, shouting, 'Get your fucking amp sorted, I'm losing money here.' This was before we'd even played a note. We recorded the backing tracks and had moved on to recording Ian when things got worse. He gave poor Ian a hell of a time, demanding that he 'sing like James Brown', among other things. Ian Curtis was a lot of things, but the Godfather of Soul he wasn't. When we'd finished recording everything and were ready to leave for the day, out of the blue the guy said that he was bringing someone in to do overdubs the following morning and we had a choice between a synth player or a sax player. We said we didn't want either, thanks, but were informed we had no choice in the matter beyond picking which one. We left feeling very dejected and walked through the centre of Manchester in stunned silence. We'd been looking forward to recording an album, but this guy was a tosser who'd turned the whole process into a nightmare from the minute we'd walked into the studio. We turned over what had happened in our minds as we walked away from the studio. No one said anything until Ian broke the silence. 'I'm not coming back tomorrow,' he said.

'But we're halfway through, Ian,' I replied. 'We might as well just finish it now and see what happens.' He thought about it for a while then reluctantly agreed, and we parted, making our separate ways home with stooped shoulders and an air of bitter disappointment.

The next day the bad vibes picked up where they'd left off. We hated the guy, and he clearly didn't give a toss about us. He probably couldn't have told you our names even after two days in the studio. We were just a commodity to be exploited and shipped out as fast as possible before he moved on to the next one.

When he'd put the overdub gun to our heads the previous day we'd chosen the synthesizer — can you imagine a Joy Division record with a sax solo? — and, sure enough, this session guy arrived and started setting up his gear. We all looked at each other, clearly thinking the same thing: a fucking session musician? Not very punk, is it? He started running through a few sounds on his synth and asked us what kind of stuff we liked. Kraftwerk and Donna Summer, we said, and his eyes lit up. He changed a couple of settings, pressed the keys and the synth started making these high-pitched *mewmewmew* sounds. He looked at us expectantly. I don't know whether it was meant to remind us of Kraftwerk or Donna Summer, but it sounded like nothing we'd ever heard before. I said, 'You can get rid of that for a start, it sounds like a fucking cat.' He straightened up, looked at us, and declared, 'That's what synths are all about, man.'

The session guy and the dickhead from the record company spent the day blasting through the album doing shit mixes of the songs we'd worked so hard to create. We got out of there as soon as we could, and dreaded hearing what it would sound like. It was clear we'd fucked up. A couple of weeks or so later, we'd taken on Rob as our manager and we told him what had happened. He pursed his lips for a moment, stood up and said, 'Right, we've got to get those tapes back.' I think we ended up having to pay something like five grand for them, and of course the guy had made copies anyway, which weren't long in coming out as a bootleg. Rob had to engage a lawyer to untangle the mess we'd got ourselves into but, thankfully, nothing like that would ever happen again.

There was one positive thing to come out of that session: the clock-watcher had a Northern Soul record he really liked called 'Keep On Keeping On' and wanted us to cover it. We told him we didn't do cover versions, but we listened to it and really liked the guitar riff. We basically lifted the riff and built our own track around it. It was 'Interzone': Ian wrote the lyrics and sang it, and it was actually pretty good. But apart from that, the whole experience had been a disaster, and an expensive one at that.

Once we'd put that incident behind us, we were ready to move on. One of the first things we did with Rob as our manager was commit properly to Factory Records. We contributed a couple of tracks to the first record ever released on Factory, *A Factory Sample*, which came out at Christmas 1978 and also featured Cabaret Voltaire, John Dowie and The Durutti Column. If I remember rightly, we'd recorded the tracks we used, 'Digital' and 'Glass', with Martin Rushent (who went on to produce The Human League's massive *Dare* album, among others), as he was looking for a band to sign to his label, a subsidiary of United Artists. We'd recorded these demos in his studio down in London and got on all right with him; he was a bit of a laugh, but he was very businesslike and not as relaxed as we'd have liked and nothing came of it in the end. So when Tony asked us to contribute a couple of tracks to *A Factory Sample*, we dug out 'Digital' and 'Glass' and handed them over for Martin Hannett to remix. We had them in the can already, so it wouldn't cost anything, and they'd never been released anywhere else. That was our first appearance on Factory.

It was a while before we'd go into the studio as a Factory band, but we kept gigging, including a tour supporting The Rezillos, and our last gig of 1978 was a special one: our first appearance in London. It would be at the Hope and Anchor in Islington, on 27 December, which would turn out to be a very strange day indeed. The Hope and Anchor was a famous pub on the circuit, a gig you had to do and a good venue to get some exposure in London. After months of try-ing, Rob had finally secured us a spot there and we were excited about what was potentially a big opportunity for us.

The problems started when I went down with a bad dose of the flu on the morning of the gig. When Steve picked me up in his car I felt like shit; I was completely spaced out and couldn't stop shivering. I grabbed a sleeping bag from home, got in the car, bedded down as best I could and we set off for London. On the way down, despite feel-ing like death warmed up, I noticed that Ian seemed to be in an odd mood. He was being unusually antagonistic, moaning about every-thing and declaring anything anyone said to be 'fucking stupid, that'. After a long drive south we arrived at the gig, set up, soundchecked and did the gig to — I'm not joking — the one man and his dog who turned up. That was the entire audience, and I don't think the dog liked us. The gig was in that strange period between Christmas and New Year when most people don't really go out, especially to a freezing-cold pub basement to see a band from the other end of the country who they'd never heard of. It was a disaster.

It would have been bad enough had I been feeling a million dollars, but I was really struggling. Every time Steve hit a cymbal the room seemed to swim and turn upside down. That a gig we'd been looking forward to had turned into such an anticlimax meant that no one was in the best of moods, so we got through it as best we could, packed the gear away and went to a little Greek restaurant afterwards, feeling pretty sorry for ourselves. Ian was still in this strange negative mood that seemed to me to be about more than just a shit gig. 'Fucking hell,' he kept saying. 'All this bloody way for nothing – have I really had to take time off work for this?' We paid the bill, piled back into the car and headed north. It had been a crap day, a crap gig – even the food in the restaurant had been crap – and we just wanted to get home as quickly as possible. We pulled on to the M1 and I wrapped my sleeping bag around me ready to sweat out the long journey home.

A short while later – we hadn't even got as far as Luton – Ian turned round to me from the front seat and said, 'Give me that sleeping bag.' I tried to ignore him – I was still feeling terrible and just wanted to get home to my own bed – when suddenly he leaned over, grabbed it and wrenched it off me. I grabbed it back, then he grabbed it again. I snatched at it, but this time he wouldn't let go and I ended up losing my grip. When I looked up I saw he'd covered his head with it and had started making this weird growling noise. I said, 'Ian, what are you fucking doing? What's this about?' The next thing we knew he'd pulled the sleeping bag off himself and started punching everything in reach, taking swings at the windscreen, the side windows, even poor Steve, who was driving. Steve pulled over on to the hard shoulder, we dragged Ian out of the car and laid him on the ground. He was shaking uncontrollably and having what we'd later learn was a full-on epileptic fit. We held him down until it subsided, and he just lay there on the tarmac, completely dazed. It was a terrifying thing to see, not least because at that stage we had no idea that Ian had epilepsy. We carried him back to the car, pulled off the M1 at the first available exit and took him straight to A&E at the nearest hospital, which was in Luton. It was a horrible night. As we waited for news of Ian, people were having their stomachs pumped and all sorts. Eventually the doctor came out to see us. The indications were that Ian had had an epileptic fit, he said, and he asked us if Ian had epilepsy. We said no, no he hasn't, because we just had no idea. It was a strange, surreal and ultimately very sad night. As we hung around the casualty department, with its aroma cocktail of floor bleach, antiseptic and vomit, we had no inkling of the impact it would have on our futures. The possible implications were lost on us in the immediate aftermath of Ian's fit: we were just baffled. One bizarre memory I have of sitting in that hospital waiting for news is how pissed off Steve was because Ian had his cigarettes. He went into the cubicle and got them out of his coat pocket. 'Never mind him,' he was saying. 'What about my cigs?' We all cracked up at this. It was a bit of light relief after a disastrous day.

Once the doctors had released Ian, we drove back the rest of the way in almost total silence. Ian spent the journey with his head against the window, looking out sightlessly at the darkness and the occasional pinprick lights of nameless passing towns.

When he saw the doctors back at home they confirmed the worst, diagnosing Ian with grand mal epilepsy. He was prescribed some very strong drugs. They didn't know nearly as much about epilepsy in the seventies as they do today, and the treatment was pretty brutal. The drugs available to the doctors then were heavy-duty pharmaceutical sledgehammers and I noticed within the space of a couple of weeks how they'd changed Ian's personality. One minute he'd be laughing and joking, the next he'd have his head in his hands, on the verge of tears: you didn't know where you were with him emotionally and neither did he.

I think people have a perception of Ian as being this gloomy, tortured poet. When you see the iconic photos of him, like those taken at TJ Davidson's by Anton Corbyn, he looks really down. A lot of people think that's what he was like all the time; that his default setting was this eloquent, dark, haunted soul, but that image doesn't sum up Ian's personality at all. He could be a great laugh, really good company. He was pretty good to take the piss out of, too, and was often the fall guy for practical jokes. For example, he wore these winklepicker shoes and skinny jeans and often we'd be in Steve's blue Cortina and Ian would get us to stop because he needed a piss. We'd pull over, he'd get out, stand close to Steve's car and start pissing, and I'd say, 'Steve, look, he's pissing down the side of your car, just pull off, quick,' and Steve would drive off, straight over his winkle-pickers. 'What are you fucking doing?' he'd shout. 'Ahh, not again! Every fucking time! Where the fuck do you expect me to stand — we're on a main road. I don't want people seeing me with my knob out!'

Most of the time Ian was a really polite, pleasant person, a pleasure to be around: funny, interesting and great company. He was best man at my first wedding (which was a very low-key occasion: we were too young and, unfortunately, the marriage didn't last, although it did produce my first son, James). But it could be a delicate emotional balancing act with Ian. If he saw something as an injustice — like at the Stiff/Chiswick night, for example — or someone wound him up, he'd reach a tipping point and blow up into these huge explosions, like a Tasmanian devil. There would always be some justification for it, they weren't irrational rages and they'd soon blow themselves out, but on the occasions he blew, he really blew. One thing he particularly hated on the road, and which always seemed to catch him out, was the kind of charges hotels levied on phone bills. He didn't realize that if you made an external call from the phone in your room they would charge you a premium rate. Whenever we checked out, Rob would present him with massive phone bills that were bigger than his weekly wage and it would always send him over the edge and he'd go absolutely fucking barmy at Rob, as if Rob was trying to rip him off.

Ian was a contradiction in so many ways. He was mad about being in a group, mad about music and mad about Joy Division making music, yet at the same time he was fearful of all those things — something that was very difficult for the rest of us to puzzle out. You didn't really know where you stood with him; whether he was in the band for life (as things turned out, we've been around a very long time), or that he was going to decide one day he didn't want to do it any more. He was unpredictable. He was so passionate about Joy Division and this being what he wanted. He loved writing the lyrics and he loved performing up there on stage. He truly thought we were the best band in the world, but at the same time he didn't know if he was still going to be there tomorrow, whether in a few weeks' time he could have walked away from it all and be running a corner shop somewhere.

I remember talking to him around the time we were recording *Closer*. He told me that the lyrics were practically writing themselves, they were coming thick, fast and fully formed, but he said he felt as if he was being pulled inexorably into a great big whirlpool. I didn't know what he meant by that. I think he may have had an epileptic fit that night; I seem to remember a cut on his head I hadn't noticed earlier, so he may have had a small fit and bashed his head. He seemed to feel that things were moving quickly and escaping his control inside and outside Joy Division. The band was really starting to take off at that stage: maybe he felt there'd been no chance to take stock, no time to stop and fully appreciate what was happening.

He was a real music fan, Ian: since his teens he'd loved The Doors, The Velvet Underground, Iggy, Bowie, Kraftwerk, Neu. Music represented an escape for him. He'd grown up and still lived in Macclesfield, a small town where there wasn't much going on. Like any kid in that situation, he had a dream of getting out, of going on to greater things, the way his musical heroes had. But here was that dream actually coming true, something that perhaps he hadn't really anticipated, and he found himself questioning everything. It was, after all, a dream that came with certain responsibilities: having to deliver to increasingly large live audiences, having to create an album of new material as good if not better than the last. Maybe he was thinking, What am I going to do if it gets even bigger? What if I can't keep producing the goods? How am I going to cope?

He was facing an intense dichotomy: he really, really wanted it, but here he was getting it and finding he wasn't sure it was what he wanted after all.

I'm sure his diagnosis only served to increase that turmoil. He must have thought that his epilepsy might take everything away from him, and felt a huge sense of responsibility to the rest of the band: with all that he was trying to cope with, he gave himself the added pressure of not wanting to let anyone down. If he packed it in, he thought, everyone else would have to pack it in too.

He did leave the band at one point after the recording of *Closer*, only for a day or so, but he did quit. He went to see Rob and told him he didn't want to do it any more and was moving away to open a bookshop in Bournemouth. He had a childhood friend who'd moved there while they were still at school and he wanted to rekindle that friendship and settle down there. Knowing Ian, I'm sure that on that particular day when he said that particular thing he believed a hundred per cent that it was what he wanted to do. Maybe it was an escape valve, maybe his wife, Debbie, had wanted him to do it, or maybe he felt he had to walk away from everything because of his illness. But later he'd feel something else, something completely different, and backtrack. I think he used to withdraw into himself, dwell upon the pressures he faced and come to a conclusion, only for the fighter inside him to emerge and persuade him not to give in to that conclusion. Then he'd end up rebelling against what he saw as his moment of weakness. The Bournemouth thing came totally out of the blue and after a day or so was never mentioned again, but it was a clear sign he was under pressure: pressure to keep coming up with new material and to keep up his intense, almost frantic performance on stage.

He never said he felt under pressure at gigs, but since his death I've read one of his letters, where he did admit to feeling increasing anxiety about maintaining his live performances. On stage, Ian was pretty full on, and I think he definitely felt the burden of having to deliver that hundred per cent performance every time, especially with the amount of gigs we were playing and, of course, especially in his state of health. It's hard enough having epilepsy, but imagine having it in the public eye like that.

The threat of fitting hung over him like the sword of Damocles. For all the drugs he was on and the treatment he was receiving, a fit could still happen at any time, even on stage. All it would take was the wrong beat or the lights flashing in a certain way and he'd be gone, on stage, in front of hundreds of people. Sometimes we'd finish the song, Steve's drums would stop, but Ian would still be dancing and we'd realise he was on the brink of a grand mal fit. By then, of course, we were much more aware than we'd been that cold December night on the hard shoulder of the M1, so we'd gently coax him off the stage to a back room as quickly as we could, where he'd start having the fit. We'd hold him down in an attempt to prevent him hurting himself until, eventually, the convulsions would subside. Then he'd tell us all to leave him alone and cry to himself, alone in a strange room in a strange town, just breaking his heart.

It's important to remember that we were all still very young when this was happening, barely into our twenties. In many ways, we were still adolescents. To be the focal point of a band that was rocketing from obscurity to stardom, a band into which you were putting your heart and soul, would be pressure enough for anyone at any age, but add being diagnosed with a serious medical condition that could manifest itself in the most public way almost without warning just when the band is really taking off (Ian's epilepsy diagnosis was confirmed between us recording our first Peel session in January '79 and his appearing on the front cover of the *NME* for the first time in August '79), not to mention the effects of what were comparatively primitive drug treatments and the turmoil of his private life, and you can only marvel at the level of pressure he must have been feeling.

At the time, we were young lads leading exciting lives, seemingly with the world at our feet. Everything was going to be fine. Everything was going to be great. Wasn't it?

Chapter Nine

Graft

In April 1979 we went into the recording studio for the sessions that would become *Unknown Pleasures* with a tangible sense of trepidation. The debacle of our previous experience was still in our minds and still giving us the horrors. Was every producer like Mr Time-Is-Money? Is that what making an album was like?

Thankfully, recording *Unknown Pleasures* would be the antithesis of what had gone before. Martin Hannett was Rob's and Tony's choice to produce our first album. We didn't have that much say in the matter and didn't know much about him, but as the extraordinary longevity of the album has borne out, he was obviously a good choice. Martin was a born maverick, a wonderful conduit of creativity and great fun to be around – most of the time. He'd produced the first Buzzcocks EP, worked with John Cooper Clarke and, when we began work on the album, he was about to have a hit single with Jilted John, so his production net was already cast pretty wide. But it was with Joy Division that he'd become most closely associated, and he did as much as anyone to help foster our unique sound.

Ian was happy with Martin as our producer and, if Ian was happy, we were happy. Ian had a great sixth sense for what was good for us and had an intuition that Martin was the right guy. I certainly noticed an immediate bond between them. For a start, Martin may have been a maverick but there was no chance of him ever asking Ian to sound like James Brown.

The immediate and lasting impact Martin had on me was that he made me completely re-evaluate the role of the recording studio. Until I worked with him I'd always thought a recording studio was nothing more than a giant tape recorder, but he made me see that the studio could be an instrument in itself. Martin's attitude was that the studio was a wonderfully creative space put at our disposal, so let's do something really cool with it.

We made the album at Strawberry Studios in Stockport, which was owned by 10CC. I'd never seen a studio like it in my life: it was packed with all sorts of gear, way over spec for a band like us. There we were, a bunch of 21-year-old punks, looking around at racks and racks of state-of-the-art gear and wondering what all the flashing lights were for. I loved it. I'd look around in awe, thinking that you could make a record just with all this, never mind the guitars.

Mad as it might sound now, it took us just three weekends to record *Unknown Pleasures*: one weekend to record the basic tracks, another to record overdubs and the third to mix it. There was no synth player making cat noises, but some of the overdubs were quite wacky, such as Martin recording smashing glass and the sound of the building's lift shaft. Another thing we did for the first time with Martin on *Unknown Pleasures*, something that would prove to have quite a legacy in the coming years, was make our very first use of a sampler. Martin had this little unit with a keyboard made by AMS and told me to plug my guitar into it and play a few notes. After that, he told me to press the keys on the keyboard and, when I did, the sound of my guitar came out of the speakers. So there we were, using samplers on our records as far back as 1978.

Typically, the first session started on the wrong foot, thanks to another issue with my guitar amp. In those days, my drink of choice was brown ale, not because I particularly liked it but because at gigs people would come into the dressing room afterwards and nick all the rider. No one, however, would nick my sweet, nutty brown ale. Anyway, no sooner had we started the first recording session than I'd knocked a full bottle of it into my amp. I braced myself for a bollocking, but Martin's reaction couldn't have been more different to the last guy's.

'Don't worry, Bernard,' he said. 'I've got a friend called Martin Usher who's a scientist. I'll get him to pop round and fix it.' Within the hour, this eccentric, lovable character arrived, a kind of slimmer, younger and bearded version of Patrick Moore with a bit of Brian Cox thrown in. He fixed the amp in no time and we were able to get the session up and running without too much of a hold-up. This was the start of a long friendship.

Once we were under way, the recording process was notably quick, and this time it wasn't because the guy in charge effectively had a meter running. The songs were all written, and had been rehearsed and honed by playing live. We knew which tempos worked and that we'd got the arrangements right. After we'd recorded our parts we stuck around for a few overdubs and then disappeared while Martin mixed it. He preferred mixing alone in the studio, essentially because he thought musicians were complete twats who had no right to be in a recording studio once they'd laid down the basic tracks.

But then again, what is the role of a record producer? Some

producers don't overly impose themselves on the songs but make sure the finished recording sounds good and is mixed well. In retrospect, I don't think this was Martin's priority: I think he saw his role in a more creative light and desired a greater input, wanting to twist the sound of the album from its original inception closer to his own vision. Which was OK as long as it sounded good too.

We didn't hear the final record until Martin had completely finished mixing it and, to be honest, when we heard it, it split the band into two camps, one loving it, the other hating it. Strawberry Studios had been built and fitted out absolutely by the book, seventies style: carpets on the walls and a really dead sound in the studio. The prevailing philosophy at the time was that you'd record everything completely dry and flat frequency-wise then add all the atmosphere electronically afterwards. It was a concept that had been taken to its limits in that studio: it was *completely* dead, there wasn't a hint of natural ambience. If you listen to the drums on a lot of disco records from that period, it's a completely dry, flat sound: there's no room ambience at all. That might be fine for disco, but it doesn't work for rock music: it makes it sound like the track has been played in a vacuum.

Paring the sound back to its bare bones in this way gave Martin a blank canvas from which to work on our album, allowing him the freedom to create his own electronic ambience. He had a device called a Marshall Time Modulator as well as an AMS delay unit that added that ambience artificially. I think it's a great idea in theory, and it could certainly work today, because the technology has advanced to a point where you can re-create natural ambience very accurately, but in those days the technology and computer power were so weedy I thought it sounded tinny. I didn't get it. I couldn't understand why you couldn't just record somewhere with its own natural feel, but Martin had seen it as an opportunity to create and record an entirely *new* sound. I guess he was just too far ahead of the technology.

He was vindicated up to a point, because the album was — and continues to be — very successful. Whether that's down to the production, the songs, the arrangements, people's perception of the band or a combination of everything, I don't know, I'm too close to it to say for certain. But the instant I heard *Unknown Pleasures* I knew I didn't like it. I felt Martin had robbed us of our power; it was as if Samson's hair had been cut.

At the same time, I found this attitude of Martin's to the studio, to use it as a great big instrument in its own right, incredibly interesting, and I admired his instinct for innovation. Samplers, for example, supposedly hadn't even been invented yet!

Ian thought the album was wonderful. I distinctly remember him declaring it a classic record straightaway. Steve was broadly non-committal but inclined towards liking it. Hooky and I didn't because we felt it had become a Martin Hannett record first and a Joy Division record second. To us, Martin had taken away the rocky aggression of our sound. You can make a comparison between what we sounded like live and what we sounded like after being fed through Martin's production process if you check out the recorded version of 'Transmission' then dig out a recording of us playing the same track live at the Les Bains Douches in Paris a few months later. It was a nice gig — there was a small swimming pool in one corner — which was recorded for French radio and mixed really well for broadcast. It's a much more aggressive sound than on *Unknown Pleasures* and provides a good illustration of what at least two of us felt had been changed radically by Martin's production.

Even though the end product wasn't powerful enough for me — the drums were too thin and weedy, and there's no way Steve's drumming is thin and weedy — just having Martin in the studio made good things happen. You played well instinctively; you had a feeling you were making something very special and forward-looking. He also made us feel very comfortable, which in the light of our past experiences was critical. He was never afraid to experiment: he'd encourage you to pick up instruments that might be lying around in the studio which you'd never have dreamed of using. On one hand we were left with an album that didn't sound like us, but on the other we loved some of the strange, curious and wonderful things he'd do in the studio.

Even if we'd been united in our dislike of the way the album had turned out, there was nothing we could have done about it, as there was no money left to re-record anything. When I played *Unknown Pleasures* for the first time, I was nonplussed by the sound and was afraid the public might not 'get' the songs because of it. Hearing it posed a question that I couldn't answer: was this album any good or not? I'd never made a proper album before, so I was very relieved when it came out to instant acclaim. I remember going into work, buying all the music papers on the way, leafing anxiously through them to the reviews section and finding them all to be glowing. More than glowing, in fact: they were gushing. For me, finally, that was the moment everything changed; that was the moment of catharsis. Thank you, all those journalists who gave the album a good review.

One aspect of the album over which Martin had no influence was the cover. The cover of *Unknown Pleasures* has become one of the most famous and instantly recognizable in history, up there with *Dark Side of the Moon* and *Sergeant Pepper.* The image itself is a graphic representation of a pulsar, the soundwaves of a dying star, which I'd found while leafing through an encyclopaedia of astronomy in Manchester's Central Library. There was something about it that just grabbed me, I can't really define what, but immediately it seemed like a perfect image for the album cover. I gave it to our designer, Peter Saville, and he took it from there. In the encyclopaedia, the image on the page was black ink on a white background, but Peter inverted the colours so it became white on black and reduced it to a much smaller size. I thought it was great. What Peter did was incredibly clever: the image is still selling on T-shirts even today, more than thirty years later.

Peter Saville is another important part of the jigsaw. Where Martin was the in-house producer at Factory, Peter was the in-house sleeve designer, and both of them were brilliant. Martin was brilliant because he was such a wild card: if you'd put us in with a normal producer we would have frozen and the album may have sunk without trace. We didn't want to do things in a 'proper' way, we wanted to fuck around and try things out in the studio, and Martin was well up for that. We were very serious about the music, really serious, but we wanted to make sure that between starting and finishing the record we had a good time too. We wanted it to be a good experience and, for most of that time, with Martin it was.

Peter was also brought in by Tony (and was in fact one of the founders of Factory with Tony and Alan Erasmus). As had been the case with Martin, we were presented with Peter as the sleeve designer but, fortunately for us, he was and remains absolutely fantastic. One thing I like about him is that he is open to ideas but has a definite authority in what he believes to be good. Our covers, both for Joy Division and New Order, have come about in different ways: sometimes we'd take an image to Peter, other times we'd all sit down with him and look through books in the studio, or he'd bring something to show us. The Italian Futurist-style cover of *Movement*, for example, was entirely Peter's creation. For *Closer* he turned up with a book of photographs of a graveyard in Italy by Bernard Pierre Wolff and we agreed on a picture of a family tomb. Somewhere in Genoa, I think it was. We had a picture from the same set on the cover of the 'Love Will Tear Us Apart' twelve-inch as well and, much to our intense annoyance, because they both came out soon after Ian died, we were accused of cashing in on his death. As if we would ever do anything like that: it tells you more about the people making the accusations than the band. Also, both those sleeves had been agreed and commissioned with Ian: they were going into production before he died, he'd been part of the process, had loved the images and given them the OK. For the seven-inch of 'Love Will Tear Us Apart' Peter had the lettering stamped out of a piece of steel, left it underground for a couple of weeks, dug it up and photographed it. This was really clever, beautiful, groundbreaking stuff. Tony was so impressed by the cover of *Closer* he had it put up as a massive billboard on Sunset Strip in Los Angeles. Of course, no one there knew who the fuck Joy Division were, but he did it anyway.

We got on really well with Peter, and still do. He cuts it fine at times, though. One day we were at Heathrow, just about to get on a plane, and he came rushing up puffing and panting, with a cigarette in his hand and saying, 'This is the sleeve for *Brotherhood*, do you like it?'

In the days of vinyl, when people bought twelve-inch records, the artwork was very important because it represented the band and its taste. Also, we were of the opinion that if you bought a record with a great sleeve you were getting two pieces of art for the price of one: the music and the artwork. It was important to us, the sleeve. When we were kids buying records we thought the choice of cover for a record was really interesting. We'd wonder what it was saying, how it worked in conjunction with the music and what it said about the band. Today's digital age has reduced the impact of a record sleeve, and I think that's a great shame, but thanks to Peter we've had some fantastic ones. To begin with, I'd quite fancied doing the album covers myself. I used to become involved to a limited extent, because it was something I was really interested in, but as soon as Peter came along I knew we were in safe hands.

For all my reservations about the sound, when it came out in June 1979 *Unknown Pleasures* was an unmitigated success. It really put us on the map and had journalists beating a path to our door. There was one peculiar incident with a journalist who came up from London to interview us at Strawberry Studios, the first interview we ever did with the national music press, and the same guy had already given the album a five-star review, so we thought we'd be all right. Of course, we were all a bit naïve, but everything seemed positive and we were ready to meet him. Bizarrely, his attitude seemed to be, 'Great joke, guys! Good one!' He'd arrived with the curious assumption that we weren't serious about what we were doing, that we'd been rumbled and he had our number: we were either a bunch of phonies or we were joking, but either way he was going to get to the bottom of it.

The interview got off to a bad start and got progressively worse, because we were all casting sidelong glances at each other as if to say, What's *this* all about? We said to him that we were perfectly serious. I think he wanted us to come clean and admit that he'd cracked the code, hold our hands up and say, It's a fair cop, well done. Then Ian started getting aggressive and I suggested relocating to the pub to give things a chance to cool down. Maybe we could start again.

When we got there, Hooky lost his rag at the journalist but then calmed down and offered to buy him a drink, and the guy ended up writing something like, 'By way of an apology, the bass player offered to buy me a drink — but I said no.' It was weird. He'd come all the way up to Stockport to interview us, but with this crazy agenda shackled to what was evidently a massive ego. Our first interview for the national music papers, and it happened to be with the worst journalist in the world. That put us off doing interviews altogether: I don't think we did another one for a very long time. It worked in our favour, though, because we then became enigmatic, withdrawn, elitist Joy Division: it suited the image that had been imposed on us. We weren't withdrawn or elitist at all – although Hooky would take it to the other extreme by having you believe that he and I were 'just a pair of northern oiks'. He may feel comfortable with that description, but I don't. OK, I may occasionally have some rather oikish habits, I enjoy the odd crude joke as much as the next man, but that doesn't mean there's nothing else to me. I grew up in a rough place, and to some extent anyone's habits are shaped by the culture they grew up in. I do swear far too much, even for my own liking, and I do have a bit of a tough shell at times, but that doesn't mean you can't get beyond it. Hooky always tried to push this sense that we were two of a kind, when, really, we couldn't be more different.

Joy Division was deadly serious: there was no ruse to rumble, no laughing up our sleeves at people being taken in by an elaborate spoof; we were real and we were genuine. We almost weren't like a band; we were more like four individuals doing our own thing with almost no direct musical interplay or discussion about our music going on between us. We were like four planets in space orbiting this sun called Joy Division, and I think that's what gave us our distinctive sound. We had no preconceptions about what we were going to make and so the sound we made was very different to what you'd hear on radio and television. It came from within us; it was absorbed from the outside but not influenced or gleaned through intense discussion. We were influenced by our individual record collections and, while we all shared a liking for certain musicians and bands, such as Lou Reed, The Velvet Underground, Kraftwerk and, from earlier days, the Stones, Neil Young and Led Zeppelin, we each had different enough musical tastes to bring a range of ideas and influences into the studio.

The other part of my life — my family life — was in a state of turmoil. Four months before we went into the studio to record *Unknown Pleasures*, in December 1978, Jimmy, my stepfather, who had already battled lung cancer once, found it had returned more virulently than before. Because my mother couldn't travel, I had to go and visit him in the hospital, where most of the time he was dosed up on morphine. One day, I went in to see Jimmy and he died in front of me, just the two of us in the room. This affected me profoundly, as well as leaving both my mother and grandmother in very challenging circumstances, and I guess this episode, in an indirect way, would come to influence my contribution to Joy Division. The music we made came from life experience, informing the interplay with our instruments. What each of us played was the sound of that combination. Put all those inner conversations together, and you ended up with a Joy Division song.

Occasionally, one of us would suggest something to someone else, but it didn't happen very often. The last time I tried it was on 'Transmission', but Hooky didn't like it. He seemed to interpret it as telling him what to do. So I gave up. It's a shame, because you would like to feel you're part of a team, all pushing in the same direction with a common goal, but for some reason I've never fathomed, it felt as if Hooky saw some kind of imagined competition going on inside the band. As the years went on, this only got worse, and I never really understood why. I felt he always tried to make out there was some kind of rivalry between us and, apparently, he still does. Even now, even though he left New Order several years ago and we've had almost zero contact since, he's still trying to perpetuate this myth that we had a rivalry dating back to when we were kids. I've been told that he dates it as far back as my having come out of school with two O levels to his one, which if it's true is bizarre. Any perceived rivalry between Hooky and me exists nowhere except inside his own head.

I wish he'd come out and spoken to me about it, but the only time it broke the surface and we had a proper row was after a New Order gig at Barrowlands, in Glasgow, about how loud he was on stage. As I've got older, I've developed tinnitus, which, if aggravated, can be like having a dentist's drill going off in your head for days on end. On stage I use a 30-watt guitar amp while he had a 1000-watt bass rig with a 'mine's bigger than yours' bass cabinet, which gives you some idea of what I was putting up with. My little Vox AC30, like The Beatles used, against this monstrosity of two six-by-four-foot cabinets just a few feet away from me on stage. It was obviously just too loud and was deafening me every night. This came to a head that night at Barrowlands, and I lost my rag and we ended up having a big row over it, smashing the dressing room up, including all the mirrors — which is a whole lot of bad luck. But that's the only time I can recall us actually having it out. The rest was suppressed for the sake of the continuation of the band, but this burning resentment he seemed to have was tiresome, palpable and pointless.

Going back to the image that had been created of us as elitist doom-mongers, there are fewer better stories to counter this than one about touring the UK with the Buzzcocks in the autumn of 1979. By then, the Buzzcocks were quite a successful band and had generously offered us a support slot, playing to large audiences at big venues, a really kind gesture for which I'll always be indebted to them. I've said before how much we owed the Buzzcocks for their support in the early days, but back then we showed our appreciation by constantly playing tricks on them. It was pretty childish really. We developed a bit of a rapport with their road crew because we travelled with them, and we were always taking the piss out of each other. In fact, the New Order song 'Love Vigilantes' came about as a result of travelling with the Buzzcocks crew on that tour. One of them was really into country music and he'd play it in the van the whole time. I remember thinking that this music was shit, but noticed how the songs all had a narrative, usually a sob story. This guy liked the really cheesy end of the country genre: there was one song I remember where the singer went through every state in America as a lyric – 'Alaska if she's seen you', 'What does Delaware?': corny as hell, but so corny it was good. Years later, I remembered that and wrote a song that had a storyline, and that was 'Love Vigilantes'.

Anyway, at one stage during the tour, the lighting guy had played a trick on me and dosed me up with some big lump of something – he said it would help me sleep. I was still a bit naïve back then and didn't know what it was, and it nearly blew my head clean off my shoulders. I got my own back by going to a fishing tackle shop, buying a load of maggots and pouring them into his lighting desk. That night, he was trying to do the lights for the Buzzcocks and all these maggots were crawling out of his desk. From there, things just escalated. At one venue we emptied all the leftover food from the gig on to the roof of the crew's van. They didn't see it when they got in, but as soon as they braked, all this half-eaten food came sliding down the windscreen.

When it came to the last night of the tour, at the Rainbow Theatre in London, the Buzzcocks' girlfriends had come down to join them, an opportunity we identified as too good to miss. We bought a dozen white mice and, when everyone was inside the venue, let them loose in their van. The poor girls went berserk when they saw them, screaming their heads off. We were waiting nearby in the car, nursing a couple of dozen fresh eggs, and as soon as we heard the screams we screeched round the corner, drove past and let them have it. Childish, I know, but we *were* children and it made us laugh.

Chapter Ten

Agecroft to Islington and that fateful day

Joy Division finished the 1970s on a high. *Unknown Pleasures* was doing well, we'd just finished a hugely enjoyable and successful tour, the band's profile was higher than it had ever been and it seemed to be growing by the day. We embarked upon the 1980s excited about what was to come. Elsewhere, things weren't quite so rosy: Margaret Thatcher had become prime minister and was about to sink her teeth into the working classes, unemployment was spiralling and, as the decade began, the British steel industry was at a standstill due to strike action. We'd just had the 'winter of discontent', the effects of which, thanks to Terry, even managed to filter down to Joy Division.

We were rehearsing at the time in a place opposite Lower Broughton Baths, next to North Salford Youth club. It wasn't the most salubrious place: when it started to get dark, rats would appear at one end of the room. We shared the space with A Certain Ratio, so made sure we put their gear at the end of the room where we'd seen the rats.

I arrived there one day to find a queue of burly-looking men standing at the foot of the staircase that led to the first-floor rehearsal room. As I was walking in, one of them stopped me and said, 'Excuse me, mate, is this where the porn film is?'

'Er, I'm sorry?' I replied.

'This is where a band called Joy Division rehearses, right?'

'Yes,' I said, unsure where this was heading. These were not only big lads, they seemed to be looking for us.

'One of our lads has a cousin called Terry,' he said. 'He said there was a porn film showing here tonight.'

I went upstairs and found the windows shrouded in blackout curtains and, in the dim light of the single bulb, saw Terry setting up the chairs in rows, cinema-style. His reaction suggested he hadn't been expecting me.

He swallowed and explained what was going on.

'It's the picket line from Agecroft Colliery,' he said. 'One of them is my cousin and, to give them a bit of a boost, I thought I'd show them this porn film.' He picked up the box. 'It's called *Eel Fuckers of Amsterdam.*'

Fellini, eat your heart out.

None of us knew anything about this, of course – we were supposed to be rehearsing, but Terry had arranged this cultural occasion and mixed up his dates. He couldn't organize a piss-up in a brewery – officially, in fact: there was an occasion where he did try to organize a party in a Manchester brewery, and it all went dreadfully wrong.

Eventually, all the miners traipsed in and sat down. To their muttered disquiet, Terry had a bit of trouble getting the projector working and in the end had to call on Steve's know-how to get it going. Then, just before the film started, we heard Ian coming up the stairs talking to someone. He was throwing out names like

Dostoyevsky, Nietzsche and Simone de Beauvoir, and when the door opened and a man walked in ahead of him we realized he was with a French journalist who'd flown over from Paris to interview him. Ian walked in and stopped dead. Where he'd expected to find us all set up and ready to rehearse, instead he found a load of miners in donkey jackets sitting in front of a makeshift screen with the lights out.

'What's going on?' he asked.

'Oh, not much,' I replied. 'These lads are striking miners and Terry's putting a porn film on to show them.'

Ian whirled round to the journalist and said, 'It's not normally like this, I promise,' just as the film flickered into life on the screen. As you can probably imagine from the title, it was utterly disgusting.

Anyway, this atmosphere of industrial unrest and social deprivation would set the tone for the forthcoming decade, but we weren't to know that at the time. Hence it was with feelings of excitement and optimism that we went into the studio in March 1980 to record our second album, *Closer*.

Martin Hannett was in the producer's chair again and this time we had a little bit more of a budget than we'd had for *Unknown Pleasures*. Because we'd moaned so much about Strawberry Sound, we were installed at Pink Floyd's Britannia Row in Islington, north London. The difference was immediately obvious: the sound wasn't dead, there was a tangible ambience to the rooms and it had great big speakers that sounded like club speakers. One strong memory I have of our first day there is the receptionist bringing us tea and sandwiches. I was gobsmacked. We were being treated like proper musicians rather than unwashed northern scum! Yes, things were definitely looking up.

I'd been growing more and more interested in synthesizers since

Unknown Pleasures and had acquired an ARP Omni as well as a little Transcendent 2000 that I'd built myself. On this album we intended to experiment with more electronic sounds and, to that end, Martin brought with him a big ARP 2600 modular synth, which was a beast. We used them on a few tracks, notably for some of the sounds on 'The Eternal' and 'Decades', while Martin made some electronic drum sounds with the 2600 that sounded amazing.

The bigger budget also meant that we had a bit more time than the six days we'd had to make *Unknown Pleasures*, which left us with more licence to experiment. We'd usually start at around four o'clock in the afternoon and keep working until dawn. It was a methodology that really suited me: working at night felt more atmospheric and there were fewer distractions; we didn't get bothered as much and could be left to our own devices. Having said that, U2 came over from Ireland to see us at one point. They were just starting out then and I think they were fans of the first album. As a result, they wanted Martin to produce their album, so they sat in on the recordings for a little while.

To me, the whole thing seemed like a great big adventure: this intriguing electronic world to experiment with and the opportunity to create new sounds we'd never thought about before. I really enjoyed working with Martin on *Closer*. He was aware of our reservations about *Unknown Pleasures* (and, of course, blamed the engineer and the studio rather than shouldering the criticism himself), so this time we went for a bigger drum sound and used more keyboards.

Ian didn't enjoy *Closer* as much as he'd enjoyed *Unknown Pleasures*. For one thing, he thought that the keyboards 'made it sound like fucking Genesis', but he was also having a bit of a difficult time in his personal life and was quite often in an antagonistic frame of mind. He'd met and started a relationship with Annik Honoré, a music journalist from Brussels who worked for the Belgian Embassy in London, and he was in a vulnerable frame of mind while we were down in the capital. It was another Ian contradiction: he felt guilty about the affair because he was married to Debbie and they had a baby girl, Natalie, only a few months old, but at the same time he still wanted to be with Annik. It wasn't like Ian to have an affair, and with this, along with his epilepsy, he was walking a dangerous path.

We were all staying together in a flat not far from the studio in which the bedrooms were at opposite ends. Steve, Hooky and Rob were in one part, while Martin, Ian and I shared the other side. Annik came and stayed for a while, but from the moment she arrived there seemed to be a bit of an 'Oh look, it's John and fucking Yoko' vibe from Rob and Hooky. They started playing all sorts of jokes on them, taking the piss and giving them grief. I felt that it was none of our business really; Ian's private life was nothing to do with the band. But Rob and Hooky wouldn't let up, and sometimes it would go a little bit too far. Inevitably, it led to a falling-out when Ian got sick of it. A bit of needle had crept in: where it had started off as being funny, the ribbing had begun to develop a bit of an edge. It went beyond the verbal: Rob and Hooky started messing about with their bed, putting cornflakes in it so when they got back late from the studio, knackered, the bedclothes would be full of them; or they'd have dismantled the bed and folded it up — all this coming at the end of a long night when we'd all been working hard in the studio and Ian could have done without shit like that.

Not surprisingly, given the constant needling from Rob and Hooky, Ian started drifting away from the band a little and began spending time with Genesis P. Orridge from Throbbing Gristle. There was also this weird Dutchman who was hanging around, and Ian started knocking about with him too. The poor guy was being pulled from pillar to post by all the piss-taking, Annik, his guilt about

Debbie and Natalie and his illness. It's no surprise he didn't have a great time recording the album.

On occasion, Rob could be quite odd back then. We'd get back to the flat about nine in the morning most days, wiped out, and one day as I was getting into bed he came in and said, 'All right, Bernard? I'm just going to sit here and read the *NME*. You don't mind, do you?'

'It's nine o'clock, Rob,' I said. 'Why don't you get some shut-eye?'

He looked at me.

'I'm going to read the fucking *NME*,' he replied, paused for a moment and added, 'And I'm going to read it out to you.'

He might have been stoned, I don't know, but sure enough he sat there and read the *NME* from front to back, every single word, including the adverts, out loud at the top of his voice.

To make things worse, Martin was there too: in our bedroom, Ian slept in the bed and Martin or I would sleep on the table or the settee. But, to my dismay, Martin didn't find Rob irritating, he seemed to find him really interesting, and I was left trying desperately to sleep between these two fucking lunatics. Martin was saying stuff like, 'Read that bit again Rob, that was fascinating,' and Rob would go back and read exactly the same thing out again. We were invariably late getting to the studio every day, which was always Rob's fault. You'd try to wake him and, even though he'd asked you to make sure he was up in time, he'd do the same thing to you every time: his two front teeth were false ones which he'd keep in a glass of water overnight by the side of the bed, and when you'd try to wake him up he'd reach for the glass, take the teeth out and fling the water over you. Every fucking day.

Despite these kinds of shenanigans, I really enjoyed making *Closer*. It was nice being in London — that was a new experience for us — and it was great having our own flat and going out to clubs, bars and restaurants. You'd notice little regional differences, even in the fish and chip shops. There was one just down the road from Britannia Row, and it had this thing called rock salmon: we had no idea what it was. They didn't have steak and kidney puddings either. There were all these little things to remind you that you weren't at home but among southerners.

The songs on *Closer* weren't quite as set in stone as they had been on *Unknown Pleasures*. Where, previously, the songs had been honed, buffed and polished with relentless live performance, this time we just had the basic formats of some of them on a cassette, while others we had played live. We'd take Martin these demos and start recording the songs properly in the studio. For the most part, we were working in a different way to *Unknown Pleasures*: at Strawberry, we'd gone in, played it live a few times and picked the best take, which was the old-school way of doing it. This time, on some of the tracks, we'd record an electronic drumbeat, say, then play our parts over that in a series of overdubs. It was an interesting experience, because we'd never done it before. It made the whole album sound fatter. All of us being there together helped as well, I think, as, apart from the needling of Ian, and Rob doing the odd mad thing, we were there as a team. Where, before, we'd popped into the studio at the weekend, this time we were all living the whole experience together and it gave it a sense of unity.

It was a great studio, too, Britannia Row. Pink Floyd certainly knew what they were doing when it came to sound. There was a range of different rooms we could experiment with; we could send sound through piped speakers and PA systems all over the building. There was one particular great big room, a snooker room, in which we put a massive PA set up with loads of microphones, and it sounded amazing. There was no real need to use artificial ambience, even if we'd wanted to: so many of the rooms sounded fantastic naturally.

Being there at night could give you an odd feeling, though: we picked up some ghostly whistles one night and recorded them. You could definitely feel a strange atmosphere sometimes. It didn't stop us messing around, though: occasionally, when we got bored, Ian and I would go into the front office and rifle through the receptionist's Rolodex. It was full of all these names and phone numbers of people who had some connection to the studio, so we'd pick a few out and ring them up at four in the morning, just to wake them up. One of them was John Peel. Like the Buzzcocks, he was someone who'd helped us on the way who ended up on the receiving end of a bit of nonsense. But that's what we were like: I guess the music was so heavy we needed to relieve the tension and, whenever we got bored, we'd just start fucking around like idiots.

Thinking back to those nights, sniggering our way through the Rolodex looking for likely victims, one hand over the mouthpiece as we'd put our ears to the receiver to hear the sleepy croak of the latest victim before collapsing in giggles, it still astonishes me to think that Ian had less than two months to live. I had no inkling that he was feeling in any way suicidal. None of us did. You look back for signs, for indicators, for missed cries for help, and maybe sometimes hindsight leads you to attach weight to incidents and words that wasn't there at the time. But while he'd become somewhat withdrawn during the recording of *Closer*, and the long studio hours and nocturnal working methods perhaps exacerbated his epilepsy a little — before returning home in early April, we played four gigs in London in the space of three days and he went into a fit on stage at one of the shows at the Rainbow — I can't recall anything that gave a hint of what was only a few weeks away. He was clearly conflicted about many things — his marriage, Annik, his medical condition, the pressures of being the front man of a successful band — but nothing at the time suggested he'd take such a drastic step.

Yet, within just days of those late-night phone pranks at Britannia Row, we got the news that he'd tried to commit suicide. We knew he was down about his health and that his relationships were cleaving him in two: it was neither woman's fault but, between Debbie and Annik, love really was tearing him apart. He had a child with Debbie, and I think he felt immensely guilty about even considering walking away from that situation. I'm sure he wanted someone, anyone, to tell him what he should do. If he'd turned to me and asked outright what I thought, stay with Debbie or go with Annik, I know that if I'd have expressed an opinion either way he'd have probably gone with that. It was as if he didn't want the responsibility of having to make the decision himself. He was in a very suggestive state of mind and seemed desperate for someone to bail him out, to make the decision for him. There was no way I could or would do that; it was none of my business. It was a decision only he could make, but he showed no willingness to make it, and I found that very strange. It wasn't just me: none of us wanted to tell him what we thought he should do, as the group was our boundary line; anything outside it was off limits. So he just went on prevaricating, turning things over and over in his mind, and it seems the method he settled upon to extricate himself from this limbo was trying to kill himself. That's never the right solution. It's always better to resolve the situation, no matter how painful.

Strange as it may sound, it wasn't until after his death that we really listened to Ian's lyrics and clearly heard the inner turmoil in them, even before any of this started, way back to his lyric writing in the early days. I can only imagine what was going on in his head. He never talked to us or indicated anything about any deep-seated problems he may have had but, sadly, it was there in his words, right from the start.

One day in early April, only a few days after getting back from

London, we all got a call from Rob to say that Ian had taken an overdose. He wasn't dead, he'd called the ambulance himself, but he was in hospital.

He stayed in overnight but came out before he was ready in order to do a scheduled gig we had in Bury. He clearly wasn't up to it, and we should have cancelled. God knows why we didn't. I think Rob probably decided that cancelling would have just made Ian even more upset — he'd have felt he'd let everyone down, the band and the audience. We had a standby singer in Alan Hempsall from Crispy Ambulance, the idea being that with Ian so frail we'd have Alan in the wings in case he couldn't get through the whole set. And of course Ian couldn't get through it. He tried, but in the end he just walked off the stage. Poor Ian, his head must have been all over the place. When Alan took his place the bottles started flying and there was a full-scale riot.

I wasn't that bothered by the violence: you got used to extreme events at punk gigs. But in the dressing room, Ian was in bits, in floods of tears, head in his hands, repeating, 'It's all my fault, all this is my fault.' Roadies were coming in bleeding from head wounds where bottles had hit them; it was an awful situation. Rather than making Ian feel less guilty, which had been Rob's intention in going ahead with the gig, it had made him feel worse.

Because of the situation with Debbie, who'd found out about Annik, Ian was staying with Tony and his wife, Lindsay, at this point but after a while I invited him to come and stay with me. I tried to talk to him about what was going on. I even tried hypnosis (I'd been reading about past-life regression therapy and tried it on Ian; see Appendix 1). We'd be up late into the night, as I'd taken to staying up until four or five in the morning since we recorded *Closer*. I'd either listen to music or watch films — a lot of Stanley Kubrick, I remember — or, when it got really late and everything had shut down, I'd sit there bored out of my skull, listening to *Truckers' Hour* on the radio, and build synthesizers.

When Ian came to stay I'd talk to him about all sorts of things, what books he liked, for example, just trying to help as best I could, keep him stimulated. At one point I asked him straight if he'd really intended to commit suicide or was it a classic cry for help. He was unequivocal. 'I definitely intended to kill myself,' he said. 'The only reason I bottled out was that I didn't think I had enough tablets and I'd heard that if you don't take enough to kill you, you can end up with brain damage.'

But you never knew if Ian really meant what he was saying. I tried to be straight with him, to pull him up. We were walking back from rehearsals one night, back to where I was living at the time, in a place called Peel Green, and I purposely took us through the big cemetery there, pointing at the gravestones saying, 'It's fucking stupid, Ian. Imagine what it would be like to see your name on one of them. I can't tell you which way to go in your life, but killing yourself definitely isn't the answer.' I was trying to make him see what a waste of a life it would have been if he'd succeeded, but I didn't get much of a response.

As human beings, we all mature physically from childhood to adolescence and then into adulthood, but our emotions lag behind. In our twenties, I think most of us still have the emotional capacity of an adolescent: our emotional maturity hasn't kept pace with our physical maturity. Your twenties are a particularly difficult period: you're not tough emotionally, you're still quite soft and malleable, and it's a period when you go through a sequence of emotional storms in your relationships. But you aren't yet equipped to deal with some of the shit that life throws at you. I think if you can make it through your twenties you can pretty much deal with anything. Sadly, Ian turned out to be one of those people who couldn't.

It wasn't just me; we all tried to steer him away from even considering suicide. We thought the best thing was to get things back to normal, as far as possible: we even did a couple of gigs, with one at Birmingham University turning out to be the last we ever played as Joy Division. We'd written two new songs while Ian was in hospital, 'In a Lonely Place' and 'Ceremony', which we thought would cheer him up, keep things moving forward and stop him from dwelling on the past.

We performed these two songs for the first time in Birmingham. After that, we were due to head off for our first ever tour of America. Everyone was really excited about it. We'd been to France, Belgium and Germany, but this was different, this was America. I went into Manchester with Ian to buy some new clothes for the tour. He bought some horrible shoes, these suede winklepickers with laces on the heels, and I said to him, 'Ian, they're like dead men's shoes.' I don't know why the fuck I said that.

Around this time, we made the video for 'Love Will Tear Us Apart'. Rob must have sensed there was something in the air, because he'd brought in a multitrack tape recorder to record the Birmingham show (it wasn't a very good show, because we couldn't hear ourselves on stage) and then make the video. He asked a guy called Harry de Mack, a sound engineer who'd been working with us for a long, long time, to record the video and asked for the live tapes he'd asked Harry to record for us at a number of recent gigs. Harry announced that he wanted a very large sum of money for them, something Rob refused to entertain. Unsurprisingly, Harry didn't show up for the video shoot. Never a band to do things the obvious way, we insisted on playing live at the recording of the video, setting up a PA at TJ Davidson's, and so making it a considerable task to fit the images to the recorded version of the song. It worked out in the end, but it turned out to be some of the last footage of Ian ever filmed.

We had friends in a band called Section 25, and they had their own problems: they were called that because one of the band members had once been sectioned by his own mother. They lived just outside Blackpool, near a river, and the weather forecast for the weekend before we were due to fly off to America was good. One of the Section 25 lads had the keys to his dad's old speedboat, so Ian and I had made plans to go over there, go out with them on it and get a bit of sunshine: to city boys like us, this sounded a great idea. We were due to fly to America on the Monday and the plan, as I remember it, was that Ian and I would go down to see Section 25 on the Saturday, hang out with them, come back on Sunday and pack, ready to leave the next day. But after a couple of weeks staying with me Ian had decided that he was going to go to his parents' house for a few days. I don't think I was doing him much good, keeping him up all bloody night, to be honest; he could keep normal hours at his parents'. Just before we were due to leave for Blackpool, I had a call from him saying he wanted to go and see Debbie before leaving for America, so he wouldn't come with me to see the guys from Section 25 after all. We arranged to meet at the airport.

I went down and had a brilliant day. The speedboat was fantastic, I learned how to water-ski — badly — and it was great, really good fun, and a beautiful sunny day. We all went back to their house afterwards and I was in the kitchen at about four o'clock in the afternoon when the phone rang. One of the band answered and said, 'Bernard, it's for you, it's Rob.'

'All right, Rob,' I said, 'how are you?'

I was just about to launch into what a great day I'd had when I heard him say something about Ian committing suicide.

'Oh, bloody hell,' I said. 'He's not tried it again, has he?'

'No, Bernard,' said Rob. 'This time he's done it, he's committed suicide. He's dead.'

The room swam in front of my eyes and I was hit full on by a wave of shock. I said again, 'What, he's *tried* it?'

'No,' Rob said. 'He's really done it, Bernard. He's dead. Ian's dead.'

Poor Rob, he had to tell me a couple of times before it sank in. I slid to the floor in shock. I didn't speak, didn't want to say a word to anyone. Section 25 really looked after me out there. Everyone was good to me, the guys from A Certain Ratio too, but I didn't really speak until the funeral. Everyone else went to see Ian in his coffin beforehand, but I couldn't face that. I wanted to remember him as he was when he was alive.

A curious thing had happened the day before Ian died. I'd been to Heaton Park in Prestwich with Simon Topping from A Certain Ratio and, again, it was a lovely sunny day. There's a large hill in Heaton Park and, as we stood at the bottom of it, a beautiful white horse came galloping over the crest. It had no rider, no saddle, it was just this amazing creature of pure white thundering down the hill towards me and Simon. The park was busy with people enjoying the sunshine, but the horse made straight for us. It stopped right in front of us, tossed its mane, dipped its head a couple of times, and we stood looking at each other for a full minute or so. Then, as quickly as it had arrived, the horse turned and ran back up and over the hill. It seemed odd even at the time but, given the events of the night that lay ahead, I wonder if it could have been some kind of omen.

Chapter Eleven

A new sound in a new town

Soon after Ian's funeral, those of us left behind had to decide what we were going to do. Were we going to carry on? The shock had been palpable and this huge presence, this vital part of everything we'd done, had suddenly been snatched away. Would it be right to continue without him? At the same time, we'd had a taste of honey; a glimpse of what life could be away from the drudgery of everyday existence in Salford. We'd all given up our jobs by this time in order to make the band work, too.

The decision we made, having weighed up all the arguments and listened to Rob's input and advice, was to carry on. In hindsight, there was never any serious question that we wouldn't. Having left our jobs, there was neither the prospect of nor desire to do anything else other than make music. We knuckled down and got through it thanks to a combination of sheer willpower and grim determination. It sounds old-fashioned, maybe it's even a bit of a cliché, but, ultimately, willpower and determination were all we had and we drew on deep reserves of both.

The first resolution we made was to play no Joy Division songs. Instead, we'd write a whole new set of songs without Ian – the songs which later became the bulk of the first New Order album, *Movement*. I think Rob wanted to avoid leaving us open to criticism of living off the legacy of Joy Division, but even though we'd made what was unquestionably a bold decision, the music press went ahead and accused us anyway. The British music press at that time was very negative, even vindictive, and they certainly didn't help us; sometimes I wondered if they were even setting out to destroy us. After what we'd just been through, it's something we could have done without.

Another problem we had was with the 'Love Will Tear Us Apart' video. Once we'd got through Ian's funeral and recovered from the shock of his death a little, we thought we'd better start collating all the recordings that were due to appear on a final Joy Division album, *Still*. In addition, 'Love Will Tear Us Apart' was moving up the charts and we needed to get the video together. We tried to get in touch with Harry de Mack, but calls went unanswered and messages unreturned: he was nowhere to be found. Eventually, Rob received a call from Harry's girlfriend insisting that we had to hand over a ridiculous sum of money for them. It was jaw-dropping. We'd known this guy for years, he'd hung out with us and he knew exactly what we'd been through, yet he still tried to pull a stunt like that. Rob struck some sort of deal with him and we got the tapes back in the end. Presumably, Harry got some blood money, hopefully with a heavyduty bit of karma attached.

Obviously, the first decision we had to make after deciding to carry on was how to replace Ian as singer. We'd considered bringing in someone new, and I'd even been approached by people in the street aware of the situation and offering their services. I remember a nice guy who was into Steely Dan coming up to me in St Anne's Square in Manchester, and that's when I realised that it would just feel wrong to bring in somebody new. There was no way we could replace Ian, he was a special person – the band was like a family and we'd just lost a close relative.

From there, it was a short step to deciding that one of us should take over the vocal duties. There was no obvious candidate, so it was agreed we'd all give it a try. We played a handful of gigs in England in the late summer of 1980 – the first was at the Beach Club in Manchester – but then Rob booked us a tour of the eastern seaboard of America and some studio time in Trenton, New Jersey, so that we could get away from the spotlight. The band, the crew, Rob and Martin flew over with us, and we all stayed amid the distinctly seventies decor of the Iroquois Hotel on West 44th Street in Manhattan. It was rundown, with a distinct fragrance of cockroach powder, but it was cheap. And hey, it was in New York, which, after England, was as exciting as it was liberating. From that base, we travelled out every day to Trenton, where we recorded 'In a Lonely Place' and 'Ceremony', the songs we'd written in an attempt to cheer Ian up. If you've ever listened to 'In a Lonely Place', it's no cheerful ditty. In fact, it's probably one of the most doom-laden tracks we'd ever written – and we'd written a few – so why we'd used it as an attempt to cheer Ian up, I've no idea. 'Ceremony', on the other hand, was a very uplifting track, filled with and enhanced by Ian's lyrics. When you listen to those lyrics, it strikes you that they're quite possibly saying, I'll show everyone, I'm going to do it this time. Isn't hindsight a great thing?

We recorded the music at Ears in Trenton, then everyone tried singing, which was a bit of a trial for all involved, and left Rob to start mulling over who should get the job. It was the live shows that would really test our vocal mettle, though, and the day after we finished recording we took all the equipment into Manhattan, ready to head out on the road. Terry, our genius roadie, and Twinny, our other roadie, had fallen out over something and weren't speaking to each other, even though they were sharing a room, and when they parked the truck across the road from the hotel, they didn't disable it. They were supposed to take the distributor cap off so no one could move it but, too distracted by giving each other daggers, neither of them did.

Tony Wilson had come over from Manchester to see how things were going and, one morning, Rob, Hooky and I, who were sharing a room, were woken by a knock on the door. In breezes Tony with a big grin on his face, saying, 'This is perfect, darlings, absolutely perfect, but you're not going to like it. You've had the truck stolen, with all your equipment in it! It's so poetic! The perfect ending!'

I think I came within a whisker of throttling him. He truly seemed to think this was a wonderful thing when it was clearly a disaster, and one laid upon existing disaster.

Rob and Hooky went straight down to the local precinct police station to report the theft. In those days, everyone had ghetto blasters with great big speakers and, sure enough, even the cop on the front desk had one, which was blasting out 'Good Times' by Chic — to which he was dancing. Rob tried to get his attention.

'Excuse me,' he said. 'We're from Manchester in England, and we've just had £47,000 of equipment stolen.'

The policeman held up his hand. 'Just wait for the record to finish, man,' he said. So the pair of them had to wait for the track to end and for him to stop dancing before they could file a report. When they arrived back at the hotel, we realized we needed to phone the insurance company, so Rob picked up the receiver and waved it around, saying, 'Let me deal with this, lads, I used to work in insurance.'

The conversation went something like this:

'Had the truck been disabled?'

'No.'

'Was the truck alarmed?'

'No.'

'Well, in that case, I'm sorry, Mr Gretton, but we can't pay out.'

Rob put the phone down and looked at us. There was a brief silence.

'You fucking dickhead,' we said. 'Why didn't you say yes?'

When the truck was eventually found, all the gear had gone and there were only two things left in it. One was a pair of skis I'd picked up from where they'd been dumped outside a house in New York (I'd just got into skiing, so I'd put them in the truck to take back to England) and the other was Pink Floyd's transformer. Terry, who was responsible for booking the gear, had booked a generator for the tour because our gear was on UK voltage and we'd be using American. In his wisdom, he'd chosen Pink Floyd's transformer, the one they used for their entire live sound and lighting set-up. It was massive. All we had to plug into it were two amps, but Terry had booked a transformer designed for stadium gigs. It was so big the thieves hadn't been able to lift it out of the van.

Years later, Steve did get his black Rogers drum kit back. The gang, which was called the Lost Tribe of Israel, believe it or not, hadn't just targeted us, they'd whipped gear from several other British bands staying at the Iroquois. By the time the police caught up with them, they had a whole warehouse full of stuff they'd nicked, but, of our gear, only Steve's kit was left.

In the meantime, we had to rush out and hire a load of new equipment and buy what we could to replace what we'd lost. Fortunately for me, West 44th Street wasn't far from all the guitar shops. I couldn't find a replacement for my special Vox amp, so I bought a

Yamaha, and then found a Gibson 335 for an amazing price. At last, I thought, a bit of bloody luck going our way. This beautifully crafted guitar was on sale for $550, a fantastic price for a Gibson, still a lot of money, but too good a deal to miss. Hooky bought a new bass and hired a six-string one, Steve hired a kit, and we were ready to go on the road.

Back at the hotel, I put my new guitar in my room facing the wall, went to bed, got up in the morning and noticed something written on the back of the headstock. I picked it up, looked at it, and saw it had 'Seconds' stamped on it. Fucking hell, I thought, now I've gone and bought a duff guitar. Sure enough, there was a big mark in the finish where the tone switch was: the drill had slipped and left behind a great big gouge. It wasn't a disaster, but having believed things were finally looking up, I started to think, What next?

Our first gig of the tour was in Hoboken, then we played Hurrah's and Tier 3 in New York, before finishing up with a gig in Boston. We were under-rehearsed and playing unfamiliar instruments, so it didn't bode well. Hooky couldn't tune the six-string bass he'd hired so he passed it over to me to have a go. I said, 'There's something wrong with this bass, Hooky, it's so tight. I'd need protective eye-wear and a crash helmet to tune it.' I was breaking strings, and they were whipping about like piano wire. We just managed to get it in tune before we went on, and when he got out there he found it was a shit instrument to play. Years later, I found out it hadn't been a six-string bass after all, it was a baritone guitar, for which you're supposed to use a completely different tuning. We had it tuned way too high; the neck was like a banana and could have snapped altogether. It must have been like playing a cheese slicer.

Instrument issues aside, everyone was worried about singing in Ian's place. I got shitfaced most nights to try and take my mind off it, but we all had a go, while Rob watched from the sidelines, stroking his chin. Fortunately for us, the audiences were great and really understanding. We got through the tour, and Rob announced that I should be the singer. I've no idea why, we must have all been as hopeless as each other, but he told me I'd got the job and, with some trepidation, I agreed to do it. I wasn't wild about the idea, but I was up for the challenge. My last memory of that tour was the final night in Boston. This guy met us afterwards, said he'd enjoyed the gig and told us he had a loft we could stay in if we didn't fancy travelling back to New York that night. He gave us sleeping bags and we all, band and crew, lay on the floor in this old factory building. It was boiling hot, so I had my shirt off, lying on the floor half in and half out of this sleeping bag, when all of a sudden I felt something scuttle across my chest. Then something else did likewise in the other direction. Then I could hear everyone else going, 'Eww, what the fuck's that?' We didn't get much sleep and couldn't get out of there quick enough in the morning. It was horrible, but it cracked us up laughing afterwards. It was either massive cockroaches or possibly mice, but it went on all night. We were serving our dues, that's for sure.

After spending a long time in the shower, we went home and recorded *Movement*. Making *Movement* was a struggle because we were in a subdued, sunken, sallow mood, understandably, with Ian's death still so fresh in our minds. We spent around six to eight months writing new songs, then travelled down to Marcus Music, a studio in London, to record the album. It was a strange time. We were working through the night and sleeping in a pretty depressing hotel during the day. London at the time was beset by rioting, at the height of which the studio bolted the doors, leaving us outside. We'd gone out for a sandwich and they wouldn't let us back in. We were banging on the doors, and the girl on reception thought we were rioters and was pretty scared and in floods of tears. Ultimately, the whole experience was difficult, and different to Joy Division because, without Ian, obviously, something was missing, never to return. It was straightforward in Joy Division: Steve played his drums, Hooky played his bass, I played guitar and keyboards and Ian sang — we all had our specific jobs. Now, the dynamic had completely shifted, everything was off-kilter, everything was different. We were having to adapt to different roles.

We felt a bit like we were in a car in which the steering wasn't quite working properly and we had lost the map. We were trying to find our feet, but the atmosphere was very down in the studio and Martin was necking quite a lot of drugs. To me, it just didn't feel right, it felt as if we were still standing in the shadow of Joy Division. I'd never sung a vocal before, so at first I based it on how Ian used to sound, because that's all I knew. Eventually, I'd find my own identity as a vocalist, but it would take time before I'd come to realize that you just need to be yourself. In those early days, I wasn't being myself and I didn't sound like myself.

I don't have fond memories of *Movement*, and it's certainly far from my favourite New Order album. I played it once or twice after it was finished and decided I didn't like it. I felt all the edges had been smoothed off and it was devoid of its own identity and uniqueness. I really missed Ian being there and his absence was something I was very aware of throughout the entire process.

I felt bad, too, because I was starting to believe we were never going to live up to people's expectations. I was convinced we needed to move forward and assert our own identity. For me, that was the only honest way of doing it. In those first months after Ian's death we were still hanging on to him; he was a crutch to get us through. You have to remember that we'd come from a place where you were told you didn't have a future, that your career prospects were zero and hence you should accept whatever you got and be happy with it. We'd disproved that by forming a successful group, we'd beaten the system to some extent, and I wanted to continue battling and beating that system. Ultimately, though, I felt *Movement* was too doom-laden and that we couldn't persist with this sound any longer. On the bright side, one of the good things that came out of this period was that we were travelling and seeing different places, especially New York, where we spent a lot of time. We met some incredible people there, including a young Jewish girl called Ruth Polsky, an independent promoter who would have put on the Joy Division tour we'd been due to start when Ian died. She was also a kind of queen of the New York club scene.

When we finally arrived in the autumn of 1980, we got on really well. She'd sussed within about a minute that we weren't these serious, earnest young men who wandered around reading Dostoyevsky and quoting Nietzsche but fun-loving guys with a healthy streak of hedonism who were up for a good time. We'd go into Manhattan every night after being in the studio and she'd take us to New York's best clubs: Danceteria, the Peppermint Lounge, the Mudd Club, Area, Tunnel, the Palladium — wherever it might be happening on a particular night. Even when she wasn't working she'd come out with us: she knew everyone in the clubs, and everywhere we went she'd give us a strip of tickets for free drinks.

We were exposed to an entirely different kind of club mentality to the one we'd experienced at home, where it was all jazz funk, sixties nights and, 'Sorry, lads, not with those trainers on.' They'd been square, stiff clubs playing old-fashioned music, venues designed more for copping off than anything else. At Pips in Manchester there were always quite a few Bryan Ferry and David Bowie wannabes: the whole thing was posey and contrived. In New York, by contrast, people were just themselves. The clubs played good, interesting, cool music and all sorts of people mingled with each other. They'd play things like 'Rock the Casbah' by The Clash and Soft Cell's

'Tainted Love' and mix it up with New York stuff, early rappers like Curtis Blow, music from Sugar Hill Records, Sharon Redd, Chic — music you'd hear over there on the big dance station Kiss FM. It was a healthy, eclectic musical mix, and you could get in wearing a pair of banana skins on your feet if you felt like it, because nobody cared what you looked like. Everyone was dead friendly and relaxed, we met a lot of nice people and had a really great time. We had a very real sense of positive cultural tourism, including a distinct advantage with the ladies, thanks to our cute English accents. Even a rough northern accent could pay dividends. It was exciting to be there. New York was — and is — a great city in which to lead a cool lifestyle and have really good fun. Perhaps not good, *clean* fun, but fun nevertheless.

I made a good friend when I was there called Frank Callari, a DJ who would go on to manage acts like Ryan Adams and Marilyn Manson but who has now unfortunately passed away. He was a big, warm-hearted guy and toured with us on one occasion. He'd send me cassettes of the New York radio stations, which blew away the English radio of the time. For a start, there were no dance music stations in England back then, and he would send me over tapes of the American ones, and they were just amazing, a real musical education. Also, I had a good friend in Berlin called Mark Reeder, who has a trance and electronica label called MFS, which stands for 'Masterminded For Success'. Back then, Mark was also Factory Records' man in Germany — he was from Manchester but had moved to Berlin in the late seventies — and he would send me twelve-inch dance records from all over Europe. Mark's still a good friend, and his is a fascinating story: he produced the last album on the old East German state record label Amiga before the Wall came down, and started MFS in late 1990 — the initials were also those of the old Ministerium für Staatssicherheit, the East German secret police better known as the Stasi, which was quite a punk thing to do when you think about it.

I'd listen to Frank's tapes and Mark's records, which, coupled with the clubs in New York, would all become big influences on me. I didn't realize this until much later, of course: as far as I was concerned, I was just having a good time, but it clearly made an impression. We all thought New York sounded like the future whereas Manchester at that time sounded like the past. Manchester had a straitjacket on, but music in New York was loose and free. London was also developing a more vibrant club culture and, a bit like Ruth Polsky in New York, an early *and* current comrade of the band Kevin Millins took us around a lot of clubs there: Heaven, Taboo, The Black Hole and other establishments and dives in Soho and beyond. Kevin had also promoted early Joy Division gigs and became a long-term friend and corruptive mentor.

It was an amazing time. All that needed to happen now was for those influences to start seeping into the music we were making after the demise of Joy Division.

Chapter Twelve

Resurrection

We knew that if we were to dissociate ourselves successfully from Joy Division, a new monicker was essential. Choosing a name for any band is a difficult thing to do: on one hand, it's just a handle with which to pick up an identity; on the other, it will stick with you for a long time — in our case, thirty years and counting — so you have to get it right. We were really struggling to come up with something effective that we all liked until, one day, Rob was reading an article in the *Guardian* that detailed how, after the fall of the Khmer Rouge, a new order had been established in Cambodia. He looked up from the paper and said, 'Lads, how about New Order?'

We turned it over in our minds. It wasn't bad.

'One thing's for sure,' he went on. 'We don't want another name with any Fascist connotations after all the hassle we had with Joy Division. New Order. It's completely neutral.'

Ahem.

In all innocence, we honestly didn't know there was a connection between Hitler and the phrase 'new order', so we pursed our lips, nodded and agreed. It had a similar vibe to 'Joy Division' and it was certainly appropriate. So we went for it.

Of course, no sooner had we announced it than everyone was saying, 'Here we go, they're at it again, they're a bunch of bloody Fascists! Why don't they just call themselves Third Reich and be done with it?' (There was even a strip in *Viz* a few years ago where one of the characters was presenting a *Top of the Pops*-style show and introduced, playing their new single, 'Blue Sunday', a band called Third Reich . . .) We'd landed ourselves in it again: yet another layer of disaster to add to the litany of disasters. We decided to stick with it, though: we knew we weren't Fascists, and at the time we were doing gigs for Rock Against Racism, but no one wrote a single word about that. Fuck everyone, we thought, fuck the world, we're going to do what we want to do and just get on with it, New Order we were, New Order we'd stay. There was just one more piece missing. When it was decided I was going to be the singer, I felt I couldn't sing and play guitar at the same time. Well, actually, I couldn't sing full stop and had really only just learnt the guitar, so to try and combine the two was just too much to take on. There'd been an incident at a Joy Division gig at Eric's in Liverpool once, where we'd been fooling around in the dressing room, things had got a little out of hand and Rob had lunged at me with a bottle. The bottle had smashed and put a deep gash in my finger — about a minute before the gig. We went on stage and there was blood all over my guitar and my shirt, and it was clear I needed to get a plaster on it at the very least. Steve's girlfriend, Gillian, who he'd met when her band, The Inadequates, were rehearsing near ours, happened to be at the gig that night, and I hissed into the wings, 'Gillian can play guitar, can't she? Just get her up for one song while I get patched up.' So that's what happened: Gillian climbed up on stage, filled in on guitar for one song and then I came back on after some running repairs to my finger.

When it became apparent that I was having problems singing and playing simultaneously, we had a meeting, decided we should get someone else in and remembered the incident at Eric's. Gillian's name was suggested — who by, I can't remember, possibly Rob — and because she'd got up that night and coped pretty well, it seemed a good solution. It was certainly much easier than the rigmarole involved in finding someone completely new. Also, her personality fitted in with the rest of us, and that was important. We asked her if she was interested, she was, and that was that, Gillian Gilbert joined New Order on keyboards and guitar, which meant I was free to concentrate on singing.

Gillian found it a bit difficult at the start, but she got better and better. The style of guitar I'd been writing was quite aggressive, and Gillian's not really like that; it was like giving a male vocal part to a girl to sing. It was hard for her to have to step into both my headspace and my shoes and interpret what I'd written. It would have been a steep learning curve for anyone. Then she had to learn to play keyboards as well, all in front of three blokes, three *blokey* blokes who were, you know, blokes . . .

So, we had the line-up and we had the name. Now we had to take the music forward. The New York influence was crucial, of course, but back in the UK there were a few places in London playing some great stuff too and we were being exposed to new types of music at just the right time, just when we needed it. In the few short years of Joy Division we'd made some dark and extreme music which I think took that sound as far as it could go, and we knew we couldn't just continue doing that for ever. In that respect, it was similar to punk, where every song would be a frantic three-, maybe four-chord thrash. It was absolutely great, you'd go and see these bands and there'd be this fantastic energy on the stage and in the audience, but within a few years it had hit a brick wall, had said what it needed to say and had nowhere else to go. It morphed into something else. The success of Joy Division had suggested we'd done something unique, something new, but, like punk, there was only so far we could take that ethos and that sound. For one thing, our music had become so incredibly dark and cold, we couldn't really get any darker or colder. And, obviously, Ian was no more.

We reached a crucial turning point at a critical time: being present for this extraordinary zeitgeist in New York and being exposed to fresh influences from Europe and the US via people like Mark Reeder, Frank Callari and Ruth Polsky. I remember quite clearly sitting in a club in New York one night, around three or four o'clock in the morning, and thinking how great it would be if we made music, electronic music, that could be played in one of these clubs.

I'd become interested in electronic music back in the Joy Division days. As a band, we loved Kraftwerk, the inventiveness they had, and we'd play 'Trans-Europe Express' through the PA before we went on stage. But we were also into disco records by people like Donna Summer and Giorgio Moroder, anything that had a new sound and felt like it was looking forward. We still loved guitars, too, though: the Velvets, Lou Reed, David Bowie, Neil Young and Iggy Pop. The first time I went round to meet Ian at his house after we gave him the singer's job, he said, 'Fucking listen to this,' put a record on, and the song was 'China Girl' by Iggy Pop from *The Idiot*. He said it had just come out that day. I was blown away; I'd not heard any of Iggy's music before and I thought it was fantastic. There was also the stuff that went back to my youth-club days: the Stones, Free, Fleetwood Mac, Santana, Led Zep, The Kinks.

Then Bowie produced the trilogy of albums he made in Berlin, which was infused with a cold austerity, something we could relate to living in Manchester, a place with a very similar vibe. We also liked the B-sides of 'Heroes' and 'Low', pieces of electronic music he'd created along with Brian Eno. I *loved* it. It was a whole new kind of music to me, one that was moving things on, looking to the future, not the past.

All these influences were converging at roughly the same time as the equipment was becoming available to put them into practice. I'd experimented with synthesizers in Joy Division, on occasion with Martin Hannett, and had a string synthesizer myself, an ARP Omni II, which I bought because I liked the look of it: I didn't really care what it sounded like. As it happened, it was a string synthesizer, which was fortunate, because I wanted one and it was the only affordable synth on which you could play more than one note at a time. Most synths at the time were super-expensive, way out of my price range, but one day I saw a magazine called *Electronics Today* that had a picture of a synthesizer on the front and the legend, 'Build this for £50' written over the top of it. I bought the magazine and the kit and for three months stayed up really late putting together my Transcendent 2000. I'd put a film on the TV, usually *2001* or *A Clockwork Orange*, or a film from the 1940s. I loved the films of Powell and Pressburger; they were the sort of films where I could turn the sound off and have these great images playing into the night as I soldered away, music on in the background.

I was also working a lot with Martin Usher, the scientist Martin Hannett had introduced me to when he came in to fix my guitar amp during the recording of *Unknown Pleasures*. Whenever I got stuck on something technical, I'd go and see him, and as well as giving me good advice he would tell me about all the latest developments in the silicon world of microchips. He wasn't interested in electronic music himself — trams were his thing — but it was Martin who'd first told me about samplers. I remember clearly him telling me, 'There's a new thing coming out called a sampler, maybe we should build one,' and I asked what it was. It turned out to be a development of the thing that I'd used in the making of *Unknown Pleasures*, that very crude, simple sampler. The technology had advanced by this stage but, generally, samplers weren't available outside universities and laboratories. Martin also told me about these amazing things called floppy disks, a revolutionary step forward that meant you could store the sounds you were creating on the samplers and use them again. Previously, as soon as you turned the machine off you'd lose everything, the memory would be wiped, but these floppy disks, Martin told me, enabled you to save the sounds you'd made and use them again. It was the future, he said, and talked me through how first of all there'd be 8-bit samplers, which would sound like long wave radio, then they'd bring in 12-bit samplers, which would sound like medium wave, and then 18- or 24-bit samplers, which would sound like FM radio. On top of everything else, Martin was getting me all fired up about the kind of technology that was coming over the horizon. (Martin never took any payment for all the help he gave me, incidentally, but we helped him out in other ways. He had an odd situation in the basement of his home in that he had a Hells Angel living down there with his motorbike. This guy was very, very keen on LSD and Martin only asked that we made a charitable contribution to his purchases.)

Despite all these developments, the first electronic dance track we recorded as New Order came about by a fortunate accident. In the summer of 1981 we went into the Marcus Music studio in London, where Steve found an Oberheim synth in the corner and tried plugging a drum machine into it. As luck would have it, the drum machine triggered the Oberheim into a rhythm that was perfectly in time with the drums and it sounded great — like Giorgio Moroder, but at a fraction of what hiring him would have cost! This seems like nothing now, but there weren't many synths that could do that in those days: usually they were played by hand like a traditional instrument, or with a crude but expensive sequencer. With this little Oberheim, however, you took the pitch from the keyboard and the rhythm from the drum machine.

We went to Martin and showed him, and the first thing he did was get Steve behind his kit to lay down a beat and record live drums. I asked how we were going to trigger the synthesizer from the drums and he told me that the VU meters on the tape machine had a test output which produced a voltage. We took a cable out of the hi-hat track, plugged it into the synthesizer — and it worked. It would start to go out of time after about thirty-two bars, but we'd just start the machine again. Back then, we didn't have a sequencer: music computers simply weren't available and there was no MIDI, which is a code that synthesizers use to talk to each other. None of that stuff had been invented yet, so for us it was all about control voltages and gate voltages. It wasn't perfect by any means — the keyboard would go out of pitch — but it just about worked, and that's how we wrote 'Everything's Gone Green', our very first tentative step into electronic dance music.

One large piece of fallout from this, however, was that it marked the end of our relationship with Martin Hannett. When we put 'Everything's Gone Green' together, we thought it was great — these big, powerful drums under this pounding *jigga jigga jigga* sound from the synthesizer. It sounded like the future and, best of all, it sounded *aggressive*, like someone kicking you in the face.

When it came to the mix, however, Martin started making it all wispy and ethereal sounding again. I remember Hooky and I were in the control room, sitting on this big long bench seat at the back. Martin didn't want us there, so what he did was tell us the engineer had diabetes and the temperature had to be kept cold in order to keep him awake, turn the air-conditioning down and try to freeze us out of the studio. He knew the vents were right above where we were sitting. We stuck it out as best we could, and I'd whisper to Hooky, 'The drum machine needs to go up, you tell him,' and Hooky would. Martin'd tut, give him a dirty look and do nothing, so after about ten minutes I'd try it, and we'd bat it between us, harassing him into keeping the sound aggressive.

In the end he got sick of this, stood up, said, 'Right, you do it, then,' and went to bed. So in the end we mixed it ourselves. Chris Nagel, the engineer, was saying, 'What are you doing? You haven't got a clue!' He was right, we didn't have a clue, but if you don't have a go at things, how are you ever going to have a clue? We were musicians, we'd written the bloody song and we knew what it was meant to sound like. So we mixed 'Everything's Gone Green' and at the same time realized we'd finally had enough of this wrestling with Martin.

There was always a contradiction with Martin: he was a catalyst and very inspiring in the studio, but when he was mixing a record, I didn't feel he was capturing the true sound of the band. Occasionally, he was spot on, and one of Martin's mixes that I *did* like was Joy Division's 'Atmosphere'. There's actually some controversy over who recorded and mixed it: we recorded it at Cargo in Rochdale, which was run by a guy called John Brierly, who had given us free or cheap studio time under the assumption that he'd be producing us. We turned up, Rob turned up, then Tony and Martin turned up. There was a big confab over the apparent mix-up and, while they were all arguing in the control room, we wrote 'Atmosphere', right there, that day, on the spot. I think the compromise was that John engineered while Martin produced, but 'Atmosphere' wasn't changed a great deal in the production. Martin put that shimmering, tinkling sound on the chorus, which sounds fantastic, but essentially it was very well engineered and geared more towards the sound we wanted, recorded on a 2-inch-valve 16-track tape recorder that gave it a really fat sound (although I've heard recent versions of it and, these days, I think it desperately needs remastering).

By that time, people had been making experimental electronic music for many years, usually in universities and laboratories, where they'd cut up audio tapes, speed them up, slow them down and put them together in disjointed pieces to create very abstract avant-garde music. These were real pioneers, and the legacy of their work was in the samplers and synthesizers that began to come on to the market in the early eighties. Among other things, they enabled you to take sounds out of the studio and on to the road to play live. I found the sheer range of possibilities offered by a synthesizer and by sound manipulation deeply intriguing, and it was that intrigue that gave birth to the ideas and music we made in New Order.

The Emulator 1 was an early sampler on which you could take pieces of music and bend and shape them. The manufacturers were so exclusive at the start that you had to make an appointment at a shop in London just to try them out, so we all trooped south to have a look at one. To help show what the Emulator 1 could do, they'd sampled the throb of a Harley Davidson engine, something Rob was particularly impressed by. He'd press the key and, instead of a conventional piano sound, a Harley engine came out of the speakers. The look on his face was one of sheer disbelief, as if this was some form of witchcraft. He was looking at it, saying, 'How the hell is that happening?'

They were keen to show us all the other synthesizers too – PPG wave synths, really good new digital technology that was still in its infancy – but Rob just kept going back to the Emulator 1 and making the motorbike noise. In the end, he made us buy it for that reason, but it turned out to be a good investment: we used it on 'Blue Monday' for some of the strings, and you could record anything you wanted on it and play it back as a sample. It made life so much simpler. Its predecessor was the Mellotron, which did a similar thing but used banks of tapes which were pulled back on a spring: when you pressed a key on the keyboard it drew a piece of quarter-inch tape over a playback head. It was very crude but gave you this wonderful, fucked-up sound. However, if you took it on tour, you needed a whole team of technicians just to keep it in tune. The Emulator 1 was a much easier thing to handle.

While I was fascinated and excited by all this incredible technology, there was some initial resistance from rest of the band. I think Steve felt a bit threatened by drum machines at first, while Hooky didn't show any interest in either the keyboards or that kind of music. Eventually, I think Steve came to find it as intriguing as he did threatening and, later on, he really embraced it, especially when it became clear we could use electronic drums as well as his live drum kit.

I did, I admit, get a little bit carried away at first. I'd been so seduced by the technology that I was even trying to persuade people to forget their real instruments and embrace electronic music completely, which was just wrong, and, obviously, the others weren't keen to go down that particular road. The upshot was that New Order became a hybrid band: not purely electronic but making a mix of electronic and guitar-based tracks, which history has shown to be a successful combination.

Fairly soon, we began to have commercial success, especially in America, and it seemed we'd created the right sound at the right time. We started to write more electronic songs, 'Bizarre Love Triangle', for example. People seemed to latch on to it, and things really began to take off. America was a great barometer for this: where at first we'd be playing to four hundred people, we started pulling in fifteen hundred, then two thousand, and every time we'd go back the crowds would just go up and up, until we were playing to twenty or thirty thousand people. In 1986, we had three tracks, 'Thieves Like Us', 'Elegia' and 'Shellshock', in a film called *Pretty In Pink*, which had been written by the same man, John Hughes, who'd written *The Breakfast Club*, which also increased our market over there. We were getting a great deal of airplay on college radio, the gigs were well received and, with the audience effectively doubling every time we went back to America, we reached a stage where we were playing massive concerts.

I was now in a contradictory situation, a little bit like the one in which Ian had found himself; one where the dreams of success were coming true but I wasn't sure if I was comfortable with it. In addition, I'd never dreamed of being a singer yet suddenly I was the frontman of a band playing to crowds of thirty thousand people. I hadn't really expected this swift transformation from highly regarded cult band to international commercial success. I'd never wanted to be part of the mainstream, yet here we were becoming part of it, with the added pressure to deliver the goods being focused on me, the semi-reluctant frontman. I can't even bloody sing yet, I'd think to myself. I'd had no vocal training and we'd never even had a producer who would tell me where I was going wrong. I started drinking far too much before gigs. Afterwards, I felt relieved I'd got through it and would drink even more. I felt I was in at the deep end. I didn't really know what to make of this success. Obviously, it has its benefits, but I was conscious that there was much more responsibility arriving with it and, suddenly, it seemed a little too much like having a proper job. And I didn't want a proper job, I'd become a musician in order to sidestep all that. But whoever said life should be easy? For most people, life is much, much more difficult than what I've just complained about. In time, I came to realize this and began to relish the challenge of becoming a proper singer. Also, I wanted to learn to write lyrics that weren't nonsense, because they *were* nonsense at the beginning. It was a massive challenge, full of contradictions, but at times it was also extremely pleasurable.

We just kept on making music and experimenting, and in doing that we created one track in particular that would elevate our situation beyond all expectation.

Chapter Thirteen

Here comes success

'Blue Monday' was a key part of our ascension of the ladder regarding electronics and electronic music. I hadn't found learning particularly interesting at school, but I found learning about how to make music, especially electronic music, captivating, because it was something you could teach yourself. 'Blue Monday' was the pinnacle of that learning process and would become the pinnacle of our commercial success too — it is the biggest-selling twelve-inch single of all time.

I'd felt there was no point in accumulating all this new equipment if we weren't going to create something unique and interesting with it. How far could we take it? What were the boundaries of possibility? Could we push them out further? By drawing together all the things we'd learned about technology, the new sounds we'd heard in New York and the records and tapes I'd been given, we had the heady combination of factors that created 'Blue Monday'.

One was the beat, which I'd first heard at a gig somewhere when a live sound mixer messed around with a delay unit and, either by accident or design, had for a few seconds added something extra to a drumbeat. Later I heard it on a Donna Summer record called 'Our Love', and wondered what else could be done with it.

We had a brand-new drum machine, one that had only just come out, an Oberheim DMX, and we linked to a little Powertran 1024 Composer sequencer I'd built. I asked Steve to programme the beat, and he added some fills and extra parts, while I thought about a bass line. I had 'You Make Me Feel (Mighty Real)' by Sylvester going round in my head, decided to attempt something inspired by it and came up with the simple bass line that underpins the track. Then Steve and I made some slight shifts in the rhythm from eighths to sixteenths to triplets, which made subtle changes to the groove. After that, we interspersed it with the kind of drum stops we'd been hearing in American dance music, the rhythmic punctuation picked up in the New York clubs, programmed it all and added a synth line over the top. When we started the sequencer, it fired up slightly out of time, which, although unintentional, sounded really nice and funky. Fucking hell, I thought, that's great, how did that happen? We'll have to do that in the studio and record it.

The next thing was that something went wrong with the drum program. We'd had this whole thing completed in one day by about four o'clock in the afternoon, and tried to back it up using a cassette machine, as you did in those days. However, instead of backing it up, it managed to wipe itself altogether and we had to start again, repro-gramming the drums from scratch. Even today, I think about how bits of it were better on the original, kind of funkier. But does that matter now? Probably not. Then I added some strings, using the Emulator 1 and the Omni, Hooky came in and put some bass on, I took the whole thing away and wrote some lyrics, and that was it — that's how 'Blue Monday' happened. It was only a day or two's work, but the result of months if not years of accumulating the influences, knowledge and technology that made this brand-new kind of music possible.

As a side effect of creating this electronic-based track with very little in the way of live instrumentation, we also dug ourselves out of a bit of a hole of our own making. In the early days, we received a great deal of criticism for not playing encores at gigs. For one thing, Rob thought that encores, like cover versions, were corny, predictable and definitely not punk. (He thought the same thing about signing autographs, because he thought they set bands on a pedestal, saying, 'You scumbags are no better than anyone else.' We thought he might have a point, so in the early days we'd never give autographs, either.) That wasn't the only reason, though. Aside from gigs, we'd occasionally go along to multimedia nights at the Scala cinema in London, or sometimes at the Beach Club in Manchester, events where they'd put a band on followed by a film, a poet, another band and finally a DJ. We'd all really enjoy these nights and thought they were the way to go. We believed that after forty minutes or so of our music people wanted something else, so we'd play for about that long and then bugger off. It never crossed our minds that not everyone thought the same way: we thought we were doing people a favour. We wouldn't leave the audience completely in the lurch: we wanted them to get their money's worth, so we'd play our set and then put a DJ on, but this didn't go down very well, especially abroad. New Zealand crowds in particular didn't like it, while in Holland, once, the place erupted when we went off and Hooky ended up getting knocked out. For the rest of that tour the promoters had to put up signs at the venues saying something like 'Please note the band only plays for forty minutes, they do not play "Love Will Tear Us Apart" and do not play encores.'

It took a full-scale riot in Boston in November 1981, just after we'd signed to Warner Brothers, to make us question the wisdom of our well-intentioned altruism when it came to encores. We played our usual thirty-five- to forty-minute set, came off and holed up in the dressing room with a few drinks. Suddenly, the door opened and in walked the police, telling us not to worry because they were there for our protection: it turned out there was a riot going on out in the auditorium because we'd played a short set and not come back for an encore. No one had told us this; it was only when the police arrived that we found out what was going on. We managed to escape with our lives, despite becoming caught up in a bit of rock-throwing outside the auditorium, which was a bit like being back in Salford.

The next morning I received a phone call from Mo Ostin, the president of Warner Brothers. 'Hey, Bernie,' he said, 'what happened last night? I hear there was a riot. You can't have the police turning up at gigs. And you only played for thirty-five minutes? Americans won't like that.'

We had a band meeting as a result, and Rob was still insistent that we shouldn't do encores. But it was all right for him: he wasn't in the firing line, he didn't have Mo ringing him up and people throwing things at him. Things had certainly shifted from the days when we were a small indie band. Where we got away with it then, now we were successful and playing to much bigger audiences. 'Blue Monday' seemed like it could be a handy compromise. We could finish the set, come off the stage, press a button and let the machines play the encore.

A few people initially didn't like 'Blue Monday', they said it sounded nothing like New Order, and I guess we lost a few fans over it – a bit like when Bob Dylan went electric. But the record was being played in clubs, and the DJs loved it because it was a floor-filler. It spread across Europe, to the point where it would reappear periodically in the charts because people would go on holiday, hear it in the clubs and come back and buy it. The success of 'Blue Monday' was a real word-of-mouth phenomenon. It didn't receive much radio play, because it wasn't very 'daytime radio', and at seven minutes plus it was long and complicated for a single. Its success became so wide-spread, though, it meant that, in the end, radio stations had to play it, but it hadn't been designed for that; essentially, it was a machine to facilitate dancing. As a song, I wouldn't say it's my favourite New Order track, but as a prompt to make you dance it's unsurpassed. Even today, more than three decades later, when 'Blue Monday' comes on in a club, people get straight up and on the floor. It still cuts it.

We produced the track at Britannia Row, making the most of the incredible speakers they had in there. They had every frequency — subsonics, ultra-subsonics: it sounded amazing, as if you were in a really good club. I'd go out to clubs and listen to the sound systems, standing near the speakers and listening to what made a record sound good. At the behest of our engineer, Michael Johnson, we hired in some specific equipment to achieve the sound, including a bloody great thing from Germany called called a Transdynamic. We went to whatever lengths we could to make the record sound as good as possible.

There were some technical barriers. 'Blue Monday' was on vinyl, for a start, which, because of the length of the track, would reduce the quality. We would have to set the equalizing levels of the track carefully to make it sound quite hard so that, by the time it had got on to vinyl and softened up a little, it would still sound tough but quite nice at the same time. We had to experiment and do test press-ings, make adjustments. Test pressings were made on acetate, a very hard plastic that would start to disintegrate after you'd played it no more than three or four times. Even acetate didn't give you a truly accurate picture of what the track would finally sound like on vinyl, though, because acetate had a harder sound. It took a lot of work to make 'Blue Monday' sound as good as it did, but it really paid off, because it went on to sell well over a million copies in the UK alone.

That's amazing in any circumstances, but even more so when you consider that we didn't really promote the record . We didn't promote anything in those days — for one thing, we didn't really know what it involved and, anyway, we couldn't really be arsed. Come to think of it, I don't think Factory ever asked us to promote anything: Rob's attitude was that, if the music was good enough, it would speak for itself.

Back then, however, if your record was doing really well, the chances were you'd have to go on *Top of the Pops*. Naturally, when faced with this great opportunity to push ourselves into the nation's living rooms and possibly open up a whole new audience, we did our best to shoot ourselves in our collective foot.

In the early days, whenever we were approached by *Top of the Pops* we told them we'd only agree to appear if we could play live. The BBC would say that wasn't possible because it wasn't a live-music programme, and Rob would just walk away.

'Blue Monday' did so well, however, that at the end of March 1983 *Top of the Pops* finally relented and allowed us to perform the track live. The potential pitfalls associated with this were numerous. Quite a lot of 'Blue Monday' was on a shaky sequencer that I'd built at home, and there was no guarantee it was going to work when we wheeled it out on *Top of the Pops*. In the end, it did hold up, but it was pretty nerve-wracking standing there trying to sing on live television in front of millions of people, half expecting the track to grind to a complete halt at any moment. It was all right for Rob to come up with the bloody philosophy, but it was us who had to play it out.

The other thing that was overlooked in our blind dedication to live performance was the gargantuan lengths we'd gone to in making 'Blue Monday' sound great on the record. To then appear on the nation's leading music show and just stick a microphone in front of it — well, let's just say it was never going to showcase the track in its best light. We were playing this hi-tech song, live, in a television studio where the directors and promoters hadn't wanted us to play live in the first place, using engineers who had never worked on live performance before. It was almost guaranteed to sound awful. Everyone else on the show would sound great, and then there'd be us, standing there playing live and sounding a bit mediocre. I think every time we performed live on *Top of the Pops* the record dropped down the charts the following week.

I guess, in retrospect, the clever thing was that, through this refusal to mime, we were promoting the band itself, not the record. Our longevity possibly bears out this theory. On the other hand, the effect on the record wasn't promotion, it was demotion. We'd succeeded in coming up with an apparently foolproof way of ensuring we sold fewer records. I kept pointing this out, but the rest of the band thought it was great. Every time I suggested we changed this utterly self-defeating policy, I'd be comprehensively outvoted. Other musicians would be slapping us on the back for sticking to our guns and playing live, while I'd stand there, eyebrows raised, pointing at the record sliding down the charts even as we spoke.

A few years later, *Top of the Pops* changed the rules and started making bands perform live instead of having them mime. It didn't last long, though: they probably came to the same conclusions I had and decided it was both too much hassle and maybe not what the programme was about. The policy they settled upon was for the *singer* to perform live while the rest of the band mimed to a backing track. As you can imagine, I was a bit pissed off about this, given it was the others who wanted to play live, while I would have been happy miming. I only had to do it a couple of times, but it was pretty annoying. The band found it most amusing, of course.

There was one other occasion around this time when I had to sing 'Blue Monday' in strange circumstances, when we had our biggest direct flirtation with the commercialization of our music. The track was going to be used as the background to an advert for the fruit drink Sunkist as part of a big UK promotion. They didn't just want to licence the song, however, they wanted me to record a special vocal for it, for which they were offering £100,000. Rob was in hospital after a breakdown at this point, and we knew he wouldn't want us to do it. He had real principles about this kind of thing and wanted the music to speak for itself. He wouldn't even sell T-shirts at gigs; he'd let other people do it. There was a guy we knew as Scottish Tommy who flogged T-shirts outside our gigs, and he felt so guilty about how much money he was making that one night he came into the dressing room waving a cheque for us, saying he felt bad about how well he was doing and wanted to give us something back. Rob came running over, saying that we didn't want it.

So, in view of the fact that Rob was incapacitated, we decided that the Sunkist ad was a good idea. I had been given the adapted lyric, in which the words went something like, 'How does it feel, when a new day has begun? When you're drinking in the sunshine, Sunkist is the one.' Not the greatest lyrics of all time by any means and, in the studio, I just couldn't sing it, I kept breaking up laughing, which would set everyone else off. Hooky was saying, 'Come on, Bernard, you've only got to sing for a minute and we'll be a hundred grand richer.' Eventually, he got a piece of cardboard, wrote '£100,000' on it in massive letters and plonked it on the mixing desk where I could see it, in order to focus my attention. I sang it eventually, Rob came out of hospital, found out what we'd done and went ballistic. 'You stupid, fucking thick, fucking Salford bastards' was, I think, the gist of it. 'Selling out as soon as my back's turned.' The first thing he did was to put the kybosh on it, and the ad was never screened.

Anyway, despite our apparent determination to achieve the opposite, 'Blue Monday' was doing very well indeed. Then one day Tony came into the studio and asked us if we wanted the good news or the bad news.

We asked for the good news.

'Well,' he said, beaming, '"Blue Monday" is racing up the charts and we're finding it hard to keep up with the demand, not just here but all round the world.'

'Great!' we said. 'So what's the bad news?'

He started laughing in exactly the same way he had in America when all the gear had been stolen.

'You know the holes in the record-sleeve design to make it look like a floppy disk?' he chuckled. 'Well, it's costing us so much to stamp the holes in the cover that we're actually losing money with every sale! Isn't it wonderful?'

Peter Saville had designed the sleeve to look like the Emulator's floppy disk, complete with the hole, which looked fantastic, but in the light of this news suddenly didn't seem like such a bright idea. I wouldn't mind, but it was a circle of bloody air that was causing the loss! Our jaws hit the floor.

'No, Tony,' we said through tight lips. 'It's not even remotely fucking wonderful.'

'Don't worry, darlings,' he said. 'It's fine. I've spoken to Peter Saville and we're going to try and change it.'

'But how many copies have we sold at a loss?'

'Oh, I think it's about a quarter of a million. Got to go, darlings. Bye!'

Chapter Fourteen

New York, London, Los Angeles, Knutsford

During the 1980s, Factory's man in New York was Michael Shamberg. We'd met Michael on our first trip and liked him immediately. Michael was — and is — a fascinating character, and produced many of New Order's early videos (one of the first things he did with us was make a film of a gig we played at the Ukrainian National Home in New York in 1981). He had a great love for film as a medium, had his head firmly in the arthouse film scene and hand-picked a host of fantastic up-and-coming directors to shoot our videos. He had quite an eye for talent, and the New Order videography is a pretty decent who's who of great modern directors: Kathryn Bigelow, who directed *Touched by the Hand of God* and won the 2009 Academy Award for Best Picture with *The Hurt Locker*, for example, while Jonathan Demme, director of *The Perfect Kiss*, made *The Silence of the Lambs* and *Philadelphia*.

Thanks in large part to Michael, ours were not your average pop videos of the time. They were little *mise-en-scènes* in themselves, with their own narratives and casts, rather than just a band miming to a song in an exotic location. In the short term, I think we probably suffered commercially a little because of that, but in that classic contradictory fashion of ours it also turned out to be a benefit. As with our determination to play live on *Top of the Pops* having a detrimental effect on our chart positions, the videos were not in the MTV mould and, much to our record company's annoyance, didn't really sell the records either. But, again, what they did sell was the *band*, because they made us stand apart from everyone else and showed that we cared about something beyond shifting units. That attitude, and the videos we made, gave us a different kind of integrity which meant we sold plenty in the long term. We didn't plan it that way of course — we didn't plan anything much — but it turned out unintentionally to be a very successful anti-strategy strategy.

Michael also had his head in the New York music world. He was well aware of and immersed in the early electro, alternative and hip-hop scene and knew many of the people making waves in it. Our next step after 'Blue Monday' was to make a dance record in New York, and Michael's recommendation for a producer was Arthur Baker. Arthur, who has over the years played his role in New Order's development and success, is a big bear of a man: think Grizzly Adams, only grizzlier. With his short fuse and big heart, Arthur clicked very well with us and remains a good friend to this day. Arthur is from Boston, of Russian-Jewish descent I believe, but is very American, very New York: he talks tough, looks tough and doesn't take any shit from anyone (well, except his wife).

Arthur was the up-and-coming big-name producer in New York and had produced a string of dance hits, such as Afrika Bambaataa's 'Planet Rock' in 1982 (I loved how he took the synth line from

Kraftwerk's 'Trans-Europe Express' and adapted it into a ground-breaking electro track) and 'Walking on Sunshine', which he released under the name Rockers Revenge (not to be confused with the Katrina and the Waves track of the same name). Arthur worked closely with a musician called John Robie, a guy who would have slotted perfectly into *The Wolf of Wall Street*, if it had been about the music business instead of the world of finance. I was already familiar with John and his C-Bank project through friends in New York, and we'd collaborate on 'Shellshock' for the *Pretty In Pink* soundtrack. Arthur also worked with Fred Zarr, who played on a lot of the great early dance records (Madonna's first album, among other things), so we were right in at the very heart of that New York scene.

When we arrived to start work with Arthur he was already occupied making a track called 'IOU' by Freeez. Freeez was basically a pick-up band from the UK that was being moulded by Arthur and John for a record that would go on to be a massive hit around the world. The problem they were having when we showed up was that the key hadn't been selected primarily with the vocalist in mind. They were struggling to find someone who could hit the high notes, and the recording was taking longer than expected. In the meantime, they parked us in Fred Zarr's studio in Brooklyn, essentially the front room of a house, and told us to knock out some ideas. Which we couldn't do.

Arthur was used to working with the kind of experienced session musicians who could churn out stuff practically on demand, but we didn't work like that, we weren't sessioneers with a long track record of hits behind us. We didn't know what the fuck we were doing and just froze. We had a much less feverish method of composition; in fact, there *was* no method: we'd just wait for inspiration to strike. We'd get together and talk about what we'd seen on television the previous night, films, books, girls or football until we got bored, then pick up our instruments and strum away until something happened.

In New York, however, we'd landed in a place that had a completely different mind-set.

At Fred Zarr's, we ended up producing tapes of little more than us going through different sounds on the synthesizer until we found a cool one, at which point I'd think, Hmm, I wish we'd never found that, because it means I've now got to do something with it. We were struggling. Arthur had put us on the spot and we didn't exactly rise to the occasion. To make matters worse, I'd come down with the flu.

Eventually, Arthur finished with Freeez, which only left us with a couple of days in the studio. The person booked in after us was James Brown. So, no pressure there. It was a real urban studio, just off Times Square, right in the heart of one of the world's fastest-paced cities, an operation with a rapid turnover that had a hint of the whole 'time is money' experience we'd had as Joy Division. It wasn't as bad as that, though, and Arthur was encouraging in his own way: his attitude was 'either come up with something or fuck off'. We were pushed, but managed to put together a track called 'Confusion' on which everyone contributed to the lyrics, largely because we only had two or three hours to come up with them. I wouldn't call them classic lyrics, but we did what we could in the time we had.

Shortly afterwards, we set off on a tour of the US and Canada. For some reason, when we went to America in the early days, Terry always used to hire Lincoln town cars. The hire places would laugh at us, saying, 'Nobody under sixty hires these.'

Normally, Hooky or Terry would drive, because I'd always had just a motorcycle licence, but a week before we left for New York I'd passed my driving test. A good thing I had, too, as it turned out that neither Terry nor Hooky had brought their licences with them, whereas I was proudly carrying my brand-new one. The problem was that I'd never driven on my own before, so my first time in charge of a car was on the streets of New York in a vehicle the shape and dimensions of a mini aircraft carrier.

I tried to look nonchalant when we picked it up, but it wasn't long after I'd got behind the wheel that the hire guy twigged I wasn't very good at driving. I drove down the ramp, aware that he was watching me, and when we reached the bottom I put my foot on the brake, and it was like someone had thrown an anchor out of the back window – the car stopped dead. Everyone in the back, the rest of the band and Rob, was thrown forward until they were practically pressed up against the windscreen in a tangle of limbs. I decided I'd better put my foot down before the guy who'd leased us the car came out and asked for it back.

As we lurched forward again, Hooky was saying, 'Fucking hell, Bernard, you can't drive!' I said that it wasn't my driving, the brakes felt really weird. He assured me it was just that American cars had power brakes and I'd get used to them, but told me to pull over nonetheless. Which I did, behind a van from which two guys emerged – carrying a body bag. As omens went, this wasn't a good one.

Still anxious, but telling myself I'd get used to it, I pointed the car towards the eastern seaboard, and off we went, my knuckles white on the wheel and my face pale as I peered through the windscreen at the speeding lanes full of huge trucks and big American cars weaving in and out. Add to that the stress of worrying about hitting the brakes too hard and turning the rest of New Order into giant, swearing human torpedoes, it was with some relief that I pulled into our New York hotel at the end of it all. When we checked back in, there was a pile of urgent messages: someone, it seemed, had been frantically trying to get hold of me since we'd left, and I recognized the phone number as that of the car hire company. When I called and said who I was, the guy on the other end said, 'Oh, my gahd! Mr Sumner! Are you OK?' I assured him that yes, I was perfectly all right, but I was a bit alarmed at

his concern for my well-being. He said, 'Mr Sumner, I'm so sorry —
we should never have given you that car. There's a serious problem
with the brakes!' He asked me to bring it in straight away and he'd
exchange it for another one, but by then we'd done hundreds of
miles. Travelling a long way in a short time unaware of whether we
could ever stop safely? It was like a parable of our musical lives.

Anyway, at the end of the tour we played in Washington, from
where we were to drive straight from the gig to a club called the
Funhouse on West 26th Street in Manhattan in order to film
the video for 'Confusion'. The Funhouse was at the heart of the New
York electro scene in 1983, a really wild place with a mainly
Hispanic crowd, all shirts off and loads of tattoos. It had floor-to-
ceiling lights shooting up, down and around the walls, and there
were punchball machines dotted around the place with guys belting
the living daylights out of them. The bouncers were enormous, like
American cars stood on end, and it was a pretty mad electric scene.
Whenever Arthur and John had put a new track together they'd
take it to the Funhouse, where the DJ Jellybean Benitez would test
its reception on the dance floor, so it was pretty cutting-edge and
made the perfect location to shoot the video.

We finished the gig in Washington, drove the 230-odd miles to
New York and went straight to the Funhouse for the shoot, arriving
at something like seven thirty in the morning. The crowd was still
rocking, but we were very late. Jellybean was OK, but Arthur was
very tense: his wife, Tina B, had been giving him grief and the atmosphere was a bit fraught. I think we were supposed to have arrived at
something like three thirty, but for whatever reason we hadn't got
there until much later and, as we arrived, the Bakers were just finishing a big argument. Arthur's wife stormed out of the club, got into
his car, rammed the car in front, then the car behind, then the car in
front again, and kept this up until they were out of the way and she

could screech away into the dawn. Arthur told me later that when he got home she threw his synthesizer at him. They're not together any more.

Anyway, finally, we were able to shoot the video. The director was a guy called Charles Sturridge, who had just made the television adaptation of Evelyn Waugh's *Brideshead Revisited* and come straight from shooting English country-house period aristocracy to this working-class Hispanic club full of tough guys and tough chicks dancing away to electro. A bit of a gear change, to say the least.

The storyline of the video is a girl finishing work at a pizza place, going home, getting ready, meeting a friend and going to the Funhouse. At the same time, Arthur is finishing a track in the studio, taking it to the club and handing it to Jellybean to play. There are also a few shots of us driving through the streets of New York in a cab — all very *Taxi Driver* — and going into the club ourselves. It's a clever video, with not just a single narrative but three, which at the same time really captured the atmosphere of the club, the scene and the kind of world in which Jellybean, Arthur and Robie were at the centre. We really bonded with Arthur. He came from quite a working-class background, just as we did, which probably helped us click. He had a real feel for beats — I've always felt Arthur would have made a great drummer if he hadn't been a producer.

There was one aspect of the New York process about which we stuck to our guns: we refused to let any session players play on our records at this stage in the process. This meant that none of the brilliant people Arthur worked with — people like John Robie and Fred Zarr — played on the tracks; just us. Arthur had suggested using musicians from his stable — after all, it was the way he worked — but we said no. If he was surprised, he didn't show it, but replied, 'OK, fine, well, you guys go off and come up with the goods but make sure they're goods with a New York sound.' This was a sound which was probably made by five people in total, and to get it right was a little like having to crack a safe. As usual, we'd made things as difficult for ourselves as we could, but I think by doing that we retained a certain amount of integrity. We might not have had a stratospheric hit record like Freeez did with 'IOU' but, ultimately, we're still around doing our own thing, so this crazy, intransigent attitude may have paid a dividend in the long run. Of course, who knows, if we'd let Arthur's crowd loose in the studio — and, to be honest, if it had been solely down to me, we would have — we might have had an absolutely stratospheric hit *and* still enjoyed the longevity we've had. After all, what's wrong with an extra pair of helping hands and additional input?

The next big step after working with Arthur was signing to Quincy Jones's Qwest label in 1985 so that it would look after our recorded output in North America. The first time I heard of Quincy's interest was when we played a benefit for the striking miners at the Royal Festival Hall in 1984. It was a pretty good gig, not least because this time it didn't involve any dodgy cinematic pornography. We were very anti-Margaret Thatcher and didn't like what she was doing to industry, especially in the north, the north-west and in Scotland. I believe we lost 150,000 jobs in the north-west alone because of her policy of asset-stripping industry and replacing it with nothing, so when the opportunity came to play a benefit for the miners, we jumped at it.

It was an occasion about as far from Quincy's world as you can imagine. Keith Allen was on the bill before us, doing a stand-up character he'd devised called 'Northern Industrial Gay'. He'd go on wearing a leather jockstrap and a miner's helmet and rub baby oil into himself. Terry must have got it into his head that, it being a miners' benefit, the audience would all be miners. Somehow, he came to the conclusion that Keith must be a miner who'd got up out of the audience and was just messing about. On Terry goes and tries to push an oiled-up Keith from the stage, with Keith trying to explain that he's the support act.

It was quite an introduction for Quincy's representative, who'd come to see us that night, but Tom Atencio was later to become our American manager. Terry used to call him Tom Percentago, but Tom is a lovely, lovely guy who's always been great for us and slotted in perfectly right from the start. It turned out to be us rather than the miners who reaped the biggest benefit of all from that gig, as we decided to sign for Qwest and gained both a manager and a record company in one night.

There were other offers on the table, we were flattered to hear, but Rob thought we'd receive more personal attention with Qwest, even though it was part of the Warner Brothers' stable rather than an indie. At the time, I think the only other artist on Quincy's label was Frank Sinatra. Ian would have liked that: he was a bit of a Frank fan.

Quincy had become one of the most important musical figures in the world at this point, having produced Michael Jackson's *Off the Wall* and *Thriller* albums, which between them have sold something north of 130 million copies.

He came over from LA to meet us. We took him to Knutsford. Over dinner there, we realized just what a really cool guy he is: to this day, I receive a Christmas card every year from Quincy and the day before I got married he rang me to wish me luck. His personal story is particularly interesting to me, too, because he also had a mother who had long-term difficulties with illness.

Whenever we played in LA he'd come and see us, and we'd go and visit him at his house in Bel Air: one night when we turned up, Natassja Kinski answered the door and cooked us dinner. I remember another occasion, when we were having a drink in his den downstairs and he said to me, 'Come and listen to this, Bernard.' He pressed play on his answering machine and it was Marlon Brando. 'Hey, Quincy,' said the voice of Colonel Kurtz, 'have you ever thought . . . about the beautiful gardenias . . . that grow . . . in the park . . .'

We liked Quincy a great deal, and his label seemed exactly the right place for us. He never put any pressure on us, didn't get in our way and even ended up remixing 'Blue Monday' for us in 1988. He made a really good job of it, as it's a very difficult track to mix (other than Quincy, Hardfloor produced a mix called '*Blauer Montag*', which I particularly liked).

In signing to Qwest, we found ourselves not only with roots in New York but in Los Angeles as well. We were made very welcome: when we first signed we were invited to the Warner Brothers' LA offices to meet the people involved and be welcomed into the family. They threw a big party for us. No one told us this; we thought we were just saying hello to a couple of people there. I remember Tom Atencio walking up to a door, grasping the handle and saying to me, 'Are you ready, Bernard?' I said, 'What for?' and he opened the door to reveal this big room full of about four hundred cheering people.

At first I found LA very alien. It's a long flight and, as you fly in, you pass over this seemingly endless cityscape of flat roofs that goes on and on; it felt like flying from Manchester to London, only with buildings the whole way. Usually, we'd stay in a hotel called the Sunset Marquis in West Hollywood, a real party hotel in the early eighties, but then, every other hotel within spitting distance had a similar reputation: John Belushi died in the Chateau Marmont just up the road around that time. On our early American sojourns we'd stay in downbeat places: there'd be AstroTurf everywhere, and when we watched TV the picture was supposed to be colour but was actually just different shades of brown. Those lower-end hotels seemed to have two types of bed as selling points — waterbeds, or beds that vibrated. Rob loved the latter kind, and he always chose a place with vibrating beds. He'd lie on it watching some terrible film on the television, drinking beer, smoking, eating heavily buttered English muffins, reaching occasionally over to a pile of quarters on the bedside table and feeding them into the slot to keep the bed vibrating. Hooky and I would wait around like vultures, because he'd pay us $15 to go and get him $30 worth of beer and some more quarters.

The next level of hotel up for Rob involved automatic revolving doors, the sort with sensors that would start the door turning as you approached. If a hotel didn't have these, Rob would pronounce it 'a shit hotel' and, next time, no matter how good or convenient a hotel it was, we'd have to stay somewhere else.

Sometimes it wasn't the hotel itself that was the issue, it could be the people we met there. I remember one time on tour in 1985 when we flew down to New Orleans. We arrived at the hotel after a long flight – and a longer night of partying – when Ruth Polsky told us all to meet downstairs at eight o'clock. None of us felt in the slightest bit sociable, but Ruth insisted we had to meet the promoter and it would be bad form if we didn't.

We all trooped downstairs at the appointed time, and at the bar we found a giant of a man with an enormous beard and a look in his eye that you felt could turn milk sour at forty paces. Ruth introduced him as the promoter, but he held up a massive, meaty hand and said, 'I'm not the promoter. I'm the promoter's representative.'

Then he turned to the barman and barked, 'Eight vodka shots.' I don't like vodka and, still feeling the effects of the previous night, was reluctant to start drinking at all, let alone something I didn't like.

'To be honest, I don't really drink vodka,' I said meekly. 'Could I get a Pernod instead, please?'

The promoter's representative turned to look at me. 'You don't understand,' he said. 'These are for me.'

He proceeded to knock back all eight vodkas, one after the other.

We sat at the bar for a while chatting to this guy, when suddenly he said, 'You,' indicating me, 'come with me, I want to take you somewhere.'

We walked out of the hotel to find police cars everywhere, sirens going, the lot. There'd been some kind of incident, but the promoter's representative was unfazed. We walked straight past the police cars and disappeared behind a wall, where he pulled out a massive bowie knife with a blade about ten inches long. Oh fuck, I thought, what's he doing?

He reached into his pocket and pulled out a wrap of strange white powder, poured some on to the blade of the knife and offered it to me, all with a dozen cops a few feet away on the other side of the wall. Perhaps it was the alcohol, I don't know, but later on I somehow felt much more confident and self-assured, and we went back to the bar, where more and more drink was taken before I suggested we get something to eat. 'No,' said the man mountain. 'We're going to meet the promoter now.'

We got into a fleet of taxis, drove out of the nice part of New Orleans and kept going into the night, watching the streetlights disappear and the houses grow farther and farther apart. Eventually, we arrived at a patch of wasteland, in the middle of which stood a solitary house floodlit by security lights and surrounded by a wire fence, around which bounded some fearsome-looking canines. A few nervous glances were exchanged as the cars stopped just long enough for us to climb out, before hightailing it back into the night as a guy unlocked the gate to let us in. The wire fence looked suddenly very flimsy as the dogs went berserk at us from behind it.

Once inside the door — and away from the dogs — we found the house quiet. There was a big spiral staircase in the middle of the living room we'd been shown into, down which came a scantily clad woman, followed by a man wearing a silk dressing gown, who we took to be the promoter. He was the absolute spit of Gomez from *The Addams Family*. 'We wanted to welcome you to our city,' he said, smiling, spreading his arms wide and insisting we had a drink. 'You like bourbon? Have some bourbon.' We didn't like bourbon but felt it best, in the circumstances, not to point this out. Then the man who'd met us at the hotel appeared with a big bag of this white stuff. He said to Gomez, 'This is the stuff left over from the Miami run.' Gomez seemed to find this agreeable and out came the bowie knife again.

I asked Gomez if he was the promoter. 'Oh no,' he said. 'Not me. I'm the promoter's representative. There are two of them, as it happens, and they live out in the swamps. Don't worry, they're coming to the gig tomorrow.'

We did the gig the following night — it wasn't a great one — and when we got back to the dressing room the man with the bowie knife arrived at the door, concerned that there was 'a problem' with our security guy. The security guy was, of course, Terry, and he wouldn't let the promoters come backstage.

A few minutes later, the promoters walked into the dressing room, and they were like no promoters we'd ever seen before: both of them were wearing caps with the confederate flag on the front, and dressed head to toe in denim. Their jeans were rolled up, there wasn't a shoe between them and their bare feet were encrusted with mud from the bayous. It really was like something out of *Deliverance*. They insisted we went back to the same house for a party, where, in the meantime, a drum kit had been set up. It was clear that we were supposed to have a jam session, but none of us could jam — we never jammed with other musicians. We never saw them again after that: maybe the next Miami run didn't go quite to plan.

Before the Sunset Marquis, we'd stayed at the Tropicana, a famous old rock 'n' roll motel in LA (The Doors apparently used to practically live there, Andy Warhol made a couple of films at the Tropicana and at one stage Tom Waits was a long-term resident). We never usually stayed in rock 'n' roll hotels, but someone had suggested it, probably Tony, who wanted us to stay in landmark hotels that famous bands had visited. (He liked the Chelsea Hotel in New York, for example, which in those days was a fucking horrible fleapit — I once stayed in a room there that was like something out of a David Lynch film.)

The Tropicana was also famous for Duke's Coffee Shop downstairs, where Hollywood stars would go and eat, slumming it, because the food was supposed to be amazing. Well, maybe it was, but the room our roadie Dave Pils, Peter Hook and I shared was right above the kitchen, and what we didn't realize until after we'd settled in was that we were sharing it with about three thousand cockroaches. We had to tuck the sheets under the mattress all the way around so the cockroaches couldn't crawl under them. There'd be what looked like a Milky Way of them all up the walls as you lay in bed, and if you went to the toilet in the middle of the night and lifted the lid you'd see them all scuttling away. Until they'd got used to you, that is, at which point sitting on the toilet became a very interesting affair.

Steve and Gillian were lucky, because they were given the room with the vodka-drinking flies. Because our room was so disgusting we'd go to theirs to party, and Steve showed me that if you put your drinks down the flies would all go for the vodka and orange, no other drink. The Tropicana was a rotten hotel — and we'd stayed in some bad ones over the years — but the people in the coffee shop below, film stars included, can have had no idea the place was infested with cockroaches. I can only begin to imagine what horrors the kitchen must have contained. At one point I complained to the guy at reception. He just started laughing and said, 'What the fuck do you want me to do about it?' It was a classy joint, that's for sure. I understand it was demolished towards the end of the eighties, and there's a chain hotel there now. For its sake, I hope the cockroaches died with the Tropicana.

This added to my mixed feelings about Los Angeles. For one thing, coming from Salford, I found the fact it was sunny all the time particularly strange. For another, being guys in our twenties, we took full advantage of the LA party scene, got ourselves in a complete mess every night and blamed the repercussions and hangovers on the city itself rather than the true culprits: ourselves.

Having had such a confused relationship with Los Angeles back then, now, years later, I have a completely different perspective and see the city with much clearer vision. It's just a nice city full of nice people.

One strong memory I have of those times is a recording session we did in LA with Arthur and John for *Pretty In Pink* in the same studio in which Fleetwood Mac had recorded *Tusk*. Just outside the studio was a lounge in which the bands could relax and unwind, which Fleetwood Mac had decorated in the style of an English stately home. It had oak-panelled walls that had been imported from England and was very sumptuous, but the drawback was that it had no windows. In an attempt to compensate for this, the ceiling had been constructed using backlit Perspex which simulated the passing of the day. When you arrived in the morning it would be yellow, then, as the day progressed, it would go white, blue, then pink, orange for the sunset and finally a darkening blue for the night. Which, strangely, sort of worked.

The studio engineer was one of those quintessential LA guys to whom everything is 'fuckin' great, man'. 'This track is fuckin' *awesome*,' he'd gush. 'The best fuckin' thing I've ever heard, and you guys are doing a fuckin' ah-*maz*-ing job.'

We weren't used to this. Being English, we were used to the engineer scowling at us through the glass for the entire duration of the session. Of course, we knew he didn't mean a single word of it, and he knew that *we* knew he didn't mean a single word of it. I think he grated more on the nerves of Arthur and John, because they were proper East Coast guys with an eye-rolling 'fuck this LA shit' attitude to such relentless vacuous positivity.

One day, the engineer started telling us how the track sounded 'fuckin' great, it's nearly fuckin' perfect, and what would make it perfect is some fuckin' percussion'. We said, 'Thanks for that, mate, but we really don't want any percussion on it if it's all the same to you.' He'd keep bringing it up, though, until eventually he said, 'Tell you what, I'll call my guy. He's fuckin' ah-*maz*-ing, he's played with everyone and would really make this track.' We finally relented – for a quiet life as much as anything – and the engineer made his call. The percussionist turned up, and he was a proper hippie: long hair, hippie clothes, Cuban heels and a canvas sack over his shoulder. He put the sack on the table and all his percussion instruments spilled out. He picked up the cabasa, unscrewed the end and tipped the contents on to the table – a small mountain of white powder. I think this was what the engineer meant by 'improving the track'. The percussionist said he had a present for us, handed us some leaves and said, 'Chew on these.' So we did. They were quite peppery, but whatever they were, they numbed our tongues and ensured we couldn't even think about eating: our appetites were hammered down for the next twenty-four hours.

Unfortunately, we were supposed to be having dinner that night with Quincy's representative, Harold Childs, a black guy from LA who was the quintessential English gentleman, to the point of smoking a pipe. He was lovely, we really liked him, but there we were, never having met each other before, dining at an upmarket restaurant, and none of us could eat a thing. This was the inaugural 'welcome to Qwest' dinner Harold had thrown for us in one of LA's top fine-dining restaurants. He'd ordered all this amazing food and we couldn't eat any of it; we just pushed it round our plates and smiled as politely as we could.

But that was LA in the mid-eighties. We had fun, and lots of it. I've matured since those days and am no longer like a kid in a sweet shop. I realized long ago that too many sweets will make your teeth drop out.

With my mother, Jimmy and grandmother on a beach in North Wales, some time in the 1960s.

My first boat. Actually I still wear that exact ame outfit for sailing.

↓ Donkey riding with my grandfather. 'Keep still and don't complain.'

↑ On holiday with my grandmother.

↗ Happy days in Alfred Street.

→ On the beach in Nassau with my son James.

↑ Lower Broughton. Amazing to think there was once a busy, thriving, happy community here. (Adventure playground on the left.)

↓ The end of Alfred Street today. Urban regeneration, eh?

Joy Division, with Mark Reeder (seated, in suit) and some extraordinary wallpaper in Berlin. January 1st 1980, Kant Kino.

Rehearsing at TJ Davidson's.

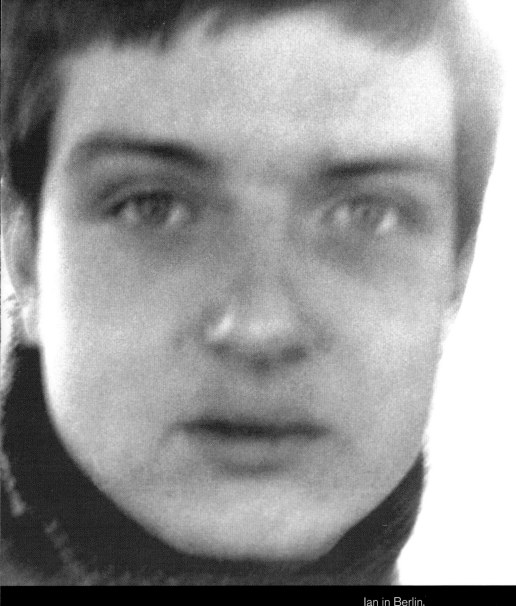
Ian in Berlin.

↑ Rob Gretton, always head and shoulders above the rest.   ↑ Steve, in camera.

↓ Talk of the devil.

← Me and Hooky, clearly enjoying ourselves.

↓ Rob feels the weight of responsibility. (Can't get this bloody shirt off!)

↑ Gillian in Ibiza.

→ You know you've made it when you share a billing with the Prince Albert Angling Society.

FORTHCOMING
EVENTS

FRI APR 19	NEW ORDER PLUS SUPPORT
SAT APR 20	COME DANCING TO STRINGS AND THINGS
MON APR 29 WED MAY 1	SCHOOLS MUSIC FESTIVAL
SAT MAY 4	TOY COLLECTORS SWOP MEET
SAT MAY 4 SUN MAY 5	ROLLER SKATING
THU MAY 16	PRINCE ALBERT ANGLING SOCIETY A.G.M.
FRI MAY 17TH	ROCK NIGHT WITH RED TAPE

↑ The Haçienda.
A club, a legend,
a money pit and, for
a while, a way of life.

→ Madonna's first
UK appearance,
at the Haçienda in
1984. Check out the
crowd – Mancunians
don't impress easily.

Chapter Fifteen

I've got an idea

While we'd been busy absorbing the influences of the clubs in New York (cleverly disguised as just going out and having a good time), closer to home, we had somehow ended up with a club of our own.

In the early eighties there had been a Factory club night once or twice a week at the Russell Club in Hulme. It was run by Tony Wilson, Alan Erasmus and a charismatic character called Alan Wise, who you may have seen introducing us on stage at gigs and festivals (see Appendix 2). The Factory Club booked a range of bands such as Cabaret Voltaire, Gang of Four, The Durutti Column, The Human League, Throbbing Gristle, Public Image Ltd, The Raincoats, Teardrop Explodes . . . at one point they even brought Suicide over from America. They were essentially bands that Tony and the two Alans found interesting, and it was always a fun night. They'd book local acts too: A Certain Ratio, Section 25 and ourselves all played at the Russell Club, and we all agreed it was a fantastic thing. Eventually, it came to an end – I've been told it was to do with a large and growing debt to the brewery, but it's also possible it had become so successful that Tony decided a couple of nights a week at the Russell wasn't enough and it was time to buy a nightclub of their own. Either way, the seeds of the Haçienda were sown in the sticky carpets of the Russell Club.

At some point in the early eighties we must have started making a fair bit of money (as a band, we were never kept informed about such trifling matters). Coincidentally, this is when talk turned to buying a club. The main lobbyists in favour of opening the Haçienda were Rob, Tony and the DJ Mike Pickering, a good friend of Rob's and someone who remains to this day a good friend of the band. In 1982 they came to us and said, 'We've found this fantastic place on Whitworth Street in Manchester. It used to be a yacht showroom and would be perfect for a club. Are you interested?' We remembered how great the old Factory club had been, visualized something similar and said yes, we were definitely interested. What we didn't appreciate before we saw the venue was the sheer scale of the place – and certainly not the extent of the costs. Neither Rob nor Tony ever showed us any financial projections or business plans: for a start, we assumed they were looking at a *part* of the building, not all of it. We were also unaware that the whole thing was a *fait accompli*, engineered by Tony.

Of the Factory directors, Alan Erasmus and Martin Hannett were against it. Having been involved in the running of the Factory night at the Russell Club, Alan was keenly aware how much time and effort would be involved and the difficulties that would have to be overcome. He knew it would detract from the core function of Factory, which was, after all, to put records out. There was a meeting at Tony's house in Didsbury and the vote was Tony and Rob in favour, Alan and Martin against. This left Peter Saville with the casting vote, but he lived in London at that point and couldn't be at the meeting. What I gather from Alan Erasmus is that Tony phoned Peter and buttered him up to the extent that he saw no alternative but to vote in favour of the Haçienda. It would have been nice if maybe the band had had the casting vote, but we weren't even aware this meeting was happening.

Under Rob's guiding hand, the then fledgling New Order, and Factory, under Tony, became partners in the project and somehow found the money for the start-up costs, presumably from our Joy Division income.

We were never told about the detail to any great extent; in fact, at one point early in the planning stages I was deputized by the band to find out from Rob and Tony exactly what was happening. It seemed to take them a little by surprise; they didn't understand why we'd want to know. They seemed genuinely mystified as to why we would be interested in where a big chunk of the money we were earning might be going. I left without much of an answer and, to a great extent, we left them to it. Our laissez-faire attitude may seem strange in retrospect: we should probably have asked some more pertinent questions, but the reason we didn't seek to become more involved at the outset was that our role was to take care of the music. Rob took care of business, and we trusted him implicitly. We knew how to write songs; he knew how to write cheques. It's possible he thought opening the club would be a great way of getting money out of Factory.

At length we were invited to have a look at the building itself. The moment we saw this huge, cavernous place it was obvious that this was never going to be a small disco with a few mirror balls: this was something on a much larger scale. The term wasn't yet invented, but this was going to be a 'super-club'. Ben Kelly, the designer, was brought in and we were shown some initial drawings. I wasn't completely convinced – I thought the whole thing looked a bit like a very large public toilet with bollards – but it reminded me a little of the clubs we'd been to in New York and was clearly a step up from the schmaltzy, Mecca disco-type establishments in the UK. This would be the first club of its kind here, a huge risk, and we were jumping in at the deep end. While we were buoyed by the zeroes-to-heroes status we had achieved with Joy Division, in retrospect, in those early days, we could well have been looking into the abyss with New Order, so it was a massive gamble. But if Rob thought it was a goer and we could afford it, then hey, why not? We liked the idea of opening a club; it seemed like a fun thing to do. We were young, we had a little money, we were very hedonistic and, as young people tend to, we thought we were bulletproof. To quote one of my own lyrics, we had 'too much to drink but not enough to lose'.

The original budget for the Haçienda was £50,000. Almost immediately, they needed another £50,000, then another £50,000, and from there the figure just kept rising. As Steve put it, 'I knew we had a 50–50 profit share deal with Factory, but I didn't realize that referred to the amounts we were spending.'

When the Haçienda opened in May 1982, a massive space with large windows in the ceiling that looked like no club that had ever gone before it, the prevailing wisdom seemed to be that 'if you build it, they will come'. There was barely any marketing, and before long no one was turning up except us and our friends. There was a big party to celebrate the first night, which was pretty well attended – and, bizarrely, featured a turn by Bernard Manning – but reality set in when it was routinely empty after that. It was too alien, too ahead of the times: the Haçienda didn't look like any other club and people were initially bemused by it. 'What the fuck *is* this place?' they thought. 'It's not even dark. And, anyway, where's the DJ?' There was no DJ booth, just a slit like a letterbox in the wall behind which the DJ played: all you could see were two eyes occasionally peering out at the dance floor. Such a large space with a high ceiling also meant the sound was horrendous: the music just bounced around the walls to the point of being practically inaudible. The sound system they'd installed had cost a fortune but the acoustics hadn't been taken into consideration and the system simply couldn't fight the building. The selling point for the lighting rig was that it wasn't going to be anything like the lights in other clubs. But it *was* going to be crap, it turned out. Right from the start, there was a catalogue of issues that just hadn't been thought through.

An early by-product of the Haçienda was that it caused a huge argument between Martin Hannett, Tony, Factory and Rob that would culminate in Martin leaving Factory altogether. Martin — who was against the idea from the start, remember — had called me one day ranting about the amount of money going into the club. 'It's a ridiculous idea!' he said. 'Just stupid! What we should be spending the money on is a Fairlight synthesizer.' One of the most exciting developments in electronic music in the early eighties, the Fairlight was the first decent computer-based instrument on the market. The drawback was that it was phenomenally expensive — you could have bought a house for the price of it. Martin fell out irrevocably with them over that, the argument escalated and there ended up being a court case, which, Factory being Factory, was given its own catalogue number (FAC61).

Things began to pick up a little for the Haçienda when we started staging live gigs. Echo and the Bunnymen, The Smiths, the Happy Mondays and The Stone Roses all played, among others, and Madonna's first ever British appearance was at the Haçienda. We played there two or three times ourselves, and the place was packed to the rafters. The club nights still weren't doing very well, however, so we rejigged things, at my behest, and installed a proper DJ booth on the balcony, recently rebuilt at great expense because of fire regulations. (If there was a way to lose money, the Hacienda would always be sure to find it.) Still, at last people could actually see the DJ at work without having to peer through a letterbox: I'm sure people must have enjoyed several nights at the Haçienda convinced we were just playing dance compilations.

The era that defined the Haçienda and sealed its place in the history of popular culture was when the acid house movement began to take hold in the mid- to late eighties. During that time the Haçienda became *the* place to go, certainly in the north of England. In my opinion, acid house truly started in the north. Contrary to popular belief, it wasn't born in Ibiza; it started in the UK and had its strongest roots in Manchester, Glasgow and London. Shoom and Spectrum opened up in London in 1987 and 1988 respectively, exciting things were happening at the Sub Club in Glasgow around the same time and, along with the Haçienda, these venues came to be the main focus of the movement. How it earned the name 'acid house', I've no idea. I think it was a daft thing to call it, but it was a handle to identify a specific kind of music; one with trademark squelchy bass sounds that sounded fantastic if you'd had an E (I presume).

Acid house was a little reminiscent of punk, except with a very different kind of music. Where punk's energy came from a three-chord thrash through distorted amplifiers, this was dance music created entirely with synthesizers and computers — and it was a fantastic thing. In fact, while acid house and the Haçienda found each other in a happy union, New Order's relationship with the scene dated back to a track we'd written, 'Ecstasy', as far back as 1982. We'd played a gig in Dallas, gone out to a club afterwards and got talking to the promoters. These were the days when *Dallas* was massive on the television and they told us that some members of the cast and crew would go to this club 'where they liked to drop an E'.

'What do you mean?' we said, baffled. 'What's an E?'

'The drug Ecstasy,' they replied. 'Haven't you heard of it?'

We hadn't. They told us all about it and how the club had been busted a few weeks earlier. When the lights came up, the police found something like a thousand tabs of E that had been hastily discarded on the floor. Ecstasy hit America as early as 1982, but apparently had not spread much further than this little scene we'd found in Texas.

Ecstasy arrived in Britain about five years later and we soon realized it was the same drug that we'd heard about in Dallas. The music here was very different, though: over there it had been electronic dance music, radically different to the tripped-out dance sound that took off like wildfire in the UK. The acid house scene became absolutely massive and the Haçienda finally took off properly. We dabbed our brows with relief at this because, the odd gig aside, the club had been really struggling.

While I'm convinced that the origins of house music lie firmly in this country rather than in Ibiza, which gets most of the credit, the Balearic island and its clubs would play an influential role in the recording of our album *Technique*. If we'd thought Ibiza was just a nice, quiet, sunny place where we could get away from it all and focus on recording what would become one of our most popular albums, we were, frankly, deluded, because when we arrived on the island in the spring of 1988 the whole Balearic beat scene was taking off.

As New Order became more successful we started to venture further afield to make albums. The official line was that there was no studio good enough in Manchester, but the real reason was that we had a whole load more fun when we went away somewhere. The thought of going to Ibiza greatly appealed to us. We'd been advised that the recording studio itself wasn't particularly good, but we were willing to risk it, mainly because the complex had a 24-hour bar with its own dedicated barman who could make stonking cocktails, there was a swimming pool and it wasn't too far away from the nightclubs. In any case, we felt we'd earned the right to make an album in a sunny place for a change, having served our dues recording in grim northern landscapes. When we got there, we found that the place was built in a Spanish hacienda style and located in a secluded spot at the end of a long, dusty road. It wasn't as good a studio as we were used to and the bedrooms were all a bit *Scarface* — everything was big and white — but it was perfectly fine and, when we arrived in the late spring, before it became oppressively hot, we looked forward to getting down to work.

We'd brought a few ideas with us which we'd written back in the UK, but what we tended — and preferred — to do was write mainly in the studio itself. We started the *Technique* process by finishing the ideas we'd brought, and we really made the most of our surroundings: I recorded the acoustic guitar part for 'Guilty Partner' outside under a tree with a microphone in front of my nylon-strung guitar while the birds twittered in the background (it was great recording outdoors because, inside, you get a really flat resonance from the building).

Steve's not a fan of the heat and the sunshine, so he spent quite a long time inside recording his drums, which left the rest of us filling in time by the pool drinking cocktails. It didn't take much longer for us to properly discover the nightlife either, at which point our productivity slowed considerably. Most of the clubs were either in Ibiza town or San Antonio, with two of the main clubs, Ku and Amnesia, on the road between them. We developed a routine of starting with a few drinks in a nice bar we'd found in a town called Santa Eulalia, a lovely spot where one night we saw Denholm Elliot enjoying a few drinks. From there, we'd move on to Ibiza town, which was more upmarket — a bit too upmarket for the likes of us, to be honest — and then we'd move on, usually to Amnesia, back then an open-air night-club. We'd get completely smashed there and stay until about 9.30 a.m., when we'd gravitate to a club called Manhattan in San Antonio before heading back to the studio at about midday, before it got too hot. (The journey back was often eventful: I remember once having to give the car keys to a farmer in a field and ask if he'd drive us the rest of the way.)

Basically, we had a great time. So great, in fact, that word filtered back to Manchester and people began flying out to visit us. Bez from the Mondays arrived at one point with a few people from the Haçienda and, for some reason, I lent him my driver's licence. Why on earth I did that I'll never know, as it was a nailed-on recipe for disaster. The first time he got behind the wheel he'd promised to come by the studio with a guy called Geoff the Chef to pick up my girlfriend Sarah and me at ten thirty, and we'd all go into town. It was a wet night and when ten o'clock became eleven o'clock, and eleven o'clock became eleven thirty with no sign of Bez, we started to become a little concerned. It was shortly after midnight when a bedraggled, soaking Geoff the Chef turned up at the door, minus both Bez and any form of vehicular transport.

'Bez has only gone and crashed the fucking car, hasn't he?' he announced, rain dripping from the end of his nose. 'It was raining so hard he said he couldn't see the road signs, so pulled over to read one and just drove straight into it instead.'

I can't say I was surprised. Bez is convinced he's a good driver but, as anyone who knows him can confirm, he really isn't. The rain had stopped by this point, so we trooped out after Geoff the Chef, walked down to the scene of the accident and found the car practically wrapped around the road sign. Bez was standing next to it, kicking it and swearing his head off, not because he'd totalled it but because he thought his night out was ruined.

Despite everything, however, we managed to get into town, where I overindulged quite spectacularly, to the point where one of the few things I remember is being carried out of a club by Sarah, Bez's girlfriend Debs, and another girl who'd come out from Manchester. Not Bez, though: he was already outside, had somehow got hold of another car and was standing next to it, grinning like a Cheshire cat and jangling the keys.

We were supposed to fly back to England the next day for a couple of weeks off, but instead of waking up at the studio ready to go to the airport with everyone else, I woke up in Bez's apartment with Sarah looking at me, worried half to death. I was in a pretty bad way, as you can imagine, and as Sarah tried to revive me I could hear Debs's voice from the next bed saying, 'Stop it, Bez, not now. Not with Bernard and Sarah in the room.'

And they say romance is dead.

It was a hell of hangover, which took until well into the evening to recede enough for Bez to drive me back to the studio. He'd clearly not learned anything from his close encounter with Spanish signage the previous night, and took anyone overtaking him as a personal affront to his honour that could only be satisfied by an immediate restoration of prime position. He also cheerfully confessed that he was white-lining it, just watching the line down the middle of the road in order to drive in a vaguely straight line. We got to the studio unscathed, but I was a complete nervous wreck by the time we arrived.

Everyone had gone back to England except the studio barman, Herman the German (who wasn't German, he was Spanish, but just happened to be called Herman), and as we pulled up outside Bez's eyes lit up and he said, 'I bet Herman the German's got some drugs.' When we walked into the bar area, we found Herman on his own and completely off his face, something Bez spotted straight away. He grabbed him by the shirt, hauled him over the counter and demanded to know where his drugs were. A terrified Herman's eyes widened to the size of dinner plates and, as soon as he'd extricated himself from Bez's clutches, he ran for it. Bez set off in hot pursuit and chased him all round the building. The screaming and shouting that accompanied the chase were more than my frayed nerves could stand, so I grabbed Sarah and we disappeared to our room. As we weren't supposed to be there for two weeks, we found the beds stripped, no towels, and our suitcases by the door. But we didn't care: we locked ourselves in and decided to lie low until the coast was clear, which could conceivably have involved the actual dismemberment of Herman the German, judging by the sounds we were hearing. (I did see Herman again, however, and was relieved to find that he'd survived his traumatic encounter with the Happy Mondays' maracas virtuoso.)

When we finally got home about three days later I picked up a copy of the *NME* and discovered that, just prior to leaving for Ibiza — indeed, the night before his flight — Bez had crashed into five cars outside the Haçienda. Which probably explained the absence of his own driver's licence when he arrived.

He really was an absolute nightmare behind the wheel. When we returned from Ibiza we finished *Technique* at Real World in Bath. Bez came down with a couple of mates and was going to drive us to a house party we'd been invited to in the town. He was late turning up because, guess what, he'd had a crash in the car and the front wing was all smashed in. 'Sorry I'm late, Bernard,' he said. 'I've had another crash, but this one wasn't my fault: someone had parked their car in the street right in the way.'

We set off on the customary white-knuckle ride, and when we turned into the street where the party was taking place Bez announced he was sure he'd been there before. When we pulled up outside the house and he emitted a lengthy string of popular swearwords, it became obvious why: of all the cars that were in and had passed through the city of Bath that night, Bez had managed to total the one belonging to the guy whose party we were going to.

Moral of the story: never get in a car with Bez, never lend him your car and definitely never lend him your driver's licence.

Back in Ibiza, Terry had the brilliant idea to add the studio to the itinerary of an 18–30s party bus tour. Goodness knows how he came up with it, but he'd gone to a hotel in San Antonio, spoken to the rep and offered them a regular weekly barbecue and the opportunity to see New Order in the studio. Sure enough, once a week, a coach would turn up dutifully at the studio packed with holidaymakers, who proceeded to eat and drink as much as they possibly could before throwing up all over the place. It sounds insane, I know, and even as I write it now I can hardly believe it myself. Back then, nothing seemed to faze us; nothing seemed wrong. No one died, so why not have a busload of hedonistic strangers let loose on the recording of an important album? I think this went on for about three weeks, until the puke got too much: we put a stop to it when we found a pancake of sick smack in the middle of the pool table.

Apart from that, we had a great time out there. With characteristic timing, we'd arrived at just the right time to immerse ourselves in Balearic beat house music. And I remember meeting my first proper E casualty in Amnesia. He was a young guy from London who was saying, 'Awite mate, checkin' aht the Balearic beats, are ya?' One of his hands was swathed in bandages and when I asked what he'd done he told me he worked in a sawmill, had one too many E's and had accidentally sawn off four fingers. He didn't even seem that bothered about it; he was having a great time. It was just the spirit of the time: nobody gave a fuck.

With all the island's distractions, we didn't get as much of the album done as we'd have liked, but we did write and record 'Fine Time', the most overtly acid house track on *Technique*. We were wrecked, though, all the time, and the whole thing cost us an absolute fortune.

We worked very hard when we got back to Real World, with only the odd foray into the clubs of London and the occasional terrorizing of the Bath locals. We had a good time while we were making the album, and I think *Technique* is a reflection of that. Not for nothing is it regarded as one of our better albums, and that's something we celebrated at the time in the best way we knew how.

Real World studios had only just opened when we arrived to put the finishing touches to *Technique*. Everything was clean, brand new; it even *smelt* new: all fresh carpet and pine. Peter Gabriel was away when we wrapped, but his studio manager, giddy with demob happiness, said to Rob, 'Now that the album's finished, would you like to have a party in the studio?' What he'd probably had in mind was a couple of crates of beer and a table laid with sandwiches and a few chicken drumsticks, but immediately Rob thought: acid house party. A massive, thumping, hedonistic acid house party. He grinned at the studio manager.

'Great idea,' he said.

Within twenty-four hours, he'd arranged for the Haçienda DJs to come down, along with a couple of coaches packed with mad Mancunians wearing bucket hats and blowing whistles. In fact, all the baggage you could imagine from the Haçienda was transplanted from Whitworth Street to this idyllic, sleepy, historic Georgian spa town. The DJs set up on the mezzanine floor of the studio and strobe lights went up. People came down from London, the record company showed up — everyone was there. We even invited some locals, and they were the ones who ended up trashing the place: someone, apparently from the rugby club, pulled a toilet cistern off the wall.

To the studio manager's horror, despite Rob's gallant attempts to placate him, the party went on all night. It was fantastic. I'll admit that I did get a little worried when I saw our publicist dragging our record plugger off somewhere with an axe in his hand and wondered whether things had possibly got a little bit out of hand, but it got to about eight thirty the next morning and everyone started piling back on the coaches to go back to Manchester. The look of relief on the studio manager's face as he watched all these mad bastards getting back on the coach was really something to see. Except, one of the coaches wouldn't start. Everyone piled off, trooped back into the studio and restarted the party until the driver could get the coach going again — about three hours later.

The level of hedonism was tremendous, but at that stage we didn't know that people could die from taking Ecstasy. We were about to find out. On rare occasions, some people can take Ecstasy once, unaware that it will have a priming effect on their immune system, which means that the second time they take the drug there can be an enormous adverse reaction. This is what led to a terrible occurrence in July 1989, when a young girl called Clare Leighton died after being taken ill inside the Haçienda. She had taken Ecstasy but despite the swift actions of club staff and the emergency services at the time, Clare died later in hospital. It was a huge tragedy, just awful. At the inquest, the coroner said the reaction Clare had experienced was extremely rare and there had only been two previous cases, both in America. From what I've learned, she'd only taken it once before, a couple of months earlier, and her immune system had reared up the second time, with desperately tragic consequences.

Obviously, we weren't selling Ecstasy at the Haçienda and the security staff at the club did their best to keep it off the premises, but it's hard to appreciate now how ubiquitous it was in those days, in pubs and clubs, at parties, even on the football terraces. I suppose it was a bit like Prohibition America in the twenties: if people want to do something badly enough, they will always find a way, no matter how hard you try to prevent it.

The acid house movement of the end of the eighties proved to be the Haçienda's peak of popularity. The capacity of this enormous venue was around sixteen hundred and, on Thursday, Friday and Saturday nights, it would be packed full of people partying and dancing. We introduced a range of themed nights which seemed to work very well: I remember Nude night on a Friday as a particularly good one, as was Hot, for which, believe it or not, a small swimming pool was constructed inside the club.

In those days, I'd spend a great deal of time at the Haç. There was an end booth in the corner, beneath the balcony, that became the preserve of Sarah, me and our friends, people like Bez, Shaun Ryder and the other Mondays. We'd all hole up there as part of a weekly routine that began with a quiet night on the Thursday, involved a bit of a blowout on a Friday and climaxed with a massive night on the Saturday, going on somewhere else afterwards till around seven in the morning, when we'd crawl into bed in a, frankly, terrible state. We had a landmark club, free booze, all our friends hung out there: it was inevitable that I'd end up at the Haçienda as often as possible. May I say, incidentally, that a certain 'Mr Haçienda' was rarely, if ever, seen there; he was never part of that scene and never demonstrated any interest in dance music whatsoever, but the rest of us would be there all the time, a gang of about fifteen or so, and there'd always be a party afterwards. When the club closed at 2 a.m. I'd generally make my way up to the DJ booth and coerce the DJ into putting more tracks on, even though the licence was clear that we had to stop at two. The crowd would still be dancing away below and, with the night in danger of continuing until sunrise, the manager would have to threaten to shut the power off and pull the plug.

Then we'd go on to somewhere else. The Kitchen in Hulme was part of a five-storey block of flats on an estate that was gradually being demolished and which some enterprising chaps had taken over and turned into a post-club venue playing primarily black music but with some techno and acid house, Detroit house, Chicago house and some Mancunian music thrown in, things like A Guy Called Gerald's 'Voodoo Ray', and 808 State. It served warm fizzy lager and similar revolting refreshments, but you paid your two quid to get in and you could stay for as long as you wanted. It was highly illegal, but the police would generally leave it alone and, as word spread, the people behind the Kitchen knocked through more and more walls of the flats in order to make the place bigger. They'd have their club nights at weekends and be smashing away with sledge-hammers for the rest of the week: eventually, they even knocked through to the floor below.

I took the Pet Shop Boys there once. Actually, I took the Pet Shop Boys to a couple of places I probably shouldn't have, and the Kitchen was one of them. When we got there, they said, 'Wow, this place is great!' but at about four o'clock in the morning this massive, weird black guy with mad, staring, bloodshot eyes arrived in a full karate outfit with a headband on with a pair of scissors shoved in it and started throwing himself around doing moves like a Vegas-era Elvis. I turned to Neil and Chris and said, 'I think we'd better go, this guy looks a little bit *too* crazy.'

Poor Neil and Chris: I'm wincing now even thinking about another night, when I took them to a really bad place. My best pals at this time were two guys called Mal and Bins. Both had at one stage found themselves temporarily on the wrong side of the law, but when I got to know them they were really nice guys (they still are). One night, Mal, Bins, Neil, Chris, Sarah and I ended up in the then notorious Moss Side district of Manchester at a blues, an illegal house party like a shebeen, run by a mutual friend of ours. Bins had connections there and, after a night at the Haçienda, thought it would be a really good idea to go. It was pretty notorious: some of the lads from the blues would drive around in cars until they could provoke the police into chasing them, then drive back to this no-go area, where they'd do a series of handbrake turns and all sorts, just to wind the police up, knowing that the area was considered so dangerous the police wouldn't dare follow them in. It was the heaviest vibe of anywhere I'd ever been, and there we were, with the Pet Shop Boys, having a party with these lads.

When we went inside there were some seriously hard-case black guys leaning against the walls, scowling into the middle distance and not making eye contact with anyone, not even each other. It's a good job we were under our mutual friend's wing, or I'm sure we would have been in serious trouble. Neil and Chris were a bit freaked out, and it got quite heavy. Sarah had a drink thrown over her head and our friend made the girl apologize to her, but the place was a tinderbox and it was time to go. You couldn't even get a taxi round there — no taxi driver would go near the place — and it certainly wasn't safe to walk to anywhere we might find one, so our friend took us round to his mother's house to make sure we were safe and called us a taxi from there. This guy really looked after us, and more than once. He's in prison now, but I still get to see him occasionally.

It just got heavier and heavier around Moss Side and the illegal party scene until, eventually, the murders started. This was the time when people started referring to Manchester as 'Gunchester': some really horrendous things happened and it would take a great deal of pain and suffering for local people before a positive change came to the area.

After the Kitchen, or wherever it might be that we'd end the night, there'd usually be a few stragglers who would crash out at my house. The next day we'd try to do what normal people did on a Sunday: read the papers, eat toast and watch *Lovejoy* and *Antiques Roadshow*. Then, as tends to happen after Sunday, there was Monday, known as 'the day after the day after' because it took so long to recover from a weekend of going at it hell for leather. While Sunday would be quite mellow, on Monday (and, occasionally, Tuesday too), you'd get the feeling you had at school when the teacher would make that horrible screeching sound with the chalk on the board. Only this was non-stop. There wasn't much you could do to ease it either: a hot bath, a walk, a run – nothing seemed to help. A glass of red wine could calm it down a little, but you couldn't really look alcohol in the eye at that stage. You'd start feeling normal again by Wednesday and vow to take it easier the coming weekend, but then on Thursday Bez or someone would call, say, 'You coming out?' and you'd be powerless to resist and, inevitably, you'd do it all over again.

Elsewhere at this time, well away from dodgy places like The Kitchen, there were raves springing up in the countryside all around Manchester. These were fantastic events. Someone would set up a PA in the middle of nowhere, put the word out and hundreds of people would troop out into the hills for a massive party. Events like Sweat It Out and Joy were organized by the Donnelly Brothers, Anthony and Chris, out on the Moors in the Ashworth Valley in the summer of 1989. Anthony and Chris were acquaintances of ours — their sister Tracey worked at Factory and the Haçienda — and their raves were among the best. They had these big PA systems powered by generators, and everyone would be there. The Donnellys' mother would be there flipping burgers: the whole thing was just brilliant, with a tremendous atmosphere. I have particularly fond memories of those nights. Nobody was hurt and there was no question of any trouble, it was just a group of people in the outdoors having a great time and doing no more harm to themselves or the surroundings than any rambler or walker. One thorn in the side of the acid-house movement — which, I must emphasize, was a very different proposition to the scene I'd introduced the Pet Shop Boys to — was James Anderton, the notorious Chief Constable of Greater Manchester Police. He was — let's be kind — a man who polarized opinion. As well as favouring a combative, heavy-handed approach to policing, he was openly political and rabidly anti-left wing, a vocal proponent of the introduction of corporal punishment, and he once described homosexuals and drug addicts who'd contracted AIDS as 'swirling in a cesspit of their own making'. He was galvanized in all of this by a deep-set religious conviction (he once told a radio interviewer that he thought God may well have been using him as a prophet), which earned him the nickname God's Cop and inspired the Mondays' song of the same name. Anderton had decided he was going to shut down anything and everything that he didn't care for — and he didn't care for a *lot*. Once he'd identified the rave scene as something to be obliterated as part of his personal holy mission, things began to change. On New Year's Eve 1989, for example, there was going to be a party in an old warehouse in Ancoats — only a small event, no more than about a hundred and fifty people — but when we arrived we found a cordon of police surrounding the building, helicopters buzzing overhead, floodlights playing over the warehouse: the lot. It was all a little excessive for a small New Year's Eve party, but it was an effective illustration of how Anderton seemed hell bent on – among other things – spoiling our fun.

Despite this, the Haçienda had been doing very well and, though the acid house explosion had played a big part in that success, the new manager we'd installed, Paul Mason, deserved quite a lot of credit. Flushed with success, in early 1989 he issued us with a bit of an ultimatum. He said, 'Look, I've turned this club around, but it's not enough for me, I want to do more. I think we should open a bar in central Manchester.' And so the Dry bar was born.

When we opened Dry I was determined not to make the same mistakes we had with the Haçienda, which had become a success almost despite itself rather than due to any great strategy decisions on the part of the management. I was a huge admirer of Danceteria in New York, one of the clubs to which our friend Ruth Polsky had introduced us (poor Ruth, incidentally, was dead by this time: knocked down and killed by a taxi outside the Limelight in 1986 at the tragically young age of thirty-one). I met Madonna at Danceteria once, very briefly (and a bit of a 'Who the fuck is this asshole?' moment for Ms Ciccone); she knew Ruth quite well and I think had even worked at the Danceteria at some point.

The great thing about Danceteria was that it ranged over several floors, with a lift that took people to a different scene and different music on each level. I thought that was brilliant. During the week, when it wasn't busy, they'd shut the upper floors so the lower floors would still be crowded, which was also a great idea. The Haçienda was rammed on Thursday, Friday and Saturday nights but completely empty the rest of the week because, with the best will in the world, you're never going to see eighteen hundred people coming through the door six nights a week. In fact, even when it wasn't empty, with a capacity that large the Haçienda needed to be well populated even to *look* busy.

When Dry was mooted, then, I suggested we go for something more like Danceteria. I'd also realized that Manchester was home to the biggest student campus in Britain so suggested placing it in a student area where we'd have a ready-made clientele right on the doorstep. I'm certainly no impresario, but it seemed to make perfect business sense.

'Oh no,' was Tony's instant response. 'We don't want to do that.'

He explained that they had already looked at some premises and were keen on one in Oldham Street. It was nowhere near the students, but was supposed to be in an area that was 'up and coming'.

Well, an up-and-coming area is all very well as long as there's some kind of timescale for the upping and the coming. In the case of Dry, this was a small detail conveniently ignored. Oldham Street is certainly up-and-coming now, but when Dry was built it was more the preserve of tramps and winos than the students and young professionals we needed to attract.

'We've found this beautiful building,' he continued. 'It's very, very long and we've worked out that we can fit the longest bar in Britain in there.'

I think this aspect in particular is what had appealed to Tony, and it was enough to confirm the decision. They'd taken Ben Kelly, who'd designed the Haçienda, to have a look and he'd found art-deco red curtain plasterwork in the walls, and got very excited about it. The die was cast. Again, just as had happened with the Haçienda, the management had been seduced by the look of the place over all other priorities and considerations. I was trying to learn from the Haçienda experience so we didn't make the same mistake twice. But guess what — we made the same mistake twice. When Dry opened in July 1989 the Haçienda crowd would meet there before heading over to the club: I think they even ran a bus between the two, which was a good idea. But from Sunday to Wednesday, when nobody went out, it was running at a dead loss: all the money it made at the end of the week was wiped out by the middle of the following week.

Also in July 1989 New Order were on a gruelling tour of America, and my relentless partying would finally catch up with me.

Chapter Sixteen

Too much drink, but not enough to lose

I started throwing up around two o'clock in the morning, and I was still throwing up at four the next afternoon. I was in Chicago, it was early July 1989 and things could have been going better.

Earlier in the evening I'd been in the back of a limo with Sarah on the way to a night out at our friend Joe Shanahan's club, Metro, in Chicago, when the coughing started and, after a few minutes, it was clear it wasn't going to stop. I asked the driver to turn around and take us back to the hotel, and we went up to our room. This relentless dry coughing carried on all night without respite. Then the vomiting started and I knew something was very wrong. I'd not even been drinking, yet there I was kneeling over the toilet in a Chicago hotel room in the middle of the night throwing up and retching long after there was nothing left to come up. By four o'clock the next day it was decided that I needed some help. I'd been ill on tour before, but never this bad.

Rob and Tom Atencio came to my room and saw the mess I was in.

Tom said straight away that I should get to the hospital over the road. Rob protested that we had a gig in Detroit the following day – which was, I suppose, understandable, because he'd have to deal with the crap my being ill would cause; but in the end Tom insisted.

I walked shakily to the lift, descended, walked across the street, got into another lift, ascended, and then bang! I was put straight into a hospital bed. The first thing the doctor told me was that I needed to stay there for a couple of days without eating anything, and that they'd need to perform an endoscopy. Rob's heart sank. As well as the gig, there was a huge party arranged in Detroit with all the local house DJs; it was going to be a massive night. He left the room, cancelled the gig and told the rest of the band and crew. The gig may have been pulled, but the flights were still booked and the party was still on and, given the choice between twiddling their thumbs in Chicago waiting for me and partying in Detroit, surprisingly, they all chose the latter option.

Rob and Tom stayed behind and came in to see me the next morning. 'You're not going to believe this,' they said, 'but there's a food festival in the street below.' Great.

When I was taken down for the endoscopy I nearly fell off the trolley when I saw the thing they produced to put down my throat. These days, the cameras they use are tiny, but this was 1989 and the contraption they were wheeling towards me was like an elephant's trunk. When he registered my alarm the doctor smiled and said, 'Don't worry, Mr Sumner, we've put a little dose of Valium in your drip. It'll be fine, you'll be very relaxed and won't feel a thing.'

Ulp. What he didn't know was that I'd been taking Valium all through the tour to help me sleep and had developed a significant tolerance to it. I said, 'Listen, Doctor, the Valium's had no effect whatsoever and I promise you I could get up off this trolley right now and run round the ward. Seriously, it's not working.' Despite my increasingly urgent pleading he just smiled sympathetically, patted my arm and assured me I really had nothing to worry about.

They put this thing down my throat, and it was absolutely disgusting, but what they found was worse. There was a network of burns, cuts and abrasions all over my stomach lining. It wasn't an ulcer but it was something very like it. The reason I was coughing was that stomach acid had been released by the abrasions, the vapours were drifting up to my throat and I was basically breathing the noxious fumes.

There was little doubt as to what had caused it: after years of relentless hard living my lifestyle was starting to catch up with me. In mitigation, I did try to put forward the incredibly spicy meal I'd eaten in Minneapolis a couple of days earlier – it really had been like swallowing lava – but I'd been burning the candle at both ends for so long the flame had finally reached the middle. I had to change something before I did myself some real damage.

Lying there with little else to do but stare at the ceiling while nearly everyone else – the band, the crew, Public Image Ltd and The Sugarcubes, who were with us on that tour – were in Detroit having a ball at the party, I had plenty of time to reflect upon and think about the implications of my situation. I was making myself ill for the sake of a money pit with a massive hole in it. I needed a break, or I was in serious danger of becoming an alcoholic, an addict of some kind or even dying.

I was hungry, weak, sore and three hundred miles from the party. The doctor had a good long talk with me, and I heard my own voice in my head say, 'Fucking hell, Bernard. What are you doing?'

I had expressed, strenuously, my concerns to Rob before all this had happened, about how I believed we needed to scale back a bit and chill things off, take stock and think about the best way to take New Order forward. They had fallen on deaf ears. I guess Rob was worrying about the money: we had to tour to keep the cash coming in to prop up the Haçienda — but my health was at stake now.

It was a stupid situation; an unsustainable one. I was going to have to take matters into my own hands. The emphasis in New Order had shifted into a seemingly endless round of gigging and touring. Hooky, in particular, loved it, much more than being in the studio, but I needed a break.

Also, I sensed that I was on the receiving end of a bit of resentment from the rest of the band either for pushing the group in an electronic direction or giving the impression somehow that I was effectively seizing the controls. To them, I say I'm sorry if I came across as a twat back then, but I was only a twat because I was feeling so much pressure.

I was pretty angry about this financial bucket with the dirty great hole in it. We were doing our bit by releasing hit records and having successful tours that made money, but the home guard seemed to have got into a situation from which they couldn't extricate themselves. I wrote the lyrics to the song 'Run' about it. In retrospect, those lyrics were about how I felt back then.

At the same time, Johnny Marr was just emerging from the fallout from the break up of The Smiths. He was pretty burnt out too, but for different reasons: in The Smiths, they'd written a huge amount of material in a very short time, and the break-up itself had been pretty acrimonious. I'd met Johnny when he'd played guitar on a session I was producing for Mike Pickering's band a few years earlier, and we'd kept in touch. Our respective situations had left us feeling a little like kindred spirits, and it wasn't long before we started writing music together as Electronic.

Electronic was very much a pressure-release valve for the two of us, because we'd both found ourselves in fraught situations. Johnny's predicament was different from mine in that The Smiths had actually split up, whereas I just needed to get a bit of distance between New Order and myself in order to revive my creative energy and come back stronger to fight another day. Also, it felt a little like the Haçienda had become a god that we all had to worship and no one was actually listening to our concerns about it. We were in a situation where the tail was effectively wagging the dog, and something needed to be done but no one seemed able to take the first step. Add that to the self-inflicted repercussions of too much partying, and something had to give. To all intents and purposes, I went on strike from New Order. Not in the brazier and donkey jacket sense, nothing that militant; I just thought I needed to demonstrate my concerns at the way things were going. It turned out that, once we'd played the Reading Festival in August 1989, we wouldn't play live again as New Order for four years.

A subtle harmonic sounding through all of this was that New Order never let other people into our closed inner circle of musicians. While this has allowed us to preserve a very distinctive sound, it's also left us open to the danger of repeating ourselves and doing the same old thing year after year.

Obviously, the longer you work with a band, the more baggage you collect through being cooped up together on buses, aeroplanes and in sweaty dressing rooms while touring, and working intensely together in studios when recording, often staying on the premises full time. With that level of intensity, it's inevitable that you'll build up little niggles with each other, little things you dislike. If you travel on a bus or a train now, there'll usually be a kid playing tinny music through his mobile phone, or some businessman on his iPhone sitting next to you, talking to Nigel in Accounts and shouting about his boring-arse business until you feel like punching him in the face. In a band, that feeling is multiplied and intensified 24/7. You go to an airport in some country or other, it's only an hour and a half after you've gone to bed, you're hungover and there's someone next to you picking their nose and playing a tape of a band you hate. With the best will in the world, eventually, that's going to get on your nerves. Even if you're lucky enough to be in a band where there are no significant egos, the tension inevitably builds up until the whole thing reaches breaking point.

There are, I think, two solutions. One was suggested to me by Billy Corgan from The Smashing Pumpkins: don't travel together as a band. At first I thought that was ridiculous – you're all supposed to be together and on the same team – but the more I think about it, the more it could make sense: if you're going to get on each other's nerves, just get together for the gigs and be pleased to see each other when you arrive.

The other solution is to go your separate ways for a while and get a breath of fresh air. That's what we did with New Order in 1989 and, to a much greater extent, between 1993 and 1998. I don't think three or four blokes and one woman who aren't related are designed to spend so much time together. It's just not natural.

I felt a need to refresh myself as a musician and learn from other players, see how they wrote songs, observe the things they did differently and the things they did the same. Our 'keep it in the family' musical policy meant that I wasn't going to find that with New Order. We'd not had any musical education beyond the 'teach yourself' books we'd bought as teenagers, and even that comprised only about 10 per cent of our musical know-how. The other 90 per cent came from our record collections, our life histories and our environment. We were also learning by playing live, but to play live effectively the hard work has to be done in the rehearsal room. To this day, I hate rehearsing. Phil and Tom love it and Steve really likes it. I don't know for sure how Gillian feels about it. It's mechanical: rehearsals are just about reactivating those brain cells that control your left and right hands and, though I know it has to be done, I find it boring, like doing push-ups. What I like most of all is the writing, the invention, and in the late eighties that creative spark needed reigniting. In Johnny, I found the perfect partner at the right time to achieve just that.

Interestingly, Johnny came from a very different angle musically. He'd written some brilliant stuff – and still does – but while I was going out clubbing in New York and Manchester, he was sitting at home practising his guitar. He found that the more he rehearsed, the luckier he became. This was a different way of arriving at success – the traditional way – and he became a very skilled musician as a result. In New Order, we did it the unorthodox way, more through instinct and inspiration. This isn't to say Johnny's playing wasn't inspired, far from it, but his was a combination of skill and inspiration. With us, the inspiration came first and the skill would come later.

I began working with Johnny on the first, eponymously titled *Electronic* album during 1988, and it was great: I could play as many synthesizers as I wanted without sensing bad vibes. Indeed, Johnny was actively encouraging me on that score, because he wanted to learn all about synthesizers as they'd been *verboten* in *Die Schmidts*. Yet while I was delighted that, certainly on that first album, Johnny was keen to learn about electronics, I was still keen for him to carry on playing brilliant guitar. I remember saying to him in the studio one day, 'Johnny, if you don't play any fucking guitar on this record, then everyone's going to blame me.'

'Yeah, OK, Bernard,' he replied, 'but what does this button do?'

Johnny is a forward-looking, open-minded musician, and he wanted to try pastures new. To a certain extent, even as one of the best guitarists this country has ever produced, he saw the world of electronic music as the future. This was literally music to my ears, but of course you can't deny – and I never would – that great music has always been made with guitars too. Although I love electronic and dance music, I also love guitar music; that's where my roots lay and it provided my early influences. If you look at some of the interviews I gave around this time, you'll never find me hectoring that electronic music was the only way forward. I was constantly reiterating that a good song is a good song no matter what instrument it's written on. It could be a guitar, it could be a synthesizer — it could be a fucking noseflute, for all I care.

Johnny and I went into the studio and just dug in. Strange as it might sound, it was probably a good four to six months before we felt truly comfortable in each other's presence: we were probably both a little bit in awe of each other at first. Once we'd broken through that barrier, however, the work started becoming fun. We had a call from Neil Tennant to say he'd heard about what we were doing and would love to be involved, so we invited him up. It so happened that around that time we'd written the backing track for 'Getting Away with It'. Neil travelled up to Johnny's home studio, we finished the track, Neil recorded the vocal and it became Electronic's first single.

I was learning a great deal. We brought in an arranger called Anne Dudley to work on the strings and I found it a fantastic experience. It was deeply interesting working with classically trained musicians and seeing the different ways in which they approached things. There was a whole range of different methodologies in play: Anne rang me one day and asked me a list of questions, whether I was an active or passive person, an introvert or an extrovert, that kind of thing (I said I was 'probably an introverted extrovert'). From my answers, she tailored the strings to suit my personality. Amazing stuff.

That's not to say, however, that I didn't occasionally get into the same old mess with Johnny that I used to get into in New Order.

Take Electronic's first promotional tour of the States, for example. In the US, Electronic were on Warner Brothers, and they brought us over for a round of publicity and interviews, beginning in New York. On arrival, we had a night off before the promotion treadmill creaked into action, so Johnny and I promptly went out on the town. It so happened there was a full-moon party taking place that night in the shadow of the World Trade Center with 3D from Massive Attack deejaying. It was an open-air rave in the heart of Manhattan beneath the Twin Towers: there was a clear sky, the full moon and we had a great time. Too great, as it turned out, because after it finished it wasn't enough and I found I'd slipped all too easily into the comfortable old suit of the New Order tours. We ended up at a small club that played soul music, but I wasn't really in the mood for soul, it was house music I was after. So when we left the club, which must have been at about three in the morning, I *still* wasn't finished, even though we had a whole range of interviews starting a few hours later. We'd not been in America for twenty-four hours and already I'd dragged Johnny under my corrupting wing. I don't think that level of partying is really part of Johnny's nature. He certainly liked a good time — he was neither saint nor angel on that score — but he wasn't as dance-club focused as I was. But hey, he was finding the world of electronic music and instruments fascinating and wanted to know more about it, so, in effect, this night was an educational expedition. A field trip, if you like. If only I could find him some house music somewhere . . .

When we came out of the soul club, there was a pickup truck parked outside with a group people in the back who I'd decided looked like they knew what was going on. I called out to them and asked if there was a party going on anywhere. A voice replied that there was and we should jump in the back of the truck. So we hopped in, the truck pulled away, and before I knew it this guy in front of me had turned round and said in broad Brummie, 'Fookin' 'ell, it's Bernard Soomner, what the fook are yow doing here?' I said we'd just arrived and were looking for a party. When I asked where we were going he said there was a house party in Harlem. So off we went.

Then someone else turned round and said, 'Fucking hell, New Order!' It turned out to be Seal. He asked what I was doing there.

'Someone told us to get to get in this truck,' I said, 'so we did.'

I looked at him and could tell he was thinking, 'Why on earth would you do that, you fucking madman?'

We arrived at the party to find it was a nice kind of chill-out thing, not quite what I was expecting but, nevertheless, a great way to wind down and finish the night. We went back to our hotel in uptown Manhattan, walking through Central Park as the dark blue of the early dawn was seen off by the sunrise. We passed people going to work as New York woke up, dusted itself down and got on with a new day. Our day was just ending, however, at eight in the morning, and when we stumbled into the foyer of the hotel we found Marcus Russell, Electronic's manager at the time, regarding us with the kind of withering look teachers reserve for disruptive pupils. Johnny and I looked at each other and, in the unforgiving glare of the cold light of day, clearly shared the same thought: what have we done? The interviews started at ten, barely two hours later, so we went to bed for an hour, got up again and, dear reader, this is I'm afraid where the narrative turns into another story involving vomit. We were in a limo doing the circuit of the New York radio stations and, as the day progressed, we felt, to put it mildly, increasingly unwell. We had a very big, bright green bag with us and, before long, were both using it to throw up into. As my hangover grew progressively worse and the limo pulled up at yet another station, I had to admit defeat.

↑ Keith Allen and John Barnes singing for England.

← My original choice of outfit for the 'World In Motion' video. Can't believe it was vetoed.

↓ Tony Wilson and Martin Hannett in the studio, with Alan Erasmus (rear, left).

↑ Arthur Baker: genius, legend and friend.

→ Rob towards the end of his unfairly short life.

Our one-time American manager, Tom Atencio. What a nice guy!

↓ That's libel, surely!

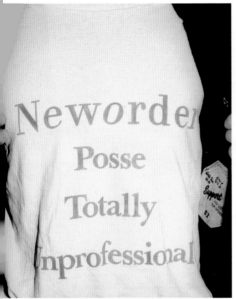

↑ Alan Erasmus, the 'quiet man' of Factory (actually he can't stop talking).

← Saint Anthony of Manchester.

↓ Two great friends, influences and co-conspirators in New York: Michael Shamberg (left) and the late Frank Callari.

← Rebecca Boulton and Andy Robinson, who somehow keep this show on the road.

↙ The incomparable Mr Alan Wise.

↓ Terry Mason, always a fish out of water.

↑ Herman the German (left, and he's actually Spanish) safe from Bez, for once.

↗ Rob and Peter Saville.

→ The glamorous world of touring.

↑ With Johnny Marr and friends. Celebrating the completion of one of our Electronic albums.

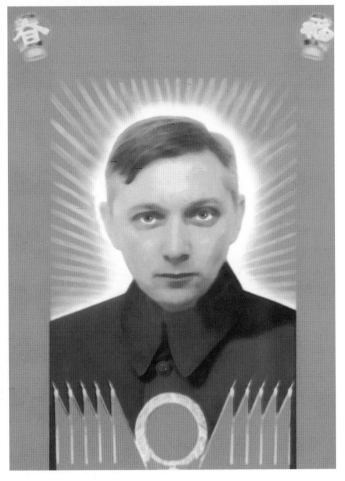

← Mark Reeder, once Factory's man in Berlin, now label owner and, it seems, head of the Chinese Communist Party.

↑ The semi-reluctant vocalist learning his craft.

← 'Did I lock the back door . . . ?'

→16   →16A   →14   →14A

↑ Who's this fresh-faced youngster?

← Off duty in Turkey.

↑ Sarah. ↗ Without whom . . . →

↙ Bad Lieutenant, in straitjacket and handcuffs.

It's a nightmare when you break down in a tunnel and have to walk out to get a mobile signal.

↑ New Order: onward and upwards.

← With Iggy at Carnegie Hall in 2014. Thank you, Mr Glass!

'Fucking hell, Johnny,' I croaked. 'I'm really sorry, but I can't move, I'm done.'

'Don't worry, Bernard,' he replied. 'I'll handle this one on my own. You just stay here.'

He disappeared into the building, and the driver said, 'You guys are on the radio, right? I'll put it on.' Much against my will, he tuned the limo radio to the appropriate station so I could hear Johnny being interviewed. After a few questions and answers, where Johnny was obviously freewheeling a little as he dealt with his own crushing hangover, I heard the presenter say, 'So, Johnny, we were expecting Ber-*nard* to be here with you today.'

Johnny started flannelling, trying to buy himself time to think up an acceptable excuse beyond 'He's outside in the limo with his head in a bag of sick.'

Johnny, bless him, did his best and actually came up with something pretty good under the circumstances.

'Oh, it's really bad news,' he said, summoning all the gravitas his stinking hangover could muster. 'Bernard's spent the night in hospital with his stomach ulcers.' This was the story we'd put out in Chicago when we'd had to cancel the Detroit gig. Good thinking, Johnny, I thought. But then the DJ said, 'Really? That's strange, because we had Seal in just before you, and he said you and Ber-*nard* were both still partying when he left you at seven o'clock this morning.'

Busted.

Somehow, we got through the rest of the interviews. Once they were finished, we had to catch a flight to Dallas and, when we got to the airport, it was teeming with people. It was a holiday weekend and it seemed half the population of the city had planned a getaway. The green bag was quite full by this stage but I was feeling no better. I sat in the doorway of the airport with the automatic doors opening and closing around me. I could see a Holiday Inn across the road. I nudged Johnny and croaked, 'Johnny, let's check in there. This hangover's not going away.' He said, 'We can't, Bernard, we've got all this promo to do.' Fair play to him, he was a trouper and I was a loser.

So I stayed sitting there on the ground as family after family passed by, looking down at me as if I was some kind of alcoholic hobo. Eventually, I summoned the energy to stagger through the airport towards security, semi-delirious, convincing myself I'd be all right if I could just get on the plane. If I got on, reclined the seat, did a bit of meditation and controlled breathing, then I'd be all right. Yes, my poor, shrivelled, hangover-fogged brain suggested, then I'd definitely be all right.

I kept up this hopeful reverie until being forced back to my senses at the security checkpoint. When I was the next person about to go through the metal detectors I realized that in my hand I was still holding the big green bag of sick. One of the security guys had sensed my discomfort and was regarding me with a vague hint of suspicion. I thought, If I dump the bag now he's going to look inside it and assume I'm some kind of lunatic carrying a bag of puke around, or, worse, conclude that I'm carrying a bomb made from some heady cocktail of volatile liquids. My only option, I realized, was to play it absolutely straight, place the bag on the conveyor belt and act as if nothing was amiss.

So that's what I did and — wouldn't you know it? — the bag passed through without incident. Maybe I looked so crazy they'd kept watching me rather than the screen, but I walked through, picked up the bag of vomit, strolled off nonchalantly as if it contained nothing more than a copy of *Newsweek*, a packet of mints and a paperback, boarded the plane and started on the road to recovery. And that was it: we didn't go out again after that. In fact, I don't think Johnny's had a drink since.

Despite our attempts to drown the promotion in puke, the

album did very well and reached number two in the UK charts. I remember being a bit disappointed with this at the time but, looking back, it was bloody good for a new band nobody had ever heard of.

We went on to make two more albums after that, *Raise the Pressure* and *Twisted Tenderness*. Working with Johnny was cool, and it was somehow more intense, it being just the two of us: it was a bit like playing badminton or passing a baton back and forth. It was either him on the spot having to come up with something, or me, and producing it ourselves added to it all. But it was a healthy kind of sink-or-swim creative pressure, and we thrived.

The premise of Electronic was that the core of the band would be kept to the two of us but we'd bring in different guest artists. On *Electronic* it had been the Pet Shop Boys, and on 1994's *Raise the Pressure* it was Karl Bartos from Kraftwerk. I'm a massive Kraftwerk fan, and always have been. I knew Karl had left Kraftwerk a few years before, thought how great it would be to work with him and wondered if he might be up for doing something.

When I contacted him, at first I think he was a bit suspicious of this strange English guy appearing out of the blue and babbling at him about making an album together, but he kindly consented to meet us in Düsseldorf and took us out for a meal (a strange combination of asparagus and ice cream, as I recall), at the conclusion of which he agreed to come over and make *Raise the Pressure* with us.

When we started work, again there was a getting-to-know-you period. All three of us were aware of our respective legacies as musicians but didn't yet know what to make of each other when we were put together in a studio. It's a strange dichotomy: you really have to make an album with someone before you know them, but at the same time you need to know them in order to make the album.

I think Karl had had a few frustrations with Kraftwerk, because their output hadn't moved as quickly as he'd have liked. In those days, there was a huge amount of programming required to obtain good results, and only one person at a time could really do that. It was a similar situation to the one I'd found with the electronic side of New Order: it was supposed to be a group effort but, obviously, only one person can use a mouse at any one time. I think he'd got fed up with all the sitting around that went with the perfectionist pace of the Kraftwerk method and decided to go it alone. It can be very easy to entrench oneself in technology, because you want to stay ahead of the game by using the very latest gear. This means learning new machines as they become available: manual work, in the sense that you're using a manual.

Unfortunately for Karl, when he came to work with Electronic on *Raise the Pressure*, we lost our engineer, Owen Morris, midstream, which, until we found Jim Spencer, left Johnny and I trying to engineer the album as well as write, arrange and play it. This inevitably slowed the whole process down.

At that time I was also participating in a fly-on-the-wall television documentary about depression that was being put together by a well-known psychologist. The premise of the show was quite interesting: the psychologist's theory echoed those of Freud and Jung, that artists were basically fucked-up people whose art was a symptom of their illness. He'd taken it a step further, however, and posited that this creative spark was specifically due to low serotonin levels. If you gave an artist Prozac, he suggested, it would raise his or her serotonin levels and, as a result, kill their art. In hindsight, participating in a programme designed to confirm this was maybe not such a great idea during the recording of an album.

I'd read a lot about Prozac. I didn't have full-blown depression, but I was certainly disposed towards it, possibly due to my family history: perhaps all the illness I'd had to witness while growing up inevitably made me a little emotionally vulnerable. Also, frankly, I'd been drinking too much, something that elevates the level of serotonin in your brain one day and depletes it the next: an unhealthy contributory factor in someone naturally prone to depression. I won't say I had a chronic manifestation of the condition. I certainly had the blues at times, and the opportunity to take Prozac and observe its effects under supervision intrigued me. I agreed to take part, began a course of Prozac and waited to see what would happen. It worked stunningly well, banishing any and all of my depressive feelings in the same way an aspirin disperses a headache.

People say there are some potentially nasty side effects of taking Prozac, that it causes suicide because of the terrible withdrawal symptoms, but that wasn't my experience at all. I didn't suffer any more withdrawal symptoms coming off Prozac than I do after a couple of paracetamol. Prozac doesn't make you feel high, or blissed out like Valium or anything like that. If you think of your moods as a sine wave, Prozac just gives you lower peaks and shallower dips, helping to keep you on a more even keel. In a chemical way, it corrects the brain chemistry to introduce more serotonin, while, cognitively, it gets you used to being in a positive frame of mind. It worked like a charm for me and I'm grateful to the programme for introducing me to it — but certainly not for anything else.

One day after the filming had finished I was driving up the motorway from somewhere down south and had Radio 1 playing in the car. The news came on at the top of the hour, and a breathless voice said, 'Bernard Sumner admits that he's been suffering from writer's block for a year and a half, but since taking Prozac he's been cured,' followed by a plug for the television programme. According to the promo, I'd apparently be laying bare my writer's-block hell in the nation's living rooms, which certainly came as news to me as I didn't have writer's block, and if I had, why would I have taken part in an experiment that might make it worse? I got home to find that a VHS of the programme had arrived and I immediately sat down to watch it. Those sine waves I mentioned that were levelled off by the Prozac? The longer I watched, the more they went right off the scale. The programme had been edited to suggest I'd been suffering from a crippling bout of writer's block and the Prozac had got me writing songs again. Completely the opposite of what I'd been told by the psychologist and nothing even close to what actually happened.

I went ballistic. I phoned the guy up, threatening legal action and all sorts, asking what the fuck was going on, why had he made up this bullshit? He was honest enough to admit the programme's producer had wanted to make it a bit juicier – I guess 'Bernard Sumner feels a bit better about things in general' wouldn't have made the Radio 1 news – so I said, 'Well, make it as juicy as you like, but if you broadcast what I've just watched then I promise you I will sue the hairs off your bollocks.' When the programme went out the following week, they had re-edited the programme, slightly, but the original version had already been sent out to the press. It did a great disservice not only to me, but also to both the drug and the psychologist, whose original concept had been sound. With the press having received the 'juicy' version, all the coverage reflected that rather than the reality of the programme as it was actually broadcast. Never again will I participate in a fly-on-the-wall documentary.

All this was going on while we were recording – perhaps appropriately – *Raise the Pressure*. We'd assumed that after all those years as a member of Kraftwerk, Karl would be Mr Electronic Music, but the music he'd really loved since he was growing up in the sixties was The Beatles and he'd thought the album would give him the opportunity to try making guitar music. It turned out to be a messy, difficult album: Karl had been frustrated by things not moving fast enough with Kraftwerk, and now here he was with Electronic finding things again creeping along at a glacial pace. In the meantime, I was battling a few demons, cleaning myself up and threatening psychologists with legal action, so it was all rather fraught, but I really liked Karl and am lucky enough still to regard him as a great friend. He lives in Hamburg now and, whenever I'm there, which isn't as often as I'd like, we'll meet up and have a great laugh together. He's got a brilliant sense of humour, knows exactly what sort of a twat I am and doesn't let me get away with anything.

I still count Johnny among my good friends too, and look back at the times with Electronic with great affection. I think we made a good team, suiting each other musically, temperamentally and socially. He's a great guy, but I have to say this — and Johnny, if you're reading this, you know it's true — he talks a *lot*. When I come off the phone to him, my ear is hot and bright red and I've barely managed to get a word in edgeways. He's such an enthusiastic person about life, and about music in particular, and is always keen to convey that enthusiasm to you at length.

He lives for music, to an extent that borders on obsession. I did try and broaden his interests a couple of times: I took him on a sailing holiday once, for the entirety of which he talked about music. Then Sarah, Johnny, Ange, his wife, and I went to a hotel in a beautiful part of the countryside where I was delighted to coax him out walking with me in the hills. It was a stunningly beautiful place but as we walked amongst this incredible scenery he stared at the ground and . . . talked about music. I've been for many meals with Johnny in some really nice restaurants over the years where, without fail, he's . . . talked about music. I've given up now, really, but he has a great sense of humour and is a really decent person. He's very observant and can sum people up very well (he does some great impressions too), and is far more disciplined than I am: I think he lives on a diet of nuts, seeds, berries and distilled water and jogs something like twenty miles a day.

Johnny is a person who's always stuck to his guns and achieves what he does through hard work. He's definitely a grafter. We both did the Lollapalooza tour in South America recently, despite his having fractured his hand just before he left. He told me he'd been out jogging, lost concentration for a moment and the next thing he knew he was on the floor, having banged his face and done serious damage to his hand. The concussion may have affected his memory slightly, because a little bird told me that he'd actually run smack into a lamp post, probably while checking himself out in a shop window.

He's great to work with and I would never rule out working with him again: we know each other well and, these days, we're both a bit more comfortable in our own skins. It's funny, in the later days of Electronic, Johnny would say that I'd become more like him while he'd become more like me. I think it's even more the case since we've stopped working together. One key difference, however, is that you'll never catch me running full tilt into a lamp post.

I've leapt ahead a little by telling the full story of Electronic, so let's navigate back to the dawn of a decade and a glorious hot summer when we provided the soundtrack as eleven men in white shirts captured the mood, hopes and dreams of a nation.

Chapter Seventeen

We're singing for England

Early in 1988, Tony had asked us to put some music together for a TV series he was making for Granada called *Best and Marsh*. It was a show that looked back to the glory days of football in the seventies — pre-dating the craze for football nostalgia that would be a feature of the nineties, so ahead of its time — which Tony presented alongside George Best and Rodney Marsh. They needed a theme tune, so Tony asked us to provide one and we were happy to oblige, even if the finished product was a little half-baked: we were about to go away on tour and only just managed to squeeze it in before we left. The rush meant that it certainly wasn't the best piece of music we've ever made and it will never appear in any lists of great television themes, but it did create a link between us and football. Someone at the Football Association must have seen the programme because, early in 1990, we received an invitation to contribute a song for England in the run-up to that summer's World Cup in Italy.

Strange as it may sound, given that 'World In Motion' turned out to be a number-one single, there was a bit of a division within the band over whether we should do it or not. When the invitation arrived we were also exploring the possibility of working with Michael Powell, the film director famous for films like *Black Narcissus*, *The Red Shoes* and *A Matter of Life and Death*. He worked closely with Emeric Pressburger, and I think I mentioned earlier what a huge fan I am of theirs: I used to have the films playing as I built synthesizers late into the night in the earliest days of New Order.

We travelled down to London to see Michael and his wife, Thelma, who was a film editor of considerable note, and hear what he had in mind. He was a lovely guy, a real character, and wore a very distinctive tartan suit. Michael's idea was to shoot a short film based on a poem called 'The Sands of Dee' by Charles Kingsley (probably most famous for writing *The Water Babies*) about a young shepherdess who is caught out by the incoming tide on the sands of the River Dee, which winds its way through Chester and out into the Irish Sea (I don't know when Michael had last been there, but there's a dirty big oil refinery there now). The estuary is a big one, where the tide comes in and goes out very quickly, which leads to the protagonist of the poem becoming stranded in the quicksand. Michael's plan was to shoot a dramatization of the poem with Tilda Swinton as the shepherdess and our music as the soundtrack ('Age of Consent', specifically, which was also the name of one of the last major films Michael made, starring James Mason) — as long as we could provide funding to the tune of about £100,000.

As a Michael Powell fan, I was really keen to work with him. Steve, also a fan, but probably not as obsessively as me, was also in favour, because he thought it was a great idea. The trouble was that it clashed with the FA's invitation, and we didn't have time to do both. It was a really tough decision, but we had to be pragmatic: doing the project with Michael would cost us a hundred grand, money there was a chance we wouldn't see again. Even Tony wrinkled his nose at the cost, but we were doing pretty well at the time and could have found the money if we'd really wanted to do it (or, more to the point, if it had been Tony's idea in the first place). In the end we went with the World Cup song.

The FA's invitation provided an interesting challenge for us. Traditionally, football songs had always been awful, usually consisting of the team lined up in matching sensible knitwear singing some kind of anthemic rubbish that was supposed to stir the loins and evoke national pride. 'Back Home', released for the 1970 World Cup, was a prime example of the phenomenon, and there'd always been the annual embarrassment of the Cup Final teams on *Top of the Pops* looking bemused beneath their perms and making token attempts to mouth vacuous, upbeat words cobbled together on the back of an envelope by some local club singer. These things always seemed badly thought out and it was almost as if they were designed to make the players look like idiots. We weren't necessarily setting out to change the face of football records, but we wanted to write a good song, one the players could get behind and enjoy being a part of.

My relationship with football had become distant in the years since I'd become a busy professional musician. I was really into it when I was younger and am a Manchester United fan — a rare one who's actually from Salford. I used to go regularly to Old Trafford as a kid to see George Best, and when United won the European Cup in 1968 I went to see them parade the trophy in Albert Square. I've mixed memories of that, however, as I was only a kid and was nearly suffocated in the crush of people. My interest had dimmed by 1990, though; I suppose I grew out of football and became interested in other things.

So I'm no football expert, but I am a lyricist, so I set out to write something different to the usual 'we're going to bring the trophy back, hurrah!' kind of thing. In order to make that happen, I enlisted a bit of help. We were all big fans of the *Comic Strip Presents* comedy series and had seen Keith Allen in one called *The Yob*, a spoof on the film *The Fly*, in which Keith is transformed from a poncey London pop-video director into a full-on football hooligan. We thought it was hilarious, Keith was brilliant in the starring role and, knowing he was a football fan, we approached him with regard to co-writing the lyrics. I didn't know Keith then: he'd appeared with us at the miners' benefit years before, had been to a party at my house once — I don't know how he'd ended up there — and I'd seen him at the Haçienda a couple of times, but we were only on nodding terms at best. It turned out, though, that bringing Keith in was exactly the right thing to do.

We wrote 'World In Motion' as we would any other track, with each of us making a contribution. Steve and Gillian worked on the first part of the song and I wrote the second, which meant that, appropriately for a football record, it's a song of two halves. We recorded the song in the glamorous surroundings of Slough, because it was close to England's training ground, which is where the players would be coming in from to record their vocal contributions. The night before the recording I'd done a guest spot for 808 State at the G-Mex on a track called 'Spanish Heart' and ended up slightly tipsy afterwards. I had a stinking hangover the next day when I was driven down with Tony and Keith and, when we arrived, I still had my head in a bucket. This probably didn't set much of an example to the footballers, but perhaps it reinforced their existing impression of musicians. The team came in — Paul Gascoigne, John Barnes, Peter Beardsley, Chris Waddle and the rest (Gazza took one look at the mixing desk and said, 'Fucking hell, man, that's a big organ') — and, if they were nervous about what lay ahead, the buckets of champagne bottles that greeted them soon had them suitably relaxed.

In the studio, we'd elaborated on one of the piano melody lines and added words to it: 'We're playing for England/ We're playing this song/ We're singing for England/ arrivederci, it's one on one,' which I thought was a great hook line. Once we were happy with that, we brought the players, Keith and the band into the studio together to record it. We'd devised a rap section in the middle of the song which Keith had written, and we asked for volunteers among the players to have a crack at it. To be fair, quite a lot of them gave it a good go, but let's just say the lads' talents lay in football and leave it at that. Famously, by far the winner of the battle of the rappers was John Barnes — he made a good job of it and was a very nice guy as well. (Steve still has a tape of the other players' efforts somewhere, which is pretty funny.)

When we made the B-side, which was an extended version of the song, we mixed it at Real World in Bath with an engineer called Richard Chappell, a born-again Christian who Terry had nicknamed Dickie the Christian. He had quite a strong West Country accent, which we thought had a certain charming quality to it, and when we asked him if he'd like to try the rap he readily consented. So that's Dickie the Christian rapping on the B-side in his lilting, fey Bath accent: it's about as far from gangsta rap as you could possibly imagine.

We got together with the players again when we filmed the video not long before the squad left for Italy. Some of it was shot at an England game when a couple of guys from Factory went down to Wembley with a camera for a pre-World Cup friendly against Uruguay, so the action footage you see in the video was specially shot, but the majority was filmed in the course of one day in Liverpool.

I was told the shoot was to be at Anfield and, for some reason, had decided the most appropriate attire for a World Cup video was an Elvis impersonator's outfit. I was working at Johnny's house on some Electronic material at the time and put on the Elvis costume there: a white flared jumpsuit covered with sequins, wig and sunglasses that gave you the full Elvis in Vegas experience, cut-price in cheap polyester. Johnny had two very large Alsatians back then and, as soon as I walked out of the studio as Elvis, they both went for me. I just about escaped with my life. I guess they weren't fans of the King.

As it was a beautiful sunny day, I drove to Anfield with the roof down. When I arrived, however, I found the stadium completely deserted. It turned out the shoot wasn't at Anfield after all, it was several miles away at Liverpool's Melwood training ground. So there I was, at Anfield, a United fan dressed as Elvis and sitting in a bright red convertible just as the schools were chucking out. Every time I pulled up at traffic lights the kids were hanging out of the bus windows shouting, 'Hey, Elvis, you twat, where are you fokkin' goin'?'

When I'd finally arrived at Melwood and amused everyone with my tale of humiliating incompetence, the director broke it to me that he didn't really think the Elvis suit worked and could I change into an England shirt instead. Why he thought that I'll never know, but there is one brief shot of me wearing it in the video, in the car, alongside Keith, who's wearing the wig.

The FA loved 'World In Motion', it was released as a single and went to number one. England travelled to Italy and reached the semi-finals — because the song had spurred them on, obviously; it's notable they've not done as well since — playing really well and only going out on penalties against West Germany.

I think 'World In Motion' really broke the mould of football songs. Football and music should, in theory, make ideal bedfellows — their fan cultures are quite similar in many ways — but, traditionally, the two had never quite gelled. It seemed to me that, in previous years, the FA had just gone to Joe and Albert from the local British Legion to put a song together, or some cheesy cabaret artiste, so it took a bit of forward thinking on their behalf to come to us. Rather than yet more cheery singalong bollocks, we made the key message simply 'express yourself', which gave the song a very different ethos. It also came at a turning point for the game. The eighties were a pretty grim time for football fans: hooliganism was rife and there'd been the terrible disasters at Bradford City, Heysel and, just a year before the World Cup, Hillsborough, but the 1990 World Cup seemed to be the catalyst for things really starting to change. Whether 'World In Motion' played a part, I couldn't really say, but the England team's success at Italia '90 certainly helped, the fanzine movement was in full swing and I think football fans began to change their mind-set and then the mind-set of the public at large. The tribalism remained to an extent — it's what fuels football culture, after all — but the violent aggression that had gone with it reduced dramatically, and that long, hot summer of 1990 was, in hindsight, a crucial watershed for football. Fans were seeing joy and beauty in the game again. In connection with this, it might be telling that Keith had wanted to call the song 'E for England . . .'

When the song became a hit, everyone assumed I was a football expert, which I'm definitely not. I do think it is the beautiful game though, and, when there's a good, exciting match on, there's nothing better. I remember the 1999 European Cup final when Manchester United played Bayern Munich. I'd like to say I was there but instead I was stuck in a London hotel room with one of the worst hangovers I've ever had waiting to go out and shoot a video at one thirty in the morning. Bayern scored after something like six minutes and then blocked the goalmouth, parked the bus, and the rest of the match consisted of United trying to break down this wall of maroon and grey until injury time, when first Teddy Sheringham and then Ole Gunnar Solskjaer scored to win the game. It was the most fantastic climax, one that showed just how exciting football can be. It wiped my hangover completely away.

While football can still be a thrilling spectacle I think there's too much money swirling around the game these days. Working-class fans are priced out and you can almost buy the trophies now. It's surely unsustainable and has changed the priorities that made the game great in the first place. Rest assured I'm not just saying that because I'm a United fan living in a house full of City fans. Really, I'm not. No, sirree.

Incidentally, on the very first day we went into the studio to work on 'World In Motion', Michael Powell died.

Chapter Eighteen

Burn bright, live long

Meanwhile, back at the Haçienda, we were starting to experience serious problems with the gangs that were springing up like enterprising small businesses across the city. This meant that we had to get tougher and tougher bouncers on the door to do what was a pretty thankless job. On one occasion in 1991, a bouncer turned away a gang member who walked off jabbing his finger and shouting, 'Right, I'm coming back and I'm coming back to shoot you, you bastard.' 'Yeah, OK, son, hurry up then,' said the bouncer, but the guy did come back — carrying a machine gun. The bouncer ran through the club with the guy hot on his heels, reached the basement and found himself tugging at an exit door which turned out to be locked. He turned round to face the gunman, who pulled the trigger, only for, to his miraculous good fortune, the gun to jam.

This was in January 1991, at which point we thought that enough was enough and shut the club down for what turned out to be five months. We were sick of it; someone was going to get seriously hurt or even killed. These guys with guns weren't joking: they meant business and they were in our club. We were having emergency meetings about all sorts of dodgy characters, while, alarmingly, it turned out the gangs were also having emergency meetings – in the club.

Although we closed voluntarily, we weren't the only ones with padlocks on the doors as the whole of Manchester, basically, closed down for a while. Anderton had shut all the after-hours party venues, and some MP trying to make a name for himself had managed to push through a bill banning any outdoor gathering of more than twenty people with the sound of a repetitive beat. Eventually, the scene shifted a few miles out of the city, to places like Blackburn, Blackpool and Quadrant Park in Bootle. I began going to Quadrant Park, which turned out to be even heavier than the Haçienda had become. It was a big club, holding about three or four thousand people, and a lot of friends from Manchester also gravitated there. It could get pretty tasty. I remember being in the toilet having a pee once when two or three big blokes came in, kicked in the door of one of the cubicles, dragged this guy out and smashed his head against the urinal where I was standing. A syringe fell out of his pocket into it. They were cops who'd been tipped off about the guy using in the toilets.

On another occasion, a load of us from the Haçienda went to a party in a block of flats in Moston. We all squeezed into the lift and stood there waiting, but the lift wouldn't move. There were about nine of us squashed in there, for a good thirty minutes, and people were starting to feel a bit panicky, worrying we were going to be stuck there all night, until the following exchange took place.

'Did you press the button?'

'No, I didn't press it.'

'I thought you'd pressed it . . .'

'I didn't press it.'

'Well I saw someone press it. It was her.'

'Don't look at me, I didn't press anything.'

'Well who pressed it then?'

Of course, it turned out no one had pressed the button; we'd all assumed somebody else had. Finally, I pushed the button, up we went and, oh, what a lovely party it turned out to be. There were no windows, for a start — we were fourteen floors up and someone had taken all the windows out, in the middle of winter, and an icy gale was whistling through the place with freezing bullets of rain. It was a right mess. I think in the end we spent more time in the lift than at the party, but strange as it sounds we did have a laugh at the time.

The Haçienda reopened in May 1991. Not long afterwards, we were just about to board a flight to New York to begin a tour when we were handed a *Manchester Evening News* by the stewardess which bore a front-page headline that read something like 'Six Hacienda Doormen Stabbed in Frenzied Knife Attack'. Our hearts sank. Here we go again.

As well as the aggravation, we as a band felt we were bankrolling the whole escapade. We'd been working hard earning money, and it was being ploughed into both the club and the label. As individuals, we were still on a token wage. We were never shown accounts (I suppose, equally, you could say we never asked to see any), nor was I ever clear in my mind what the band was earning from record sales. When we went on tour, we'd see a big wedge of money for that but, otherwise, we were on a basic hundred pounds a week with absolutely no idea how many albums we'd sold. We had a platinum-selling album in America in the compilation collection *Substance* — and I only know that because I was presented with a platinum disc by the American label — but the way we'd set things up all the income gleaned from record sales was going into the Haçienda rather than coming to us.

But, you know what? We weren't all that bothered, because life was fun and we were young. We didn't really want much anyway: if I had a car to get around in and somewhere to live, I was happy. The band was making good music, my life was great and I'd pretty much got everything I wanted, which in terms of buying things wasn't much. We trusted Rob implicitly — we had utter faith that, money-wise, he'd do the right thing. He did do the right thing too in his own way; he'd just got it wrong when it came to the Haçienda and, once he'd been sucked into the gravitational pull of the black hole on Whitworth Street, he couldn't get out of it again.

As well as its now-legendary money troubles, the violence focused on the Haçienda refused to go away and so did the gangs who gravitated towards the club. We learned that one of the gangs was even setting up its base in the Gay Traitor bar downstairs (it featured a large portrait of Anthony Blunt, who, like Tony, had been to Cambridge University). The whole thing was becoming heavier and heavier: we'd had the machine-gun incident, the knife attack and, on another occasion, a bouncer had been shot in the leg. Sarah had been physically threatened too: she went to pick something up from the Haçienda in my car one day and emerged to find someone sitting on the bonnet, a particularly nasty man known as 'White Tony', a well-known gangster, long dead now. I think there was some kind of connection between him and the Moors Murders — he was a cousin of one of the victims — but he was a really vicious scumbag. Sarah asked him to get off the car.

'Talk to me like that again and I'll take your fucking eye out,' he said.

She went back into the club and told one of the bouncers, who eventually managed to persuade White Tony to remove his backside from the bonnet and warned Sarah to drive straight home. If anyone followed her, he said, she was to drive to a police station. White Tony was a dangerous, volatile, violent man who'd made plenty of enemies.

In many ways, it wasn't a pleasant time. As well as the Haçienda issues, I also had to deal with the death of my mother. After Jimmy died, my grandmother had moved into the bungalow in Swinton that my mother had shared with him. They could help each other, but it was extremely difficult for both of them: my mother could see and direct my grandmother, who was still completely blind, to reach things she couldn't. Being away so often with the band, I couldn't be around to help as much as I'd have liked, but I'd drive over whenever I could. A few years after Jimmy died, though, my mother met someone new: a very nice man called Eric. He collected miniature cars and had a camper van of which he was very proud, and he was very good to both my mother and grandmother, but in the late summer of 1991 my mother passed away.

Quite a strange thing happened on the night she died: I had a dream in which I saw her slump forward in her wheelchair and, in it, I knew she was dead. It was very weird — one of those particularly vivid dreams that stays with you for the rest of the day. I was walking through our local town with Sarah and the kids the following day when a car nearly ran us all over, the driver sticking two fingers up at us as he passed. I told Sarah to take the kids and walk on, went to find this guy and we ended up having a brawl in a street full of shoppers on a busy Saturday afternoon that ended up in the local papers. It's not something I'm proud of, but he'd nearly killed my wife and kids, and I'm nobody's fool.

It was a weird day all round. I'd woken up after a lucid dream about my mum dying, which affected my mood for the whole day, got up, gone out for breakfast and ended up rolling around in the street with this complete stranger. Then, when I got home, I received a call to tell me my mum had died in exactly the way I'd seen in my dream.

Back at the Haçienda, as you can imagine, our bouncers needed to be pretty handy. Some of them were part of a crime family overseen by the Noonan Brothers — and these were supposed to be the good guys. That's how heavy the situation had become. We were musicians — making records and playing gigs was our business — yet we were having to deal with gangs, guns and crime families with whom even the police weren't keen to become involved. We tried so hard to do the right thing, but the whole scene had turned sour and I'd had enough; enough of having to attend crisis meetings, enough of the pressure, enough of the endless tours. I just wanted to make music.

Apparently, Rob wanted us to keep touring in order to raise capital for the Haçienda, but I knew we would be effectively burning money that way, as it was clear to anyone that the ship was going down. Only ego was keeping the whole thing even vaguely afloat. When we'd returned from the gruelling 1993 tour — our first for four years — a meeting was arranged at Manchester Town Hall to inform us that an opportunity had come up to buy the building. Would you believe it, by sheer chance it would cost almost exactly the amount we had just earned across the Atlantic. It was explained carefully to us that the owners would sell the building to someone else if we didn't buy it there and then and we'd lose everything. The band was effectively over a barrel. To nobody's great surprise, it later transpired they needed more money than they had originally asked for to complete the purchase, so, given the apparent urgency of the situation, a bridging loan was taken out to make up the shortfall, with a whopping interest rate attached to it. Only once the loan had been secured did it become clear that a mortgage to buy the building was out of the question because of the state of Factory's accounts.

The organization was already leaking money like an elephant with cystitis, and now we'd been left with a loan that cost double what the building's already extortionate rent had been. Another key business decision had completely backfired.

We looked at the situation as it stood in 1993: machine guns, knives, bouncers getting stabbed, dealing with the police (who hated us), gangs, violence – and after all that we were still making a loss, even with the acid-house explosion. It was clear the Haçienda was never going to work. We'd given it a good go, we thought, but it was just doomed to fail. Rob, however, was a gambler. I'm not – I did the lottery about three times when it first started and didn't win anything, so that was it for me – but knowing Rob as I did, I knew it was his nature to risk carrying on, with the relentless optimism that luck would change and things would turn around. I couldn't rely on luck and optimism, however. For a number of reasons, things had to change.

At the Reading Festival on 29 August 1993 we finished what had been a barnstorming set with 'Blue Monday'. As the familiar opening drumbeats thumped out of the PA to a rapturous roar of recognition from the huge crowd, we were to all appearances a band at the peak of its powers with the world at our feet. Our new album, *Republic*, had been released a few weeks earlier and gone to number one in the charts, just as its predecessor, *Technique*, had done, while 'Regret' had reached number four in the singles charts. Yet, when the final notes of 'Blue Monday' echoed around the Berkshire sky that night and we walked off stage with the cheering of the crowd ringing in our ears, it would be another five years, almost to the day, before we played together again. As ever with New Order, we didn't really do things the conventional way.

The Reading Festival had come at the end of a particularly gruelling tour schedule that was close to burning me out. Every summer, it seemed, we'd criss-cross America, and every summer things were getting bigger. The early days, when we'd play small club venues to five hundred people, sleep at someone's house and move on to the next gig, seemed like a different world. In those days, everything had been both manageable and enjoyable. I had no desire to be famous; I wasn't even that bothered about chart success. It was great if it happened, but I hadn't set out actively to pursue it. For me, being in a band was mostly about the creativity and the lifestyle: I was lucky enough to do something I loved – creating music – for a living. As long as that continued, it was all right by me. World domination was not on my personal agenda, because I've seen people have a taste of success, become addicted to it and end up just wanting more and more. Keep chasing that particular dragon and one day you'll find yourself with a tough comedown. In my experience, if you take it easy, appreciate what you're doing and what it provides, it can last a long time. Burn bright or live long, that's the simple choice.

I cared very much about the music, though. I found writing it utterly fascinating, and the creative process is something that's always held me in its thrall. I never wanted to give that up, but I was becoming very unhappy.

As you might remember, before becoming a musician I'd been prevented from going to art college by circumstances beyond my control, something that had frustrated my attempts to make a living from art, which, at the time, was the only escape I could see from the beaten-down frustration of working-class life in northern England. Then the world of music suddenly opened up in front of me, transforming my life like nothing else ever could. I'd moved from finding myself parked in one of life's culs-de-sac, thwarted by society, to being paid for doing something I love. This was my *living*. I felt incredibly lucky, and still do.

The other aspect of being a musician that I enjoyed before we became a huge commercial success was the social interaction: meeting people at gigs and travelling to a range of different countries. Take America as just one example. Americans were really friendly, they spoke the same language and it was usually sunny and warm. The cities we played in were generally interesting and the music coming out of those cities was often tremendous. It wasn't just America either: I'd seen all sorts of countries and cities all around the world. It was a transient lifestyle, granted, but I made some good friends along the way.

As the years went by, the social side of things increased at the same rate as our popularity, so a New Order gig would become more and more like a party. We'd do the show and have people back to the dressing room afterwards. Thanks to our regular tours, we'd built up groups of friends in each city, and they'd come along expecting a party: they'd bring their friends, and their friends would bring their friends, and everyone would wind up backstage after the gig. By the time we reached the acid-house period, we had smoke machines, decks and strobes *in the dressing room*. Then we'd move on to a club, maybe two, and finish up by bringing the club back to the hotel, where we'd finish the party as the sun climbed into the sky. It was like this every night — every fucking night — and if, for whatever reason, it didn't turn out that way, even for just one night, you'd feel disappointed.

At that age, though, you think you're invincible and you don't think about the toll that level of hedonism is taking. I felt we needed a managed retreat from this itinerant lifestyle and to spend more time at home: for one thing, my son Dylan had been born the previous year and I wanted to be around a bit more — for him and for my other son, James, now ten. I'd felt the strong gravitational pull of home and, inevitably, this had created friction with the band and the management, who wanted to tour, especially Hooky. He didn't seem to mind being away from home for long periods, he seemed to relish it even, but the novelty of long tours had long ago started to wear thin for me. It wasn't that I wanted to stop playing live altogether, not at all; I just didn't want to prolong this endless litany of planes, hotels and venues we seemed to be locked into. Outside factors influenced this: Rob, I'm sure, was always trying to keep us out on the road because the organization as a whole needed money coming in. Without the regular income from the tours, it was harder to prop up the Haçienda.

While I could appreciate all this, I had to make sure my priorities were right. I knew that if we kept touring at the rate we were I was putting my health at risk and that I'd have only myself to blame. I had caned it as hard as I could, and no one but me is responsible for that, but I challenge anyone in that environment not to join in, to eschew the clubs, the limos, the drinks, the people you meet, and to go to bed early with a book instead. It's nigh on impossible; it was just too easy to be swept along by the whole travelling circus of New Order on tour. I'm not complaining either — I *loved* it, it was really good fun — but it was having the unfortunate side effect of making me ill.

The after-effects seemed to hit me more than anyone else too. At airports in the mornings, I'd be running off to be sick in the toilets while the others were all eating and drinking as if nothing was amiss. We'd have been partying just as hard as each other, but yours truly seemed to be the one copping most of the consequences. And they were starting to exact a price.

There were issues away from the road as well: Factory's notorious financial difficulties were particularly acute at this time. For the first time ever, they had another very successful group on the roster: the

Happy Mondays had really taken off and were selling a lot of records. The problem was that Factory had to finance the making of records by both us and the Mondays as well as keeping the Haçienda going. Things were fine when the records were out there and selling, but when both bands were in the studio at the same time it meant a lot of money was going out and there'd be a significant amount of time before the resultant record sales would come in.

In those days, studio time for us and the Mondays could be very expensive. On top of that outlay, the Hacienda was haemorrhaging money at a terrific rate. In the middle of all this we'd been trying to make *Republic*, working away in the studio, all the while wondering if the studio bills were being paid. It was embarrassing for us having to work with engineers, given the possibility their time wouldn't be paid for. At one point, Gillian came up with the suggestion that we should go on strike until Factory had sorted a few things out. It was an idea that gained traction among the band — but it would have been a very long strike.

There was friction developing within the band, too. We were by now writing more and more electronic music, things like 'The Perfect Kiss'. As I mentioned earlier, Steve had, I think, initially felt that his status as drummer was being challenged: the nature of dance music dictates that a lot of the beats are programmed rather than played. Hooky probably also felt that his status as a bass player was being challenged for similar reasons. As Karl Bartos had noticed with Kraftwerk, when you're writing electronic music, only one person can sit at the computer at a time, leaving everyone else sitting around waiting. This also gave the erroneous impression that one person was running the whole show. They weren't: it was just a one-person activity that happened to take up a lot of time.

Despite all this, the music was really working for us. Now that we were a successful band playing to larger audiences, though, a lot of things had to change. We'd have to go on stage at 9 p.m. instead of 11 p.m., as we used to, for example, and we had to play encores and full 90-minute sets where, in previous years, we might have done forty, if you were lucky. We were in constant demand for interviews, there were meetings about all sorts of things and we rarely had any time to ourselves. I may sound like I'm begrudging the success, but I'm not: if people are paying a lot of money to come and see you at a big venue, you want to make it worth their while; and the bigger you become, the more demands on your time there are. But I could see things becoming visibly more corporate. There were far more suits in the dressing room after shows than there used to be and I sensed that this juggernaut of success was going to be hard to slow down.

Chapter Nineteen

The tempest

Having a gun waved in my face proved an effective way of convincing me that things needed to change. On this particular night, after the Haçienda closed we'd ended up at a reggae party at a youth club in Moss Side. We arrived to find a large crowd of people jostling bad-temperedly at the door trying to get in, so not a good sign. Then I saw a friend of ours who had, let's say, a certain amount of local influence. The crowd cleared for him and he took us inside, where, as we stood just inside the door, we could see a guy with a beard and a bright orange jacket trying to get out the same time a couple of hundred people were trying to get in. He was being a pain in the arse, quite frankly, pushing people out of the way, and in the end someone socked him in the face.

We thought no more about it, walked past a kitchen hatch and saw they were serving delicious-looking West Indian food. I bought a portion of chicken and dumplings and was standing up eating it out of a white polystyrene tray when I had what appeared to be a strange hallucination in my peripheral vision: it looked like all the people had turned into bulrushes, and were blowing against the walls. When I looked up, I realized this was no hallucination: everyone in the place was pressed hard against the walls, leaving the only people in the middle of the floor Mr Dickhead White Guy here with his tray of chicken, and a man in a balaclava and a bright orange jacket who happened to be brandishing a very large revolver. It was the guy who'd been punched. As disguises go, it was pretty ineffective, but it was the enormous gun in his hand, the one that everyone but me had clocked immediately, that was of more immediate concern. He was pacing around, looking for the person who'd punched him earlier and, as he passed, he waved the gun inches away from my face. I don't think he looked at me, he was only interested in finding his assailant, but when he disappeared into another room I turned to Sarah and said, 'I think we'd best go home now.' When we got there, we found that Sarah's father had been taken ill earlier in the evening and rushed to hospital, so we went straight there and remained with him for the rest of the night.

All in all, that night totally freaked me out. I'd had enough.

On top of this, I was asking myself some important questions. Did I want this pressure? Was this lifestyle making *me* happier, or just feeding my ego? Was giving myself a big pat on the back for commercial success healthy? I took time to weigh up the important things and realized that, for me, happiness is about finding the right balance between public and private life, work and home, music and family. There were money worries at Factory even though they had two of the most successful bands of the era on the books. New Order was in a tricky place creatively, yet people loved that music: it was working. Whichever way you turned, there seemed to be contradictions, and I was struggling with them.

Hooky was different. He loved the success and the trappings that went with it. He enjoyed the adulation, thrived on it. I enjoy it, of course, but only up to a point: it's not the core of my existence. Also, I kept thinking back to how part of the message of punk was essentially 'Fuck stardom': keep your feet on the ground and don't take yourself too seriously. Yet here we were, in danger of rising above our station and watching things drift away from our origins.

I decided I didn't want to go out on the road as much any more. This was a problem for Hooky: I think it got in the way of his ambitions, and he resented me for it. For my part, I still felt I was getting bad vibes for pushing the band in the direction of electronic music, even though we were all reaping the benefits.

This had all come to a head just before *Republic* was released. Hooky, in particular, felt I had been taking over the creative side by writing the electronic songs on *Technique*. I said that they should all write stuff and I'd just concentrate on the vocals and we'd see if we could get the old equilibrium back that way. We were back at Real World, where Peter Gabriel had what was known as 'The Pagoda' to serve as a writing room. I'd sit in there writing lyrics while the band fed me the material they were working on. I'd be happier with some parts of the songs than others. Stephen Hague, the producer, would come in to see what progress I was making and I'd say something like, 'Well, the chorus is great but I don't think the verse works.' I'd ask him to get the others to work on the verse while I worked on another song. Then, a week or so later, he'd ask me about the first song, and I'd say, 'Well, they haven't got back to me with the reworked verse yet.' We were left with this bizarre political situation where everything was going through Stephen, which meant the whole process ground almost to a halt. Add to that the fact that I didn't think some of the material was quite strong enough, and it made the writing and recording of that album very difficult indeed. The vibe between the whole band had deteriorated and I wasn't enjoying it any more. I needed a break. We all did.

So, in 1993, we stopped working together as New Order for a while. While we never split up, it would be the best part of five years after that Reading show before we'd all stand on the same stage again.

The Haçienda situation limped on until 1994, and a meeting at which Steve, Gillian and I said we were heartily sick of it. Enough was enough and the three of us informed everyone else that we weren't putting any more of our money into the club, because it was over. We needed to just let it go down. Rob and Hooky said they thought we could still turn it around and, even if we weren't going to invest any more, they were going to keep it going. I pointed out that we were all in the same band and we were in the majority. Everything we did was decided democratically and we'd decided that we didn't want to keep the whole disastrous escapade going any longer. We said that if they insisted on carrying on, it was their decision, but that it was obvious to anyone that they'd be wasting their time and money. But I still kept my shares in the Haçienda albeit as a sleeping partner. After all the money I'd invested I thought it was the right thing to do.

Despite this, the two of them kept at it for another two or three fruitless years, and the club sank further and further into dire financial straits. I don't know how they were raising the money, but the pair of them were getting into a right state. As the rest of us had come to realize, the Haçienda was a problem that couldn't be fixed and the only thing to do was shut it down, but they stubbornly persevered — even though they had to close the club temporarily again in 1997 due to yet more drug-related incidents.

Within weeks of reopening, the death knell finally sounded for the Haçienda. In June, some lad — I think he was from Liverpool — was chatting up a girl in the club who turned out to be the girlfriend of a gang member. This didn't go down too well. As he left and walked across Whitworth Street, another member of the gang came up behind him and whacked him over the back of the head with a cosh. The guy went down in the road like a sack of spuds, whereupon the gang member got into his car and drove over him.

It just so happened that a minibus full of magistrates, who'd come to observe how things were going now the club had reopened, had just pulled up at that moment, and the whole thing played out right in front of them. I've heard that some of them were even splattered with blood.

Unsurprisingly, witnessing this horrific event didn't make them particularly well disposed towards the Haçienda, and that was it: they closed it down for good.

That's not the end of the Haçienda story, though. When it went into liquidation, there was a meeting I wasn't invited to with the accountants. Rob and Hooky were there and it was decided that any money left over from the sale of the building and the interiors would go first to them to reimburse them for the extra money they'd invested after we'd turned off our financial spigots. Once that was done there was no money left to pay the rest of us back the hundreds of thousands of pounds we'd invested over the years. They got money back for the disastrous period they'd overseen at their own risk, but we didn't receive anything at all. Steve, Gillian, the Factory directors and I, we got sweet fuck-all. I've heard it mistakenly said that we wrote off our financial interest when we refused to put any more funds in. In fact I was sure to keep all my shares in the Haçienda and I effectively became a sleeping partner. After all the money I had invested this seemed like the best course of action and the right thing to do. I just refused to keep pouring money into what was clearly a yawning chasm of financial disaster.

Hooky complained to me that Rob had received more money

than he had out of the settlement and that Rob had been able to put a lot more money into the Haçienda. He said he was suspicious about where Rob had found this money and felt strongly that we should sack him. Hooky called a band meeting at which he declared that Rob had to go, but after everything that had happened, all the time we'd spent together and the fact that, for all his faults, I think and hope Rob meant well, we decided he was one of us, and we didn't abandon our own. Hooky was the only one in favour. If we fired Rob, we thought, what would he do after all this time working with us? What else *could* he do? The rest of us felt that, whatever had happened, we trusted Rob, so he remained part of the team and we stuck together.

Recently, I read through some of the documentation, and I think Rob *had* put more money in and therefore potentially had the right to receive more money than Hooky. But, as is customary when it comes to matters New Order, it's very complicated. Rob was paid as our manager but he was also, I believe, paid as a director of Factory. I think Rob must have ploughed both his New Order and any Factory money he might have got into the Haçienda. It seems Rob did put more in (and could have made more money had the Haçienda done well), but we received nothing and Factory itself went down in 1992 owing us royalties.

I think when the three of us voiced our considered opinion that the Haçienda should close and we intended to put no more money in, that got interpreted as us not wanting it any more. But I still owned shares. And Steve, Gillian and I had put a great deal of money into the Haçienda over the years. Hooky even claims that I stopped going to meetings. I did stop going to the ones about whether to sell cheeseburgers as well as normal burgers, but I never stopped going to the important meetings — the ones where important strategic decisions, security and police issues were discussed.

A year after the Haçienda had closed, early in the summer of 1998, we all got together after receiving an offer from Vince Power of the Mean Fiddler organization to play the Phoenix Festival in Stratford-upon-Avon. By that time, we'd suppressed the bad things that had happened and were focusing on the good things. Vince's offer felt like the opportunity for a fresh start, and we'd be going back to what we did best: creating music. The band hadn't split up; if we had, we'd have said so. We'd just stopped working together for a while and concentrated on other projects.

Vince had always been good to us, and we got on very well with him, so we decided to take him up on his offer. We'd had a meeting in Rob's office, during which we'd talked about what had gone wrong and how we'd reached that point. There was a sense of the air being cleared and a genuine attitude of goodwill. I came out of that meeting feeling very positive, and the band started working together again. I had one commitment outside of New Order that I had to fulfil – the release and promotion of the Electronic album *Twisted Tenderness* – but after that I was free to concentrate on New Order again. In the event, the Phoenix Festival didn't happen. Vince proposed moving us on to the Reading Festival bill later in the summer, and we headlined that instead. As our previous gig had also been at Reading, in 1993, this created a nice symmetry, and it was brilliant, we had a fantastic gig.

Things were looking good as 1998 became 1999, but then, in May of that year, Rob died suddenly from a heart attack.

Rob's health had always been a complicated set of scenarios, particularly after a breakdown he'd had back in 1983. We'd aroused the interest of the Inland Revenue back then and when Rough Trade's American arm went bust, they owed us a great deal of Joy Division royalties – something in the region of £600,000 according to Rob. On advice we believed that we only had to pay tax on moneys received and, as we'd not received the money from Rough Trade America by the time they went to the wall, we didn't owe any tax on that figure. The Inland Revenue thought otherwise, however, and we were called in for a series of increasingly daunting meetings.

The tax man knew something we didn't: how much money was coming into the organization. However much it was, it was significantly more than was reflected by the wages we were receiving. No one in the organization was paid much – I think we were all on about a hundred quid a week at that stage – which was OK for Tony, because he had a job working for Granada. Alan Erasmus, to the outside world, the quiet director of Factory (although he actually came up with a lot of ideas), said to me recently that whenever he asked for a pay rise or dividend from Tony, he would quote Karl Marx: 'From each according to his ability, to each according to his need, darling.' (I'm not sure the 'darling' was in Marx's version.)

At the meetings, on the Revenue's side was a good cop/ bad cop act comprising a dour Scotsman called Mr Munro (bad cop) and his sidekick, who looked a little like Jeremy Beadle (good cop). I think they believed we'd been stashing thousands of pounds away in Swiss bank accounts or something, but we hadn't – we weren't clever enough, for a start. We pointed out that we hadn't received any money from Rough Trade because they'd folded, so surely didn't owe any tax. Mr Munro took great delight in informing us this wasn't the case and we were required to pay tax on moneys *earned*, not just moneys received. So, even though we were the victims of Rough Trade's collapse, the Inland Revenue was convinced we still had to pay tax on money we'd never received. It was a very serious situation indeed, and there was a genuine danger of everything collapsing around our ears. We even had to get our chequebook stubs together and list all our furniture and possessions in preparation for the possibility of bailiffs arriving at our doors. In fact, I think they did call at

Rob's once: he really thought he was going to lose everything.

Eventually, we hired a top tax lawyer called Paddy Grafton-Green who came into a meeting with us and informed Mr Munro that there was no tax owing because the disputed figure could be written off as promotional costs pertaining to the Haçienda, closed his brief-case, stood up and led us all out of the room in triumph. We were off the hook, thank goodness, but the whole process really took its toll on Rob. I noticed in the meetings that, when he held a cup of tea, his hands would be shaking quite badly. He was pretty tough about most things and didn't show much interest in money, but these shakes got worse with each meeting, and he began doing odd things. One day he came into rehearsals with Terry, sat us all down and produced a bunch of newspaper clippings.

He turned to Terry and said, 'Terry, what is my brain?'

'A super-computer, Rob,' said Terry.

'That's right, Terry, my brain is a super-computer,' he said. 'I've been analysing the situation and have researched all these newspaper clippings.'

They were all things like, 'MAN ELECTROCUTED BY LAWNMOWER'; all sorts of mad stories which he apparently thought had some relevance towards the tax situation. It was crazy.

Eventually Rob had a breakdown and ended up in hospital for quite some time. It was very upsetting to see him like that. At the time of the tax investigation, the Haçienda was already losing money, which gave Rob a double dose of stress, as cash he'd been counting on hadn't come in while, at the same time, the tax man was hammering on the door and threatening to cast us and our families out on the street.

He'd been under enormous levels of stress and become very ill. As had happened with Ian after his epilepsy diagnosis, Rob was put on some pretty heavy-duty psychoactive drugs and, to me, he was never quite the same again. He lost a certain amount of his endearing 'Jack the lad' quality and, while he did make a recovery, I don't believe it was a complete one. A few years later he had problems with an overactive thyroid gland (the doctors later cut it in half, leaving him with an underactive one) and perhaps, in hindsight, this had made some kind of contribution towards his breakdown. An overactive thyroid produces too much adrenalin, so he may well have been having panic attacks. I remember saying to him just before one gig in America, 'I'm a bit nervous tonight, Rob, you should feel my heart.' He said, 'Never mind feeling your heart, look at mine.' He opened his jacket and I could actually see it beating beneath his shirt.

On top of that, he never really looked after himself. He drank a lot of beer and didn't eat healthily, never took exercise and spent quite a lot of time in the pub.

I didn't know at the time that he had a heart issue, and wonder whether, again, that could have been related to his thyroid problem. Either way, we were all deeply, deeply shocked when he died. He was a father figure to us all — we were really young when he became our manager and benefited from his being a little older than us. He always stopped us from being complete twats.

It had been his decision to go with Factory, where Tony and he were like two wings on the same bird. I think, politically, they thought the same way, in very socialist terms, and they had quite a similar sense of humour. Even though Tony went to Cambridge, he was a Salford lad at heart; Rob came from Wythenshawe and, despite being outwardly very different characters, they shared the same sensibilities.

Rob always gave us moral guidance. Not that we were immoral people, of course, but he supplied us with a crucial roadmap of principles. He also taught us about independence, staying in Manchester and doing things that were good for Manchester. He gave us directional and musical encouragement, and I'll always be grateful to him for all this.

One thing he didn't do was rein in the chaos. He didn't see money as important and therefore didn't see losing money as important. When the likes of Mr Munro are looking levelly at you across a table and raising a quizzical eyebrow, however, it obviously becomes *very* important. There comes a point when you have to leave behind the endearingly naïve, shambolically amateurish approach, because success precludes being as cheerfully anarchistic as we once were. Tony loved the anarchy, but he had his job at Granada to keep him anchored. Rob's whole world was guided by his instinctive sense of principled anarchy, and, as we grew more successful, perhaps it was not recalibrated as much as it should have been.

Rob had a gift for injecting levity into a difficult situation at just the right moment and was a great laugh. He instilled in us the confidence that we didn't have to rely on anyone else because we were *good enough*. The business side could have been taken care of better, but we'd never have become remotely the force we became without Rob's guiding hand.

He was a big City fan and when he died he was due to be buried at the Southern Cemetery in Manchester. His widow, Lesley, was told by the cemetery manager that he had a great plot for Rob, right next to legendary Manchester United Manager Sir Matt Busby. That didn't go down too well, so another one had to be quickly found — although if Rob had had his way I imagine Sir Matt would have had to move.

My last memory of Rob is speaking to him at rehearsals shortly before his death. New Order were working together again and he was really up about that, but he said that he had to go to a funeral a couple of days later. He was dreading it, he said, as he always cried at funerals. That was the last thing he ever said to me. Rob's death was tragic, unexpected and I still miss him to this day. We all cried at his funeral.

Once we'd started to recover from this terrible blow things began to go from strength to strength. We'd started writing again and continued the tradition of keeping things in the family when Rob's assistants, Rebecca Boulton and Andy Robinson, took over as co-managers of the band. Rob's were big shoes to fill so Andy and Rebecca filled one each. This ensured a seamless progression and both continue to do an amazing job, for the band and for each of us as individuals.

Even my relationship with Hooky appeared to be back on a friendly footing, but it didn't last. One day he turned round to me and announced, almost as an aside, 'Oh, by the way, I've bought the Haçienda name from the receivers.'

'Oh, really?' I said. 'How much for?'

'I'm not telling you.'

What he would tell me was that, having bought the name, he'd cut a deal with the construction company who were going to build apartments on the site and he'd sold them the right to use the Haçienda name for the apartment block.

I was stunned. We'd just got back together, and were trying to keep everything positive, and then Hooky had done this extraordinary thing. He'd not discussed it with any of us or suggested we all buy the name together as a band, he'd just gone off and done it himself.

As I saw it, there were two ways forward: either let what he'd done ruin everything again, just when things were on the up, or try to ignore it and carry on. For the greater good, I chose the latter option, but it didn't sit well with me. I recall Rob coming to see us at Steve's studio around the time the club went down. Alan Erasmus had noticed that the opportunity had arisen to buy the name of the

Haçienda. Rob asked us whether he should buy it on behalf of everyone, and Steve, Gillian and I said yes, with Steve adding that we should always own the name if possible. Rob never mentioned it again, I presumed it was all in hand and we went back to making music. To be honest, I really didn't want to think about the bloody Haçienda again.

Anyway, I'm conscious that I've made a great deal of the club's extraordinary story sound negative, but please don't think it was all doom and gloom. Like many people, I have a host of great memories of the Haçienda — for one thing, it's where I met Sarah, my wife — and there were plenty of positives, which have left me with lots of good memories. I think it was also part of Rob and Tony's noble plan to make Manchester a better place; to create a vibrant city by having a vibrant music scene. They wanted to improve the scene for DJs, dancers, musicians, promoters — the whole range of people involved — and the knock-on effect would be the improvement of the city for everyone. It was quite an achievement, even if a series of poor decisions ensured the club was never destined to succeed financially. It was a wonderful dream, and one that came true to a great extent, but one in which the heart too often overruled the head.

Chapter Twenty

'It's a disturbing story, there's no way round it'

If the combined story of Joy Division, New Order, Factory and the Hacienda has often seemed stranger than fiction, then it's probably no surprise there have been two major feature films made about it.

The first was *24 Hour Party People*, directed by Michael Winterbottom and released in the spring of 2002. It was an amusing look at what went on behind the scenes at Factory and the Haçienda, focusing on Tony as the central character. Steve Coogan played Tony and did so very, very well indeed. I think they were friends before the film, which must have helped his performance. I already knew Steve could do a very good impression of Tony and thought he captured him in brilliant caricature on screen. In real life, Tony was almost a caricature of himself: flamboyant, charismatic and (often unintentionally) funny, and that really comes across in Steve's portrayal of him. In some ways, Tony must have been fairly easy to play, yet at the same time he was such a big personality it would have been a major challenge for any actor to pitch him right: Steve had it pretty much spot on and was the perfect choice for the role.

John Simm played me, and people often ask me if I thought he'd captured me accurately. I can't really answer that, because I can't see myself from the outside. The only time I see myself is in the mirror, and I don't tend to say much then. At some point after the filming, I bumped into Steve and John at the Press Club in Manchester and, as I was talking to Steve, I became aware that John was watching me very intently. Even though the film had already been shot, I think he was still studying me to see if he'd got me right. I managed to turn the tables on him in a way, when I pulled him on stage with me to sing 'Digital' at a gig we did in Finsbury Park that summer. He was very reluctant at first but was soon joining me at the microphone, eyes closed and belting out, 'Day in, day out' as if his life depended on it.

I liked Steve and John, I thought they were great guys and am a big fan of their work. I'm really pleased John played me and equally pleased that Steve played Tony: such great casting helped the film-makers really capture the essence of the insanity that was Factory. With all the moaning I've done in these pages – and I know I've done quite a bit, but hey, at least *some* of it is justifiable! – about the stress, the pain and the financial crises, it's easy to overlook how much fun we had. If *24 Hour Party People* hadn't captured both that and the prevailing anarchy of the times, it wouldn't have been half as good a film. The Sex Pistols sang about anarchy in the UK but, for better or worse, we lived it. People who've seen *24 Hour Party People* often ask me if it was really like that and I always answer no. They look a little disappointed until I add that, in reality, it was much more extreme.

In retrospect, if we'd got our shit together in a more conventional way, we might have become more successful. But maybe if we'd gone about things in a more traditional manner we wouldn't be going strong and enjoying the kind of success we still are today. And I'm sure we wouldn't have had half as much fun. And, for us, the scales were always loaded heavily towards the fun end of the spectrum.

The film also gave us a unique and wonderful opportunity to relive a little bit of that fun, because they rebuilt the Haçienda for it. It was a very Factory and New Order situation: the Haçienda building itself was scheduled for demolition just before they began shooting, so the producers had to construct a brand new one entirely from scratch. It was deliciously ironic, because Tony's slogan with regard to the club had always been, 'The Haçienda must be built.' In everything he said or wrote about it, that's the phrase he'd always use, borrowed from the radical organization of avant-garde social revolutionaries the Situationist International. Five years after the doors had closed for the last time, the motto came to pass: the Haçienda had to be built. Just as the real Haçienda was being pulled down, another one was going up inside a warehouse at Ancoats.

When filming had finished, they threw a party there for the cast, crew and all the old Haçienda heads: the bands, the DJs, everyone. I walked in and was stunned: it was exactly the same as the interior of the Haçienda, right down to the last detail. It was breathtaking, like stepping back in time. That night was a great one on many levels, but particularly because we'd never marked the passing of the Haçienda when it closed. The end, when it finally came, had been sudden and, with the bad feeling, we hadn't felt like celebrating its legacy at the time. But this was different: it was much later, a feature film was celebrating that legacy and the party turned out to be a fitting celebration of all that had gone before. I'm really glad the film gave us that: it was important to us. That night was a little like walking through a dream. No amount of receivers or bailiffs can ever repossess the memories of what were very special times. To me, no matter how many Haçienda theme nights might still go on today, that party was the final chapter, the night the sun finally set behind the Haçienda, and it should be left to rest in peace.

The story hasn't all been fun, of course, and Anton Corbijn's 2007 film *Control* reflected that. A very different entity altogether from *24 Hour Party People*, *Control* took on a part of the tale that lay firmly on the other side of the coin.

Control was specifically a Joy Division film, with Ian as the central character, based on a book written by his widow, Debbie, called *Touching from a Distance*. I've read Debbie's book and, while it is the story of what happened, inevitably it's a view of events seen from her perspective, which was, understandably, not an entirely objective one. Debbie saw one side of Ian, we saw another, and none of us saw the full story. Ian was never a completely open book — none of us are; we all have a bit of a private corner in our souls to which we like to retreat, and rightly so. Despite this potential pitfall, however, I thought the film generally captured the Ian we knew very effectively.

Again, I'm asked if *Control* portrays the story and the times with any degree of accuracy, and I reply that it does — except we lived it in colour, of course (also, while they were shooting *Control*, there was an incredible heatwave; it was unbelievably hot, which was certainly nothing like it was in 1977). The portrayal of Ian by Sam Riley at the heart of the film is very accurate indeed, I was very pleased with how James Anthony Pearson portrayed me and I thought the entire cast did a really good job. Anton Corbijn had taken a lot of the most famous Joy Division and early New Order photographs — including the one on the cover of this book — and we'd known him from the very early days. There were other great photographers around, too, notably Kevin Cummins, but Anton had moved to England from his native Netherlands for love — not for a girl, but for the music of Joy Division. The music had captivated him in a way that compelled him to up sticks and emigrate. Anton was a fan, he'd been around while much of the story had played out, and he's a brilliant photographer, so it was entirely fitting that he should make the film. It was beautifully shot, as you would expect from Anton. The actors even learned to play Joy Division songs and sounded better in the film than we did on the albums! The footage in the film is much more like the sound I'd wanted on record, but hey, that's digital technology for you.

For obvious reasons, Ian's suicide overshadowed some of the humour and light-heartedness that underpinned day-to-day life in Joy Division, and obviously the music was pretty heavy and dark too. But, as I've said before, we were the products of our upbringings and of Manchester itself. I believe very strongly that you're shaped to some extent by your environment and, visually, ours was a brutal and barren place to grow up, something that was reflected inevitably in the music of Joy Division. Way back then, we were also reacting against what we were hearing on the radio, music to which we just couldn't relate. We didn't like it, our friends at school didn't like it, yet it was everywhere: every time you switched on the radio it would be schmaltzy ballads and acts like Chicory Tip, The Sweet, Tina Charles and Showaddywaddy, the musical equivalent of junk food being force-fed to a sleepwalking nation, and we thought we'd better do something about it. *Control* captures the difficulty of our battle to achieve a positive outcome from the hand life had dealt us. It captures the atmosphere of Macclesfield, too: it was shot in the town and even used Ian and Debbie's real home, the very place where Ian killed himself.

It's a disturbing story, there's no way around that. It doesn't have a happy ending and there's no way around that either. I've given Ian's death a lot of thought over the years and I sincerely believe that any other outcome was out of the question. We all tried talking him out of it, we did everything we possibly could, but he was a very self-willed person, had set himself on a particular road and he wasn't going to make a detour for anyone. Again, that's something that I think the film captures very well.

Both films are great portrayals and retellings of two very different aspects of a long, varied and fascinating story. We had very little direct input: I think we may have seen an early script for *24 Hour Party People*, but that was pretty much the extent of our involvement, partly because we were busy making *Get Ready* at the time. For *Control*, we all read through the script, fact-checking with Anton, pointing out things that didn't happen or things we wouldn't have said. We were involved with the soundtrack too but, beyond that, we just let them get on with it.

I wonder what Ian would have made of the films. He would, I think, have liked to know he'd been remembered. Most good people do, and Ian was a good person. I think he made a huge mistake when he killed himself. He was in the midst of an emotional hurricane whose eye passed over him that night, and had he lived to grow older he would have taken a different path in life. He'd have calmed down, settled down and I think would have stopped performing and become a writer.

As a band, as individuals and as an organization, New Order doesn't normally mark the anniversaries of Ian's death in a public fashion, because we don't want to commercialize it. I prefer to mourn away from the glare of publicity, believing that's the dignified and proper way. What happened to Ian has always been so public I prefer to set aside a quiet moment in private to remember him, particularly on the anniversary.

The same goes for Rob, Martin Hannett (who'd died of heart failure in 1991) and, of course, Tony too, who contracted renal cancer and died aged only fifty-seven in the summer of 2007, just a few weeks before *Control* was released. Tony was one of those people who would never have suited growing old, because he was so inherently young in spirit. He was immersed in youth culture and music and in injecting life into Manchester, attempting a literal rejuvenation of the city. Tony was so shot through with dynamism and ebullience that when he was taken ill it came as a great shock to us all: we had assumed that nothing could bring him down and that he'd go on for ever.

After the demise of Factory, Tony had tried to start Factory Too (I first wrote 'Factory had tried to start Tony Too' there, which is a Freudian reversal I think he would have enjoyed), but it didn't work. I think the landscape of the city had changed: that particular story had reached its end, it had been told, and perhaps it was time for a new one to begin.

When he was taken ill, Tony was living in a loft apartment not far from the Haçienda, just across the road from where TJ Davidson's used to be. He'd stopped working full-time at Granada and was spending most of his days walking his dog and chilling out when he learned he'd contracted this horrible disease. Ultimately, it would defeat him and he died in hospital on 10 August 2007. The last time I saw him was at my wedding to Sarah in July, and it's hard to think he had only a matter of weeks to live that day. The spirit of Tony is still tangible in Manchester, along with those of Rob, Ian and Martin. If pressed, I'd say the two biggest champions of Manchester were Tony and Rob. I think they succeeded in what they'd set out to do: the city has changed for the better. An indelible layer has been added to its history, a story that will never now be forgotten.

When the news broke that Tony had died they lowered the flag over Manchester Town Hall to half-mast. I think he would have liked that.

I'm eternally grateful to Tony because, if it wasn't for him, I wouldn't be living the life I am now. I think my life would have been pretty dull without Tony Wilson in it.

Chapter Twenty-one

'No matter what you say or who you are, it's what you do that matters'

St Catherine's Court in Bath, where we convened to start work on recording *Waiting for the Sirens' Call* in 2005, is a beautiful, peaceful place. The current house dates back to the early sixteenth century when, after the Dissolution of the Monasteries, exacerbated by Henry VIII's desire for a divorce, the house passed to John Malt, Henry's tailor, whose daughter Audrey was Henry's illegitimate daughter. The actress Jane Seymour bought it in the eighties but after her own divorce in the early nineties converted the house and rented it out as a recording studio.

If being in a band really is like a marriage, this centuries-old legacy of nuptial dispute made St Catherine's Court the ideal place for New Order. Although we didn't know it at the time, events with their origins there would ultimately lead to Hooky leaving the band for good.

I found it a magnificent place, if a little bit creepy. Steve's room was panelled in dark wood, with a painting in one corner of a forbidding-looking couple dressed in Elizabethan clothes, a painting that was hard to escape as it was visible in the many mirrors that hung around the room. Beside his four-poster bed was an antique baby's cot with a doll in it. Apparently, the skeleton of a baby had been discovered behind one of the fireplaces during a renovation in the sixties and, as a result, you weren't supposed to remove the doll from the cot. Now, call me a wimp if you want, but that room wasn't for me. I took the Joan Collins room instead.

Everything seemed fine when we arrived. We were trying different producers for this album, and things had been going pretty well. We did notice that Hooky was getting very boisterous, particularly when we were out for meals. Sometimes he was funny, but sometimes you could see people at other tables looking a little uncomfortable. With Hooky, there seemed to be an aura of resentment underpinning his behaviour and at St Catherine's Court there were indications of things beginning to rise to the surface. Looking back, there were strong indications of what lay in store that I didn't necessarily pick up on at the time.

After quite a few weeks at St Catherine's Court we moved back to Peter Gabriel's Real World studios in Wiltshire. Initially we worked in a different way than we did on our previous album, 2001's *Get Ready*, with the band jamming ideas and me concentrating on the vocals and lyrics. On *Get Ready* I'd spent a lot of time in the studio, working and reworking the guitar parts, while the vocals stayed much the same as I had written them at home, but on *Waiting for the Sirens' Call*, it was essentially the other way around. It wouldn't be my preferred way of working, as I don't regard myself purely as a vocalist: for me the music usually comes first. But I was happy to work in this situation so long as I also had a shot at writing some music at some point which, to be fair, I did: I'd begun writing late at night back at St Catherine's Court.

As ever, we weren't doing things the conventional way. It's certainly different being in New Order. It was different being in Joy Division too. Things happen — sometimes quite odd things. One of them happened at Real World during the making of *Waiting for the Sirens' Call*. We'd finished recording for the night and I'd gone to bed but, soon afterwards, I could hear a strange noise coming from outside: a kind of snapping sound. I went over to the window and there on a hilltop was this huge barn and house on fire. I went outside for a better look and found Hooky already there, swaying slightly. I suggested that we go over for a closer look.

It was a really bad fire and the emergency services were already there when we arrived. We could hear shouting coming from the house, so we parked the car in a field nearby and tried to get as close as we could. The next thing we knew a guy was running straight at us, screaming his head off and brandishing a massive piece of wood. Unexpected, to say the least. I turned around and saw Hooky legging it down the hill as fast as he could. I ran back to the car, jumped in and started the engine, just as this madman appeared near the entrance to the field. I skidded past him, just getting away in time and, in true action-film style, looked into my rear-view mirror to see him running after the car, shouting and waving this big bloody log about.

The next thing I knew there was a huge explosion and flames right behind me — possibly a gas bottle going up — and something hit the back of my car. To this day, I'll never know if it was the log, a piece of gas bottle or the guy's head.

Alas, this wasn't to be the only explosion during the making of *Waiting for the Sirens' Call*. Everyone would stay down at the studio during the week and we'd all go home at weekends, although, sometimes, I'd stay later on a Friday with Andy Robinson, who'd help me with some of the engineering. One week I came back on the Monday and it was immediately obvious there was a really weird atmosphere. I'd arrived last in mid-afternoon and walked in to find everyone tense and jittery. I asked what was going on and someone said, 'Hooky's had a few and he's going mad. He said Andy had told him you don't want anyone to play on any of your stuff'. This was complete nonsense: I hadn't said anything like it. I don't know what Andy had said to him or whether Hooky had misinterpreted something but, either way, it obviously needed sorting out. I found Andy, who told me he and Hooky had been tidying up the studio and he'd told Hooky I'd said one particular track didn't need any more bass than it already had. Hooky had decided I'd said 'I don't want anyone else to play on my stuff,' and gone off like a factory siren.

I found Hooky in his room, told him I'd heard what had happened and explained there was no way I'd said that to Andy and was sorry if he'd thought otherwise. He seemed to accept this, but was still absolutely furious. He seemed to have it in for Andy after that. Even though Andy apologized, it seemed his card was marked from that day on.

There was also an incident when Peter Saville came to visit us and out of nowhere Hooky launched into this tirade against the poor guy, calling him a parasite and all sorts of names. It was horrible, totally uncalled for and totally unjustified: Peter Saville is the nicest, most inoffensive guy you could wish to meet and to this day I've no idea where it came from. It was mystifying at the time but turned out in hindsight to be a genuine watershed moment.

After the recording was finished we moved on to the mixing stage, at Olympic Studios in Barnes, south-west London. We started working on the first mix with Jim Spencer, our engineer, and almost immediately Hooky became particularly belligerent about the bass drum on one of the tracks. He'd been out to the pub for the Bloody

Mary he always had at about four o'clock, and when he came back he started going on about it, insisting that it needed to come up in the mix. I told him it was fine, but he wouldn't have it. 'No, it needs to go up,' he said. 'Jim, what do you think?' This was Jim's first mix of the album, but he agreed that it was fine. So Hooky wheeled round to Steve. 'Steve,' he said, 'you're the drummer, it's your bass drum, what do you think?' 'The bass drum's fine,' Steve assured him. Hooky went quiet for a moment, fixed his eye on me and said, 'Typical. You know what they're like, just siding with you. They always just side with you.' I said, 'Hang on a minute, nobody's "siding" with anyone. Steve's the drummer and Jim's the engineer and they're both saying the bass drum is fine at the level it is. That's pretty convincing, isn't it?' He wouldn't let it go, though, and any time anyone asked about the mix he'd reply, 'The bass drum needs to go up.' This went on for most of the night, and to say it was irritating is an understatement.

I know this sort of incident happens with most bands, but it was the sheer irrational intransigence, this railing against everyone else in the room at the slightest opportunity, that was odd. This incident encapsulated the situation and atmosphere at the time. Reading between the beats – excuse the pun – I'm sure it was nothing to do with the bass-drum levels, it was more about Hooky wanting to be in charge. I felt the issue was control, who was the boss man. I'm certainly not like that and, as a band, we're a democracy, always have been, always will be. It's something that was instigated by Rob years ago in Joy Division: if we had a dispute, it was resolved by vote – no arguments, no tantrums – that was how it was. No one person is in charge and never will be.

One Monday after that we were due to start work, but there was no sign of Hooky. I asked where he was and someone said he'd checked himself into the Priory. I suppose the fact that we all drank a lot and had done for years meant we hadn't really spotted that

Hooky was struggling with it. Fair play to him for recognizing the problem and addressing it, but it came like a bolt from the blue to the rest of the band. He'd not talked to any of us about it, let alone mentioned that he was thinking of going into rehab. In retrospect, this may have explained some of his more recent extreme behaviour.

While, obviously, we were pleased for him that he was getting himself sorted out, we still had an album to complete, and his sudden absence made this tricky. On some of the tracks his bass was still in a bit of a mess because it was only half finished. The engineer had to try and figure out where he thought Hooky would want it but then got a load of grief later for not getting it right.

I'd like to say that when he emerged from rehab Hooky was his old self, with a new perspective on life and what's important, but the sad truth is that I can't. To me he seemed to come out of the Priory very uptight. One theory we discussed was that the drink had kept a lid on it all, that all his demons had been subdued by the alcohol, as if it was a pressure valve, and now they'd been unleashed.

We welcomed him back, wished him well, got on with rehearsing to tour the album and went out on the road. It was then that I started noticing him doing some odd things. He wouldn't sit near me on a plane, for example, and I'd sometimes catch him giving me strange looks. Then, on other occasions, he'd be all right. There didn't seem to be any logic or reason behind it.

It was around this time that he started his 'celebrity deejaying'. He'd begun doing 'New Order' after-show parties on a regular basis to earn more money, because, despite the money we were earning from the tour being pretty healthy, it somehow wasn't enough for him. I didn't really like him doing it, to be honest; I thought he was cashing in and it was all something of an ego-feeding exercise. Ultimately, it was up to him, though, and as long as it didn't interfere with the band then, as far as I was concerned, he could get on with it.

DJing is something I have done only a handful of times, nearly always as a favour for friends, but for Hooky it suddenly became a big thing, even though he'd never really shown any interest in dance music.

Things moved up a notch when we went to Japan to do the Fuji Festival in July 2005. We'd had a very good year; we'd played a lot of gigs and festivals throughout the spring and summer in Europe and America and things had gone pretty well. Fuji was our last show for a few months and it seemed like a nice way to round off what had mostly been an enjoyable and successful time. We were staying in the Park Hyatt Hotel in Tokyo, the hotel where *Lost In Translation* was shot, and a night or two before we played we went up to the Peak Bar for a drink and a meal (without Steve: he's got no head for heights and had decided that the Peak Bar, high above the ground and with floor-to-ceiling windows looking out at the Tokyo skyline, wasn't for him). We were in buoyant mood because everything looked positive: the gigs we'd done had gone well and we'd pulled in some massive crowds. I was quite relaxed about everything and in a good mood — we all were — but as soon as we'd gathered around the table with a few drinks, out of nowhere Hooky launched into this un-provoked, finger-jabbing diatribe against me, accusing me of fucking up his past, intending to fuck up his future and telling me that I was responsible for everything that had ever gone wrong with New Order. It was all my fault and we could have been a much bigger band if it hadn't been for me. We weren't doing enough gigs because of me, I'd been holding him back and he'd had enough of it.

I was completely taken aback. For one thing, I thought, Hang on, I finished that album, we all did, pulling together while you were in rehab. And we could have been bigger? We were up there in that bar to celebrate how in that last bunch of gigs we'd played to hundreds of thousands of people across three continents. But no, it wasn't enough for him: my life was somehow getting in the way of his, and that was that. He was seething. I felt like letting him have it with both barrels, but we had an important gig to do, the last of a long run before taking a break with our families, so I didn't want to ruin things with a full-blown argument. I think, in reality, his problem was something within himself but he'd somehow externalized it by blaming me for everything. It seemed to me that he couldn't understand why I didn't think like him and how I couldn't *want* as much as he did. When he projected his personality upon me, it came back with a negative and he didn't like it.

We're back to this supposed 'rivalry' that Hooky seems to believe exists between us. A rivalry is by definition a two-way thing, but in this case it's all coming from one direction. Whatever the origins of his issues with me, it was clear from his outburst in Tokyo that, for him, things had come to a head. It seemed that if he couldn't get what he wanted then, well, we were all bastards. But I was the biggest bastard.

We did a few gigs in Britain and Europe in the summer of 2006 and Hooky would occasionally give Andy and Rebecca a hard time, such as when we were playing in Newcastle and he told them he'd drive himself there. When he found out they were sending a car to take Steve home after the gig he went berserk at Rebecca because they'd not got him one, even though he'd specifically told them he didn't need one. All he saw was them looking after Steve but not him.

Odd outbursts like this aside, things generally chugged along in New Order world until the autumn of 2006, when we went on tour to South America. There was an increasingly tangible tension on that tour which centred on Hooky and his attitude to me. I kept catching him giving me looks that seemed to say, You know *exactly* why I'm so angry — but I didn't, I absolutely didn't. I really had no idea what this guy had against me and why.

In South America, Hooky was deejaying until 4 a.m. most nights at his after-show parties, and one night Sarge, our security guy, had told him we were leaving at half past eight the next morning. But Sarge had got it wrong, we weren't leaving until later in the day, so when Hooky got up after four hours' sleep to check out, he found nobody else there. He went mad. But he didn't go mad at Sarge, he called Andy and Rebecca, screaming at them about having got up so early for no reason when it clearly had nothing to do with them.

There were a few of these weird little eruptions offstage, but then strange things started happening *on* stage as well. For some time he'd been in the habit of spraying slogans on his bass amps, stuff like 'Salford Rules' — which was strange, as he hasn't lived in Salford for years — but I never usually saw them because, on stage, I was at the microphone and his amps were behind me to my left. It was left to the roadies to pull me to one side and tell me what he'd been spraying on the amps over the space of three gigs in South America. The first one was 'Two little boys met at school'; the next was 'And then they fell out'; and the night after that it was 'And now they hate each other.' Pretty strange stuff: I wasn't very happy with him, to say the least, but I certainly didn't hate the guy. If he had a problem, which he clearly did, if that really was how he saw it, why spray it on his amps instead of talking to me about it?

Then he'd persistently stand right in front of me on stage while I was singing. It was getting beyond strange now. The roadies are telling me about the amp thing, I'm getting daggers off him all the time, Andy and Rebecca are getting abuse off him, and now he's doing this. The bigger the gig, the more he was doing it. In addition, if the show was being filmed, he'd make sure he stood in the way of any cameras trained on me. He was also doing it to Phil, our guitarist. It was just ridiculous. It was a hard tour anyhow: our regular sound engineer wasn't able to do it and his stand-in couldn't cope with what was at that time a stupendously complicated live set-up, and I couldn't hear myself on stage. Add to that an airline strike creating delays of five hours or more at some of the airports, and there were already significant levels of stress. By that stage, I'd had enough and just wanted to finish the tour and get home.

Then *Control* happened. We'd been working on the soundtrack, and that caused even more friction with Hooky. The brief from Anton Corbijn was that he wanted some ambient background music behind the film, so I thought I'd start the ball rolling with a few soundscapes and then get everyone else to play on them. I think Hooky, meanwhile, was envisaging the whole band going into a studio and jamming to the visuals. Some of the scenes, like the one showing Ian on the night of his suicide, were very delicate and had to be handled carefully and a jamming session probably would not have fulfilled the ambient brief we'd had from Anton.

We'd played a gig at the Civic Hall in Wolverhampton just before the 2006 South America tour, a really good gig. When we came off stage I told Hooky that I was going to work on *Control* that week and suggested he came round and worked on it with me. He said he couldn't because he was deejaying. I reminded him that we were leaving for South America the following week so only had a limited amount of time. 'Well I can't help that,' he snapped. 'I'm busy.'

Control was due to be shown at the Cannes Film Festival in May 2007. We'd not gigged since the South American tour so it was the first time we'd been in the spotlight for a while and we were looking forward to it. Being screened at Cannes is a great honour for any film: we were delighted to be out there, and delighted for Anton. It turned out the film would pick up a clutch of awards at the festival, so it was all really exciting and positive.

At least it should have been.

Four days before the screening, word came back to us that Hooky had done an interview on Clint Boon's show on XFM and taken it upon himself to announce that New Order had split up. More specifically, he said that the two of us would not be working together again.

None of us knew about this announcement.

If a band splits up, it's usually a pretty basic prerequisite for the members of that band to know it's happening. Of course we hadn't split up. We've never split up. Even through the years when we were all working on different projects we were still New Order. What on earth was he playing at? When a band splits everyone agrees to it and goes their separate ways. The only person going their separate way in this instance was Peter Hook and it was entirely of his own volition. I was furious. Not just at *what* he'd done but that he'd chosen to do it right before Cannes, hijacking Anton's and the film's big occasion. I was so angry I couldn't even speak to Hooky. I didn't want to stay in the same hotel as him, I didn't want to set eyes on him. After thirty years together and all we'd been through, I thought what he'd done was disgraceful.

It also meant that when we got to the festival and did interviews that were supposed to be about the film, we were bombarded instead with questions about New Order, apparently, breaking up. Our reason for being there in Cannes — supporting the film and supporting Anton — had been completely undermined. It was a deeply uncool thing to do.

Steve and I were doing interviews together — we refused to do them with Hooky — and just kept saying that we had no idea what he was talking about, that we knew only as much as they did and that they had better ask Peter Hook. They all trooped off to Hooky and he was asked the same questions. Afterwards, back in the UK, he felt like he'd been allowed to make a fool of himself and fired Rebecca.

Given the media frenzy that followed, and in the interests of the fans who were, understandably, concerned, we put out a statement in order to set things straight:

After thirty years in a band together we are very disappointed that Hooky has decided to go to the press and announce unilaterally that New Order have split up. We would have hoped that he could have approached us personally first. He does not speak for all the band, therefore we can only assume he no longer wants to be a part of New Order. Whatever happens, musically or otherwise, New Order have *not* split up, they continue to exist. New Order will be making no further comment about this matter.

We wanted to — indeed, we had to — carry on, but circumstances intervened. For one thing, Gillian had just been diagnosed with breast cancer and Steve really needed to be with her. Also, after Japan and South America and the previous few years, which had seen a progressive intensity take over New Order again, I needed to do something else for a while. I went on to work with Jake Evans, Phil Cunningham, Alex James and three drummers: Carl Jackson, Jack Mitchell and, when Gillian had successfully completed her treatment, Steve, in a band called Bad Lieutenant. We wrote an album called, perhaps appropriately, *Never Cry Another Tear*: I needed a break from all the stress and to work on something positive, with people who didn't come with any baggage. Bad Lieutenant was a really pleasant experience and that contributed to what I think is a good album.

While this was going on, we did have meetings with Hooky. Although he'd left the band, it was a little more complicated than him just walking off into the sunset with his bass slung over his shoulder, as we were still shackled to him in a business sense. Things had moved on a bit from the days when we could resolve band departures with a box of Milk Tray, a slap on the back and a cheery 'All the best, mate.' There were a couple of discussions — sour affairs, let's say — about how the business side of things should move forward. Before one of these meetings — I think there were two — our manager had learned that Lesley, Rob's widow, owned half the Haçienda name. This was news to me, as I thought Hooky owned it all. He'd certainly left me with that impression and had never mentioned anything about Rob's involvement in the purchase. Lesley wanted to offload her share, because she simply couldn't deal with Hooky any more. Technically, he had first refusal but, even though he'd indicated he wanted it, Lesley was prepared to let us, the other members, have Rob's half for nothing instead — or at least no sum of money was discussed at the time.

He'd sacked Andy and Rebecca by this stage, accusing them of favouritism and claiming they always agreed with me. I think, really, the problem was that when he said jump they didn't always jump; instead, they would make the most logical decision in each circumstance. In addition, I suspect he still saw everything through the prism of the imaginary power struggle he'd conjured up between the two of us and examined everything Andy and Rebecca did from that perspective.

At the end of the second meeting, we said, 'Oh, by the way, we believe you're trying to buy Lesley's share of the Haçienda name?'

'Yes,' he said, a little surprised that we knew. 'That's right, I am.'

'Well, we want it,' we said. 'Considering all the money and hours we put into the Haçienda over the years, we feel we have a right to at least part of the name.'

He flew into an incredible rage, shouting and screaming at us, losing it completely. I tried to ask why he thought he had a right to it while we, apparently, had none.

'You didn't go through those three years of hell!' he bellowed, jabbing his finger at me.

'Hang on,' I said. 'That was entirely your choice. We went through *twelve* years of hell before that, which was why we finally wanted it to stop. Have you forgotten about that?'

In fact, I had remained a shareholder until the bitter end. Hooky stood up, bellowed at us a bit more and stormed out, slamming the door near off its hinges and leaving us all sitting there looking at each other open-mouthed.

There were a few moments' silence.

'That went well,' said Steve.

That was the moment I decided I didn't want anything more to do with the guy. I still feel that way today, even though it's several years since he left the band. The business side of things is done through our management and third parties. His 'Fuck you, I'm having that' attitude was just too much for me to bear any more after much provocation accumulated over a period of — what? — thirty years or more. When you're in a band, everyone needs to pull in the same direction and want what's best for the whole, not the individual. No one is bigger than the band and it's vital everyone thinks that way. We're a team. That's the most important thing. If the strikers in a football team aren't playing for the benefit of the whole side, if one won't pass to the other or goes for goal when there are team mates in a much better position because their personal ambition has crept ahead of their sense of the team ethic, then it's to the detriment of the whole outfit and, by extension, to the supporters too. It's exactly the same in a band.

This denouement had come in three distinct stages. First, his buying the Haçienda name, which we felt belonged to all of us. Second, his claiming that New Order had split up, when it was clear to anyone that we hadn't. The final straw was this tornado of self-righteous rage at our audacity in feeling we had a right to 50 per cent of 'his' Haçienda.

I finally accepted there was no reasoning with him. He just wouldn't listen to anything that didn't suit his agenda, an agenda that appeared to us to be nothing more than looking after number one. His behaviour in general had become intolerable, but over the Haçienda in particular we felt he'd effectively stolen a large part of our heritage and, frankly, enough was enough. As I've said before, I'm nobody's fool.

While he was still a member of New Order Hooky had put together a band called Freebass with Andy Rourke and Mani from The Stone Roses, which had quietly imploded, and not long after that we discovered he'd formed another band, with the sole intention of touring *Unknown Pleasures* played from start to finish. He was doing exactly what he'd done with the Haçienda to an album with which Steve and I had been intimately involved. He didn't ask us or tell us about it — as usual, we had to find out via the press — but I'd also heard through a little bird that he planned to work his way chronologically through all the Joy Division albums and then all the New Order albums. I've heard him claim he did this because I was playing New Order and Joy Division songs at Bad Lieutenant gigs, which is true. But out of a set of, say, fifteen songs, we would only play maybe three or four songs per group — and we only had one album's worth of material ourselves. Obviously, he doesn't have to account to us for his every move now he's no longer in New Order, but this was different: *Unknown Pleasures* was hallowed ground and something all three of us had helped to create and all three of us hold dear.

Peter Hook has said a lot of stupid things about me, especially since he left the band. I'm sure I don't hear about them all — and I certainly don't go looking for them — but I've done my best not to respond, as most of them don't deserve the dignity of a response. I've neither the desire for nor the intention of being drawn into a public slanging match with him, but it's difficult sometimes, especially with some of the more outlandish claims and slurs, calling me highly offensive names in the press. He still seems determined to perpetuate this imaginary rivalry but New Order have moved on, and I've moved on. He left of his own volition and is now doing his own thing. Good luck to him. I hope he finds the happiness and fulfilment on his own which it seems he couldn't as a member of New Order. We're happier with the way things are now; I hope he is too.

For all my disagreements with Hooky, I've always said that the work he did on bass was really great and something that played a big role in creating our unique sound. It's a shame that his frustration, his perceived thwarted ambitions or whatever it was that led to his departure had come to stand in the way of his talents as a bass player. I'd never say anything bad about his playing: there's no doubt about it, he's really good. Whatever talents you have, however, you still have to live with and have respect for other people, especially those with whom you work closely. That's a huge part of being in a band. I'm in no way perfect myself, of course, and openly admit that on occasions I've been a right miserable scumbag. It's usually been the result of some binge or other, but not always, and in any case, I'm not sure how much of a defence that is. However, I've learned that if you don't give respect to or lose the respect of your peers, then eventually things are going to go very wrong indeed. No matter what you say or who you are, it's what you do that matters. Your actions will ultimately betray your true nature.

For the stranger on the street or even a diehard Joy Division and New Order fan, it must be hard to decide what's really going on, because of course they can't see things from the inside. All I can say is: just do the maths. Everyone else in the band is still here. Virtually everyone involved with the management side, the entire crew and backroom staff, they're all still here too. Some people made an effort to at least stay on civil terms with him after he left the band, but it was just thrown back in their faces. It's quite sad in a way, because he's lost out on so much. He was a big part of this incredible journey but threw it all away and alienated a lot of people in the process, some of whom he'd known and worked with for decades.

While I feel strongly that people deserve a clarification of the circumstances that surrounded Hooky's departure from New Order — and I've gone into great detail here in order to set the record straight — I don't really want to dwell on it further, because everything's been so positive since he left the band. My final word on the subject is this: when assessing the situation Peter Hook created back in 2007 and its subsequent fallout, I think the best thing to do is not listen to what he says but to look at what he does.

Chapter Twenty-two

The epilogue

We were coming to the end of 'Love Will Tear Us Apart' on stage at Carnegie Hall when a whirling dervish, shirtless beneath a dark grey suit and with lank, blond-highlighted locks flying, appeared next to me at the microphone. He stabbed his own mic at his right cheek, looked me right in the eye and joined me in singing, 'Love, love will tear us apart again' in a baritone growl that seemed to emanate from somewhere beneath the stage and possibly below the earth's crust itself.

I've had some pretty vivid dreams in my time, but performing 'Love Will Tear Us Apart' with Iggy Pop, one of my musical heroes and a huge influence on the music I've made, on stage at arguably the most prestigious venue in the world was no nocturnal fantasy. It was March 2014, it was real, it was happening. The final notes of the song faded away into the surge of the crowd's roar, and before I'd even had the chance to lift my guitar over my head, Iggy was walking towards me, creasing his face into a huge smile and locking me in a back-thumping embrace. Over his shoulder in the wings I could see Philip Glass smiling, applauding and nodding his approval.

Alfred Street to Carnegie Hall had been quite a journey. How on earth did I get here?

I'd really enjoyed working on the Bad Lieutenant album *Never Cry Another Tear*. As had happened with Electronic, it was great to work and record with other musicians and play gigs with another good, tight live band. We'd written a really good set of songs, released an album of which I'm very proud and gone down a storm live wherever we'd played. I'd found the whole thing a positive and rewarding experience — apart from two disastrous attempts to tour America, that is.

The first time, in 2009, we'd had to pull the tour literally as we were about to leave when last-minute issues with our visas emerged. It was happening to a lot of bands at that time, I think, but the news that we weren't going after all only reached us when we were on the platform at the railway station about to set off for London to pick up our passports and head across the Atlantic. It was as infuriating as it was devastating. We were determined not to let down the people who'd bought tickets, however, and rescheduled the tour for a year later, adding the Coachella festival to the itinerary too. Again there was a visa problem, but just a delay on mine this time, so the rest of the band travelled to London slightly ahead of me while Rebecca also went down to ensure my visa came through without a hitch. She was due to pick it up early in the morning and the plan was that I'd meet her at Euston, pick up my passport and visa and head off to Heathrow to fly out to the States.

The phone rang early that morning. Sarah answered and came into the bedroom holding the receiver just as I was zipping up my bag ready to go.

'Who's that?' I said, irritated. 'I can't hang about, I've got a train to catch.'

'Actually,' she said, 'you're not going anywhere.'

'What?' I replied.

'It's Rebecca on the phone. You're not going to believe this, but a volcano has erupted in Iceland and the ash cloud means that all flights have been grounded until further notice.'

She was right: I couldn't believe it. Not again.

Rebecca said I should still go to London to wait until the situation became clearer, and I ended up checking into a hotel in Paddington packed with similarly stranded and anxious would-be travellers. All across Europe it was the same story: Johnny Marr and his band were stuck at a ferry port in Rotterdam and there were many more bands who couldn't make it over to Coachella. After a day or two of waiting, it became clear we'd have to pull the tour again. To all the people that bought tickets for gigs on either or both those tours, I can't emphasize enough how sorry I am. It's scant consolation, I'm sure, but the band felt as bad about it as you did. If anything, it broke our spirits and pretty much hastened the end of the Bad Lieutenant project.

Bad Lieutenant had been a fresh start for me in a way, but when it had run its natural course I was ready to start working with New Order again. I wasn't the only one, either: it was soon obvious to the rest of us what we wanted and needed to do. I think Steve summed it up well when he said he wasn't prepared to throw away thirty years of his life because one person had thrown their toys out of the pram. On top of this, when an old friend in desperate circumstances needed our help, the catalyst we needed for New Order to resume finally presented itself.

Michael Shamberg, who you'll remember as the man responsible for our pioneering early videos, had been spending a lot of time on this side of the Atlantic, particularly in Paris and Beirut. We'd kept in touch with him over the years and had always been happy to help whenever he needed it. In the late eighties he'd made a film called

Salvation, for which we provided the music, including 'Touched by the Hand of God'. We were under intense time pressure at that point and did all the songs for the film in one night, handing the final versions to a courier at eight o'clock in the morning because we'd never let Michael down. More recently, he'd made *Souvenir in Paris*, which starred Kristin Scott Thomas, and spent some time in Lebanon producing a film called *P.S. Beirut*. However, Michael had left Beirut with a mystery illness so serious that he'd fallen into a coma in hospital in London. He emerged from the coma after a time but was still incredibly ill and relying on support from UK-based friends and his partner, Miranda. After a series of tests, the doctors concluded it was some kind of viral brain illness – the effects looked to me like those of motor neurone disease – and Michael spent a lot of time in London until he was well enough to return to New York. He was by no means recovered, however, and still required constant care. In 2011, we heard that Michael was really ill again and his medical bills were crippling him (we all know what the American welfare state is like: there isn't one). We wanted to help.

My thoughts turned to how we might be able to best help him. Bad Lieutenant were playing much smaller gigs and the amount of records we were selling wasn't massive. Realistically, *Never Cry Another Tear* had reached the end of its life cycle, and my time with the band had given me the opportunity to take stock away from New Order to the point where I could see the wood for the trees again. Steve and Gillian had been spending most of their time looking after their daughter, whose medical condition required care, and Gillian herself had fought and now won her battle with breast cancer. She was ready to come back into the throng for the first time since 2001, and was keen to do so because it was a part of her life that she loved and had missed; and so was Steve. I could see where the future lay. It was time for New Order to start working again.

With Hooky having moved on to pursue his own projects, we needed a new bass player, and the obvious choice was Tom Chapman. Tom had been involved with Bad Lieutenant, playing our live shows and appearing on a couple of tracks on the album. Our original bass player, Alex James from Blur, lives down south in the Cotswolds, while we're up north – where, you know, the real men live – and there was just too much to-ing and fro-ing up and down the country carting gear backwards and forwards for Alex. Jake Evans, who played guitar on the album, also played bass on some of the tracks and clearly he couldn't play both guitar and bass live. Tom got the job. When he came in to audition I think we gave him the impression that we'd already auditioned about twenty bass players when we were actually only auditioning him. Tom's a really nice person, which was important, and he plays really well. He fits in perfectly. When we asked him to join New Order, it can't have been as straightforward a decision as it might have seemed: after all, he had some pretty big shoes to fill. But Tom has a very sanguine attitude towards life and the transition was absolutely seamless, for us and for him. He's a very flexible musician too: as well as all the old material, he's capable of playing in a range of different styles, something that brings us an extra dimension.

Phil Cunningham was also keen to get going again. Phil had arrived in 2001 when Gillian had to take her sabbatical. I knew Phil through Johnny; he'd been in a very successful band called Marion, who were part of the Britpop scene in the nineties and had then done some live television work with us in Electronic. Next, he slid in as an extra pair of hands for Johnny Marr when we did a very guitar-based album in *Twisted Tenderness*, so when Gillian had to take a back seat it was logical that Phil should step in. He fits in really well with the rest of the band: he's got an easy-going person-ality, he's a good person to be around, a good person to have around and he's a very good guitarist. Also, Tom's arrival was a fillip for Philip — for one thing they're good friends anyway, but it also meant that, after a decade in New Order, he was no longer 'the new bloke'.

Once we had everyone on board, we scheduled three concerts, two of them in continental Europe. Our first gig in five years would be at the Ancienne Belgique in Brussels on 17 October, with another at the Bataclan in Paris the following night (our agent Ian had told us the Bataclan was the hottest place in town to play, and he was right about that — it was unbelievably fucking hot: in its eighty- to a hundred-year history, they'd never got round to putting in any ventilation). The third gig was at the Troxy in London in December, a lovely venue, which allowed us to recoup the costs of the other two gigs and ensure we could give all the proceeds to Michael. All these shows went wonderfully well and we got a great live album out of the Troxy show.

The first two gigs in particular garnered a lot of attention and, as soon as they were announced, Rebecca and Andy began receiving calls from agents and promoters around the world asking if we'd play. It was overwhelming and instantaneous: before the Troxy show in December we even managed to fit in three South American concerts. South American crowds are amazing: they sure wear their hearts on their sleeves, and the gigs were as great as the caipirinhas.

In 2012, the whole thing snowballed and we were inundated with offers: I think we played fifty concerts in a year — including the London Olympics closing ceremony concert in Hyde Park — as part of what, effectively, turned into a world tour. It was the busiest year for touring I'd done in a long time, possibly the busiest ever. We played at the Ultra Music Festival in Miami, an amazing event in the Bay Park area in front of the skyscrapers, on to which video images were projected. We toured Britain, Europe, Japan, Korea, Australia,

New Zealand, and finished the year with a string of dates in the US and Canada.

I know some people had wondered whether one of the original members of the band leaving might cool interest in the band a little, especially among the fans, but the gigs were incredibly well-received — the initial three sold out in a matter of minutes. Everything about New Order was positive again: the gigs were all successful (we won an award for the best festival performance of the year for our live show at the Festival No. 6 in Portmeirion in 2012), the vibe was good and we were having fun again. I've not enjoyed touring as much in many years. We still try and help out Michael whenever he can, he's still not very well, but as with the miners' benefit in 1984, it seemed that, while benefiting others, by happy coincidence we'd also ended up benefiting ourselves.

Early in 2014, a letter arrived from Philip Glass asking if I and two members of the band would go over for an annual concert he stages to benefit an organization called Tibet House, which lobbies for the preservation of Tibetan culture and awareness of its situation. I had a bit of affinity for Tibet because, when I was a teenager, my cousin Steve and I read avidly the work of a Tibetan monk called Tuesday Lobsang Rampa, which became a bit of a bible for us. The books contained a great deal of moral and spiritual guidance: how you should conduct yourself, for example, the effects of drug taking on the soul and how the Tibetans used spiritual teaching to improve themselves and their minds. Steve and I were pretty enthralled by this and, when we read of how the monks in the Himalayas drank hot butter tea, we tried to make some ourselves. Let's just say we only tried it once. Take it from me, butter works much better on toast.

I'd also read in my comic books about Tibetan monks with amazing powers acquired through meditation: one was levitation; another was that they could put a blanket soaked in icy water over themselves and it would turn to steam. Also — in comic books at least — they could run incredible distances by using a special technique of superhuman strides that enabled them to cover great distances in a short time. Tibet seemed like it must be a magical place. It certainly sounded different to Salford.

So when I received the letter from Philip explaining how the organization was dedicated to the preservation of Tibetan culture, my teenage Tibetan learnings came flooding back and it really piqued my interest. (It later transpired, incidentally, that Lobsang Rampa was actually a plumber from Plymouth called Cyril. When questioned about him, the Dalai Lama said something along the lines of 'While we do not accept Lobsang Rampa as a true Tibetan monk, we applaud anyone that spreads the message about our nation,' which was pretty gracious of him.)

Whatever the nature of the occasion, the opportunity to work with Philip Glass is a no-brainer for any musician. Philip is one of our finest contemporary composers and I've been a fan of his for a long time. I remember being in London recording a good few years ago, and every night we'd return from the studio to the flat we were staying in to watch *Koyaanisqatsi*, an absolutely hypnotic combination of images and music for which Philip had written the most fantastic soundtrack. Since then, I've explored his other work, and it's incredible stuff. Occasionally, I've heard criticism that it's too repetitive, but look at club music, house music, r 'n' b: it's *all* repetitive, and there can be a great beauty in repetition. Philip's music isn't simply repetitive, though; his pieces evolve slowly, like a wave approaching the shore, subtly changing shape and form as they build to a climax. I find his music as evocative to listen to as watching the ocean; seeing the waves build and build then break on the sand. The crashing of waves is repetitive, but each is different, each builds in its own way with its own energy and harmonics, and Philip's music works in exactly the same way.

I spoke to Philip on the phone — I think he actually called me, from a Mexican airport — and he explained a bit more about the content and context of the evening. The Tibet House concert has been an annual event for more than twenty-five years now, he told me, and has always had a strong theme of collaboration. He said that he'd like us to collaborate with some of the other musicians involved: Patti Smith, The National and, perhaps most excitingly for me, Iggy Pop. He told me Patti's band was available if we needed them and the Scorchio Quartet would be there too.

This gave me an idea. A Manchester poet called Mike Garry had written a fantastic poem about Tony Wilson called 'Saint Anthony'. The string arranger Joe Duddell, who's probably best known for his work with Elbow, had taken the New Order song 'Your Silent Face' and arranged it for a string quartet with Mike reading the poem over the top of it. I really liked it: we performed it at an amazing gig at the Jodrell Bank Observatory in 2013, in the shadow of the enormous Lovell Telescope, and it went down fantastically well.

I sent the poem over to Philip, and he loved it. He told me Allen Ginsberg had been a big part of the event until his death in 1997 and jumped at the idea of having some poetry on the night as a way of continuing Allen's legacy. When I contacted Mike and told him all this, he nearly fell off his chair.

As for collaboration with the other artists, I had another idea. We'd written a song called 'Californian Grass' which appeared on the *Lost Sirens* album of songs we'd recorded while writing *Waiting for the Sirens' Call*. We'd written far more songs than we needed, deliberately so, the idea being that we'd write two albums at once and not have to go away again to record for a long time. The album that became *Lost Sirens* was therefore designed to be the album that followed *Waiting for the Sirens' Call*. Obviously, in the meantime, certain things had changed, which meant that *Lost Sirens* didn't come out until 2013, a decade after the songs had been recorded. It saddens me a little that *Lost Sirens* is thought of as an album of out-takes from *Waiting for the Sirens' Call*, because it really isn't, it's actually a second, unfinished album — unfinished because, among other issues, Hooky had refused to come into the studio and finish it and then dragged his heels over its release.

I'd written 'Californian Grass' in my home studio. The way we normally work is to write, arrange and record the music first, coming up with a track that sounds good as an instrumental. When that track has reached a level where I feel inspired to take it further, I'll bring it back to the little room I use in my house as a studio, burn the midnight oil and write some melodies, lyrics and vocals over the top of it. I wrestled a bit with 'Californian Grass', because it happened to be in an awkward key for me: it was pitched pretty low. I'm a high tenor (some might have you believe that at certain stages of my career I've been a *very* high tenor), but the verses in particular were a struggle for my vocal register. I distinctly remember sitting in my studio late one night and thinking, It's a bit Iggy, that vocal, it's exactly the kind of phrasing and pitch he'd use.

When I learned that Iggy was also doing the Tibet House concert a light bulb went on over my head. I wondered whether he'd be interested in collaborating on 'Californian Grass'. After all, his music was partly responsible for the band and I being around today. You might recall that the first time I went round to Ian's house after giving him the job of singer, the first time we spent any significant time together, he played me Iggy's version of 'China Girl' from *The Idiot*, which had been released that very day. I'd been blown away by it and been a fan of Iggy's ever since. He's always been a key influence from the early days of Joy Division and I thought working with him would be incredibly exciting.

Feeling slightly nervous, I sent the song over to Iggy to see what he thought. He came back pretty much immediately and said, 'Sure, I can sing that, Ber-*nard*; the key's kinda sweet.' I thought, Yeah, it is fucking sweet because I wrote it with you in mind! I was thrilled that he'd agreed to do it. In addition, on the night, Philip would join us on stage too to play the piano on it: an amazing experience that drew together different aspects of and influences from my musical past.

The rehearsals were almost as magical as the concert itself. Finding myself sitting on a sofa next to Iggy Pop watching Patti Smith singing a beautiful version of 'Perfect Day' while Philip Glass looked on was pretty mind-blowing, it must be said. Rehearsal time was at a premium, however. When we — Tom, Phil and me — first arrived, Philip had come over and said, 'We've given you guys four songs, as you've travelled by far the furthest of any of the acts,' which was very fair of him, but we only had twenty minutes' rehearsal. We'd rehearsed 'Saint Anthony' at my house with Mike and an English quartet before we left and it had sounded great but, even so, rehearsal time was pretty tight. We had another rehearsal at Carnegie Hall itself, before which we received a call to say we had seven minutes — enough for about a song and a half — which sounded pretty daunting. As it turned out, we did have a decent rehearsal and, when the time came for the show itself, everything went like clockwork.

We did 'Saint Anthony' first, then Iggy came on to sing 'California Grass'. When he walked out, it was like having a sun joining us on stage, this huge smile and warm presence, a jerking, twisting dynamo of enormous, room-filling charisma — and of course that voice, sounding like it was coming up from the gates of hell. I think he actually sang an octave lower than the one I couldn't reach: it was like his voice was coming from under the ground.

We finished up where we came in at the start of this chapter, with him joining us on 'Transmission' and 'Love Will Tear Us Apart'. There are some moments in life when everything seems joyfully complete and you look around and think, I could die right now and that would be just fine. This was one of them.

But that would have brought the whole story to an end, when the story is far from over. There's still much to be done, and New Order continues to go from strength to strength: we're playing concerts in parts of the world we've never explored before, our live reputation just keeps on getting better and the invitations for gigs and festivals continue to roll in. I think we're a better live band now than we've ever been. Our live set-up is technically fantastic, with visuals playing on a screen behind us, and our set list is a really good mix of the hits people want to hear, a few tracks that people wouldn't necessarily expect us to play live and reinventions of some of the standards in order to keep things fresh.

My favourite song to play live is 'Temptation'. It's one of New Order's oldest songs, dating back to 1981, yet over the years it's evolved and developed on stage into the stomping, thunderous nine-minute behemoth we play today as the climax of our live set.

We recorded it in London at a studio near the Post Office Tower on a day when it was snowing heavily. While I was recording the vocal Rob snuck into the studio and stuck a snowball down the back of my shirt. You can hear that on the long version of the song: all the whooping and shouting is the result of Rob's handful of snow going down my back, which is a wonderful memory to hear on the record but, even so, I think 'Temptation' is a much more powerful song live than it ever could be in the studio. It's neither our most famous song nor our most commercially successful, yet it draws people in and has become the pinnacle of the entire set. There's something about the repetition and the emotion it involves, the simplicity of the structure and the words that make 'Temptation' a very spiritual song for me. I don't think I can explain why, there's just a tangible sense when I'm singing it that makes it feel to me like a prayer. It's transcendent, exultant and seems to draw the crowd and the band together like no other song. 'Temptation' is one song that I never, ever tire of playing because of that, and also because it unfolds a little like a film; there are shifting scenes within the song that carry the crowd with them.

I love playing 'Love Will Tear Us Apart', too. In fact, I can't think of a song that I *don't* like playing live, even ones I've played hundreds of times. We mix the set up and throw in a few unexpected songs from left field, but obviously there are people coming to a New Order gig expecting and wanting to hear certain songs and we have to play them or people will be disappointed. I conducted a phone interview with a Peruvian journalist recently with the promoter also on the line acting as interpreter. The journalist asked something about 'Blue Monday' but it was a bad line and when I asked the promoter to repeat it he replied, 'He said that if you don't play "Blue Monday" in Lima they'll lynch you.'

As I write, we're working on new material and the mood in the camp is buoyant. New Order continues to evolve. First Phil a decade ago and, most recently, Tom have come in and are both great presences on and off the stage. Tom has filled a difficult position in the New Order narrative and he's making a great contribution to the live shows — the fans have really taken to him too — which I hope will continue in the recording studio. In addition, Gillian's keyboard playing has progressed greatly since we began playing live again; she's just getting better and better. I think she's become much more confident in herself as a live performer since her sabbatical and grows in stature with each tour.

The cast is in place, the mix is right, the chemistry is right. Playing live has been a real pleasure since we did those two gigs for Michael in

2011, and I can honestly say this has been the most enjoyable period in which to be a member of New Order.

Away from the group, I'm in a good place too. I'm happy, lucky and content and, as a band, we've found a sensible balance between touring and life at home. I'm also fortunate to have a particular interest away from music which this balance allows me to pursue. I find the sea very calming and love the way it appears to be alive. I remember clearly the first time I ever saw the sea, on holiday in Rhyl one summer when I was a very young child. I was running up a sand dune, wondering what was on the other side, reached the top and found myself looking down at this vast expanse of water that stretched all the way to the horizon. I was smitten. My life had been defined by narrow boundaries and the streets of Lower Broughton. Yet, here, I felt as if the shackles were being cast off, and the uninterrupted horizon made it feel as if I could see for ever. As the sunlight sparkled on the surface in millions of ever-shifting shards I felt an immediate kinship that has stayed with me to this day. I even remember standing there with this vast, rippling, twinkling expanse in front of me and saying out loud to myself, 'My sea!'

When I take time away from music I like to have something to occupy my mind, something that doesn't involve playing or programming or writing lyrics, something that allows that part of my brain to rest and recharge. I find being on a boat perfect in that respect: it's a million miles from studios, dressing rooms and being on stage in front of all those people, it keeps my brain and my hands occupied and it's something I love doing very much. When sailing, you harness nature — the wind, the tides and the currents — to take you from place to place. You have to respect the weather and the sea: you're in their realm, right at the heart of nature, and they're completely in charge. I enjoy the planning, the navigating, the course-plotting and the monitoring of weather charts, but most of all

I enjoy sitting at night on my boat beneath a clear sky untainted by light pollution, lying on my back, perhaps with a little drink in my hand, listening to some music or the faint ripple of the waves against the hull, looking up and seeing this vast canopy of thousands and thousands of stars.

I've sailed frequently along the west coast of Scotland, which when the weather is in your favour is a stunning and wild place to sail. I once sailed from the small island of Canna, south-west of the Isle of Skye, to Barra in the Western Isles, and we had to leave early. My son Dylan had begrudgingly agreed to get up and help me raise the anchor but, after that, he was 'going back to bed'. This left me sailing the 47-foot yacht on my own while the wind was blowing up.

About an hour later we reached the western tip of the island and, with everyone else down below still asleep, there was a sudden almighty double crunch from below, as if I'd hit a rock. I looked around me, but the sea was rough and I couldn't see anything. I checked my charts and there didn't seem to be anything on the sea bed that would present a problem. I pulled the boards up to look down into the hull and they were dry. I figured that if I went back to Canna there was nothing there — no facilities, no divers to inspect the hull — so I called the coastguard on the radio, told him what had happened and he confirmed that there were no rocks or wrecks in my position. I decided to continue to Barra, pulling the boards up every ten minutes to make sure we weren't taking on water, and the coastguard asked me to radio him again when I approached the island, which was now about thirty miles away. Everyone was up by now and I must admit it was a little disconcerting, but we took on no water and things seemed fine.

I called the coastguard again as we approached Barra, and he said that another sailor had contacted him to say he'd passed through the area where we'd had our collision and seen several sharks close to the surface. When we moored I found a diver, asked him to go down and check the hull and, sure enough, there was the imprint of a large shark with gill marks in the slime on the bottom. It was probably a basking shark, which can grow up to thirty feet in length and weigh up to four tons. The boat was OK, but I needed a wee dram after that particular trip. For one thing, I've met enough sharks in the music business over the years: I didn't need them turning up under my boat.

I sailed across the Atlantic a couple of years ago, a journey of three thousand miles down the coast of Africa and then west across the Atlantic to the Caribbean. It was incredible. It took us three weeks and was like being on another planet the entire time we were out of sight of land. When you're that far out at sea and there's nothing around you in every direction but the horizon, it's an extraordinary feeling, one that helps you see your own life from a distance and gain a sense of what it means, as well as giving you an appreciation of just how huge the world really is.

I'm lucky enough to have seen a good deal of that world. I've travelled to many continents and seen many fantastic places and met countless amazing people, most of whom have been fans of the bands I've played in and the music I've made. Maybe all bands think this way, but I think New Order fans are special. They feel a spiritual connection to the band or, more specifically, to the music we make. Many of them have grown up with the music of New Order: I often hear the phrase, 'Your music has been the soundtrack to my life.' Well, it's been the soundtrack to my life too. It's helped to define me as much as it's helped to define you. If you're feeling down, music can be a great healer, and if you're feeling up it helps to keep you there. The best music will form a tangible bond with the listener, conveying the emotions felt by the composer that compelled them to write it in the first place. A piece of music is a composer speaking straight to you, from their heart to yours, and it's a fabulous, vital thing. I have a real sense of how that has happened for our fans, because it's happened to me too with the music I love.

New Order fans range across a whole spectrum of demographics. Every gig is different. We played T in the Park in Scotland a year or so ago, and it was like playing to an army that was about to storm a citadel. Our shows today can range from seeing loads of teenage girls at the front to an older crowd of rock fans or more of a dance crowd: because our music encompasses different styles, it has a wide appeal, which earns us a wide and varied following.

It's a dog-dead cliché but, without the audience being so passionate about our music, I wouldn't be sitting here writing this book now. I think I can speak for the whole band here in saying how incredibly grateful we are for the loyalty our fans have shown us over the years we've been together. It's truly touching.

Things are better than they have been for a very long time and I have to say I enjoy the whole experience much more now I realize that the only thing to fear about being on stage is falling off it. I'm enjoying my life and my work more than ever before. I'm looking after myself better, I've given up getting fucked up all the time and, as Jimmy Cliff sang, I can see clearly now the rain has gone.

Shit does happen in life, but you can get over it. Don't let it defeat you.

And, with that, I think we'll leave my story there.

Postscript

Yes, we were hedonists; yes, we got drunk; and yes, we were off our faces a lot of the time. Big deal, yeah yeah, blah-de-blah, so what? That's almost a conformist attitude for a musician. It's not the main theme of this book, as that story has been told by others many times before.

This book is about what it means to be truly alive. It's about operating outside the system and beating it. It's about surviving catastrophe. It's about hanging on to some of the things you once valued as a kid and how, along with that, just having fun can lead to — and in fact is — success. You just have to take a few steps back from life occasionally to see things the way they ought to be.

Bernard Sumner, June 2014

Appendix One:
Ian Curtis and Bernard Sumner
hypnosis recording

Around the time of Ian's epilepsy diagnosis, I'd been reading a book on hypnotic regression. It described how regression therapy could be used to pull out something trapped in a past life that caused problems in this life, and I thought I'd give it go: it would make a good party trick, if nothing else. As kids in Alfred Street, we'd messed about with hypnotism, and there seemed to be something in it, so, intrigued by the possibilities, I tried it on a couple of people. Sure enough, they'd begin to talk about what appeared to be a past life.

I first tried it on Ian when we were bored one day at the rehearsals. He came out with some stuff that sounded very interesting but, afterwards, he had absolutely no recollection of what he'd talked about.

When he stayed at my house a couple of weeks before he died, we'd stay up late, talking about everything under the sun. One night I said, 'Shall we try the hypnotic regression again, only we'll record it this time so you can hear it back afterwards?' Straightaway, he was up for it, so I put him under again (he was really easy to put under) and recorded what he said. I'd never tried it more than once with the same person before and the startling thing was that Ian said exactly the same things he'd said at the rehearsal room.

The full transcript of the tape, which I still have to this day, has never been published before.

This is what he said.

[Tape begins]

Ian   . . . just down the road from where I were.

Bernard   What's your friend called?

Ian   Tony.

Bernard   What does he look like?

Ian   [exhales] He's got like . . . light coloured hair.

Bernard   What are you doing there?

Ian   Sat . . . sat down, on the kerb. Got lollipop sticks, or some-
           thing sticks, digging, like, cracks in the . . . in the pavement,
           like. Not grass, some kind of like . . . moss, green moss
           over the top of it. Digging it out, between the pavement.

Bernard   Are there any cars in the street?

Ian   Just way down the road.

Bernard   Do you know what colour they are?

Ian   Dark blue.

Bernard   What are the houses like?

Ian   All the same.

Bernard   Have they got gardens?

Ian   Yeah.

Bernard   How old are you?

Ian   Five.

Bernard   Do you know what the date is?

Ian   Fifteenth of July.

Bernard   Just relax . . . You're very secure . . . deep sleep. Very deep
           sleep. Hear my voice. [inaudible] . . . don't care. You need

	to go to a time when you were three years old. Any time, when you were three years old. Tell me what you see.
Ian	My auntie. In the garden. My granddad's here.
Bernard	What's your auntie's name?
Ian	Nell.
Bernard	And what you doing there?
Ian	Playing. Sat in the garden. They've got a dog.
Bernard	What does the dog look like?
Ian	It's very . . . very hairy, all over its eyes. Looks the same from the back as it does from the front.
Bernard	Is your auntie in the garden there with you?
Ian	Yeah. And my uncle. My dad. My mum.
Bernard	What, have you gone to visit?
Ian	Yeah.
Bernard	Do you like your auntie?
Ian	Yeah.
Bernard	Can you see yourself?
Ian	Yeah.
Bernard	What do you look like?
Ian	Small, and fat. Round. Round face. Not fat, chubby. Plump, my mum says.
Bernard	Your mum said you're plump?
Ian	That's what they al . . . y'know . . . not . . . not really, I suppose. It's what they said.
Bernard	OK. Just sleep again. Still remaining at the age of three . . . you understand? Now just sleep. Don't pay any attention to any noises whatsoever. Just wait. Just sleep. Just relax, and wait. You're totally secure. I want you to go back to when you were two, and any time during which you were two, any memory that you can remember.
Ian	Sat on the rug at home . . .
Bernard	At your mum and dad's home?

Ian   Yeah.

Bernard   Can you describe the room?

Ian   Yes. A fire, coal fire, a strange metal thing, I think maybe
           for lighting it. I don't think it works, it could come off.
           Then there's two chairs and a settee. Television. Carpet's
           red and beige. Rug's red.

Bernard   What colour wallpaper?

Ian   S'like a pattern, goldy. There's a table, a sideboard under
           the window, there's two windows facing each other.
           Bernardrown tiles round the edge of the carpet.

Bernard   Now, do you know what the date is? Can you tell me
           what date it is?

Ian   Er . . . no.

Bernard   How old are you?

Ian   Two.

Bernard   Two years old. I want you to go back even further, to when
           you were one. When you were one year old. Anything
           when you were one year old.

Ian   Just . . . ceiling.

Bernard   Ceiling?

Ian   In my mum and dad's bedroom.

Bernard   Are your mum and dad there?

Ian   No. My nanna.

Bernard   Your nanna?

Ian   Mm, just looking at me.

Bernard   Are you lying down?

Ian   Yeah.

Bernard   In bed?

Ian   Yeah, I think so.

Bernard   Can you see any pattern on the ceiling?

Ian   [murmur, inaudible]

Bernard   Can you see the wall?

Ian	No . . . something in the way.
Bernard	What, between you and the wall?
Ian	Mm.
Bernard	Describe what it is in the way.
Ian	I don't know, it's white . . . can't reach it.
Bernard	Can you describe yourself?
Ian	Mmm . . . just can't . . . can't see . . . tired.
Bernard	Drowsy.
Ian	Mmm.
Bernard	Just relax and listen to my voice. Go deeper into the sleep. Go deeper into the sleep but listen to my voice. Now I want you to go further back in time to before you were born. Before you were born. Tell me the first image you see.
Ian	Trees.
Bernard	Trees.
Ian	Lots of trees.
Bernard	Just relax. No harm can come to you. Whatever you see, whatever happens, no harm can come to you, I promise you. I just want you to be totally relaxed and tell me everything you see.
Ian	Trees are all around.
Bernard	It's a forest?
Ian	I think so.
Bernard	Do you know the place?
Ian	No.
Bernard	Are there any people there?
Ian	No, it's just me.
Bernard	Do you know why you're there?
Ian	Mmm . . .
Bernard	Think carefully. Plenty of time.
Ian	I feel tired, in my legs, as if I've been walking . . . for quite a while. I don't think I've always been . . . been here.

Bernard So you've walked from another place.

Ian   Yeah.

Bernard Do you remember where you've walked from?

Ian   Er...a house. [pause] I think I'm lost.

Bernard You're lost? OK, just relax. Go further back, to another time, further back to another set of memories. Don't worry, no harm can come to you, just relax. Go back to a further set of memories and tell me what you see.

Ian   [pause] ... sat ... oh. Sat ... just sat down.

Bernard Where are you sat down?

Ian   Just...at home.

Bernard Where is home? What can you see?

Ian   Just reading.

Bernard What are you reading?

Ian   A book about...erm...it's about laws.

Bernard A book about laws?

Ian   Mmm.

Bernard What language is the book wrote in?

Ian   English.

Bernard Do you know how old you are?

Ian   Twenty-eight.

Bernard Twenty-eight? Say that again.

Ian   Twenty-eight.

Bernard Why are you reading the book about laws?

Ian   I've been reading it...for a couple of days...and going over bits and making notes ... I'm keeping notes.

Bernard Why, is it part of your job, or something?

Ian   Something I ... I do at night.

Bernard Is it night-time now?

Ian   Yeah.

Bernard Is there a light in your room?

Ian   Yeah.

Bernard Describe it to me.

Ian The brightest, comes from the fire. I'm close to the fire. [inaudible]

Bernard Do you live on your own?

Ian No.

Bernard Who do you live with?

Ian I'm married.

Bernard What's your wife's name?

Ian [pause] [murmur]

Bernard What's your name?

Ian John.

Bernard Sorry?

Ian John.

Bernard John. What's your second name?

Ian [pause]

Bernard Are you living in England?

Ian . . . yeah.

Bernard What else can you see?

Ian I can . . . it's very dark. I can see . . . what, from the window?

Bernard Yeah.

Ian The street below.

Bernard I want you to go to the next day. The daytime. And what do you see now?

Ian Er . . . lots of people around.

Bernard How are they dressed? Pick one person out and describe how he's dressed.

Ian Shirt . . . or, or coat . . . trousers, shoes . . . hat.

Bernard What kind of a hat?

Ian Not very high.

Bernard Is there a name for that type of hat?

Ian I think there is but I . . . I'm not sure, I never wear . . . not sure . . .

Bernard How do people travel about in the town below?

Ian   Coach.

Bernard Apart from walking.

Ian   Coach.

Bernard Coach. How does the coach move?

Ian   Wheels, it's drawn along.

Bernard Drawn along? By what?

Ian   Horse.

B   Do you know what date it is?

Ian   Date . . . it's in April.

Bernard What year?

Ian   April . . . April the fourth.

Bernard What year is it?

Ian   1835.

Bernard Say that aloud.

Ian   1835.

Bernard 1835. So, do you work?

Ian   Yeah.

Bernard What is your profession, your job?

Ian   I just work in an office.

Bernard What type of office? What is their business?

Ian   Provide books for shops, schools . . . mainly shops.

Bernard Do you like reading?

Ian   Yeah . . . yeah. I don't like the job.

Bernard Why don't you like the job?

Ian   It doesn't seem to be get . . . getting . . . it's a very small
         business . . . just a whole family.

Bernard What's the name of the firm?

Ian   Heyman.

Bernard Heyman? What city are they based in?

Ian   London.

Bernard Is that the city where you are now?

Ian	No.
Bernard	Is that the city where you work?
Ian	Yeah.
Bernard	You work in London. What street is the . . . is the office where you work?
Ian	[whispers] Street . . .
Bernard	What's it called, the street?
Ian	It's no main street, it's . . . it's hard . . . it's behind . . . a set of buildings. An open . . . like an open yard.
Bernard	Is it near any major street?
Ian	[murmurs]
Bernard	What area of London is it in?
Ian	Just outside the city.
Bernard	Just outside the city.
Ian	Westminster.
Bernard	Have you always lived in London?
Ian	No.
Bernard	Where did you used to live?
Ian	My parents lived . . . for a while . . . in Southampton.
Bernard	Southampton. Did you like it there?
Ian	No . . . ships . . . quayside . . .
Bernard	What made you go to London?
Ian	Decent work.
Bernard	How old were you when you went to London?
Ian	Nineteen.
Bernard	How old were you when you got married?
Ian	Twenty . . . twenty-two.
Bernard	Right, I want you to go back in time. Further back into your memory. Further and further back. But relax, it's all very easy. Plenty of time. Further back into your memory to a time before that. Relax and allow it to come to you. Further back into your memory. Further back through

	time, until you rest upon something. Now go deeper into a sleep. Go deeper into a sleep. Hear only my voice. Only my voice. And where are you?
Ian	I'm in a room.
Bernard	What's the room like?
Ian	Completely empty . . . door's locked . . . the window's high.
Bernard	What is your name?
Ian	Just . . .
Bernard	What's the name?
Ian	Justin.
Bernard	Say it louder.
Ian	Justin.
Bernard	Justin. What nationality are you?
Ian	I was born . . . in England. But . . . when I was very small . . . my parents moved to the Netherlands.
Bernard	How old are you?
Ian	Forty—
Bernard	[interrupts] Forty . . .
Ian	. . . nine . . . or maybe forty-eight. Not too sure . . . forget . . .
Bernard	Do you know what year it is?
Ian	It's . . . sixteen . . . forty . . . three . . . or two, the year before.
Bernard	Say that louder.
Ian	Sixteen forty thr— . . . two . . . maybe lost count.
Bernard	So what are you doing in the room, why are you there?
Ian	Waiting.
Bernard	Who for?
Ian	No one. Here for good . . . no way out.
Bernard	Why have you been put there?
Ian	I don't . . . believe . . . I should. Crimes . . . wrongfully . . . done in the first place. The wars . . .

Bernard You mean . . . you've been wrongfully accused of
         committing a crime?
Ian   [pause] . . . fought . . . for the wrong side.
Bernard You fought for the wrong side.
Ian   Yeah.
Bernard You mean in a war?
Ian   [murmurs — inaudible]
Bernard` A battle?
Ian   [murmurs — inudible]
Bernard What was the fight over?
Ian   . . . all the same . . . fight for whoever . . . that's . . . who . . .
Bernard You mean for money?
Ian   No . . . for . . . whatever values . . . would seem to be right
         at the time.
Bernard Who were you fighting for last? What were the reasons?
Ian   I can't remember any more . . . it's useless anyway.
Bernard Why?
Ian   It won't change . . .
Bernard So how old are you?
Ian   Forty-eight, forty-nine.
Bernard How long have you been locked up for?
Ian   At least four . . . maybe longer.
Bernard Right, we need to go deeper into the sleep. Relax. Just
         relax. We'll go further and further. Ten years on. Ten years
         on in time. Just relax. Totally relax. Same person, ten years
         on in time, tell me what you see.
Ian   Nothing.
Bernard You can't see anything? Nothing at all?
Ian   No.
Bernard Right. Go five years on in time, from when you was in the
         room.
Ian   C — can't see anything.

Bernard	OK, go back to the room. Can you see that? Go on one year in time. What do you see?
Ian	Just the room.
Bernard	What do you feel?
Ian	I'd say . . . ill . . . cold . . .
Bernard	Is it in England, the room?
Ian	It's not.
Bernard	Where is it?
Ian	In France.
Bernard	Is it winter? Or summer?
Ian	It's winter. All . . . cold. Not summer.
Bernard	Do you ever speak to anyone?
Ian	No.
Bernard	What about the people who bring you your meals?
Ian	They just put them through . . . open the door . . . one . . . places it inside of the door . . . [inaudible]
Bernard	What are they dressed in, the people who . . .?
Ian	Don't know, just . . . they wear normal clothes.
Bernard	What do you mean, normal clothes?
Ian	Trousers, boots . . .
Bernard	What have you got on?
Ian	Like . . . a jacket . . . it's wearing very thin.
Bernard	Are you a tall man, or a short man?
Ian	I'd say tall.
Bernard	What colour's your hair?
Ian	Dark, almost black . . . raven, very, very dark.
Bernard	Go on a year in time. Year in time. Tell me what you see . . . Just relax and allow it to come to you.
Ian	[faintly] Walls.
Bernard	What do you see?
Ian	Walls.
Bernard	You're still in the same place? Where are you now?

Ian	I'm in a room . . . looks the same . . . there's a different smell, it's different.
Bernard	How does it smell?
Ian	I . . . I don't know.
Bernard	Are there other people there?
Ian	Yeah.
Bernard	Do you know why you've been moved?
Ian	I think . . . I have a fever.
Bernard	Is it a hospital, where you are? For the sick?
Ian	There are other people here . . . fever.
Bernard	What language are they speaking?
Ian	In French.
Bernard	Can you speak French?
Ian	No. I . . . can hear it . . . and can understand almost . . .
Bernard	What languages do you speak?
Ian	English is the language I . . . I use.
Bernard	How old are you now?
Ian	Um . . . fifty . . . I dunno . . . fifty-one? Don't . . . know any more.
Bernard	So you've been kept prisoner in France. Do you know where in France? The district?
Ian	I . . . Lyon.
Bernard	Lyon?
Ian	Mmm.
Bernard	Is it for fighting against the French?
Ian	[faintly] Yeah.
Bernard	When you fought, what weapons did you use?
Ian	We use . . . [faintly] swords . . .
Bernard	What?
Ian	Sword . . . blade . . . pistols.
Bernard	Were you ever injured in a fight?
Ian	Yeah.

Bernard   Where were you hit?

Ian   In the leg.

Bernard   Which leg?

Ian   Twice in the right, once in the left . . . and . . . cuts on both
          arms . . . sides . . . all healed.

Bernard   What battle was that in?

Ian   It was in . . . France . . . and in . . . in Spain . . . and . . . they
          weren't battles . . . fights.

Bernard   Fights? So was it an army you'd been fighting for?

Ian   Sometimes. Spain . . . where our army brought together
          . . . to fight . . . internally.

Bernard   The family you come from, is it a noble family?

Ian   No . . . not . . .

Bernard   What is the family name?

Ian   . . . not, not poor, though.

Bernard   What is the family name?

Ian   Father's . . . English . . . it's Cheacott.

Bernard   It's what?

Ian   Cheacott.

Bernard   Tea cup?

Ian   Mother . . . was . . . Flemish.

Bernard   Flemish?

Ian   Mm. I forget the maiden name. Seems . . . a long time since
          . . .

Bernard   Relax. Just listen only to my voice, no other noises, my
          voice.

[Tape pauses]

Bernard   What is your name?

Ian   Justin.

Bernard   Justin. Is there any memory in your life which particularly
          stands out, that you think about?

Ian   Just friends, people, good friends . . .

Bernard	Have you ever had any profession?
Ian	Not since I was very, very young.
Bernard	Where do you get your income from? Where do you get your money from?
Ian	Seem to save . . . require . . . a high salary. Whatever, lodgings, food, always provided.
Bernard	Why do they provide it?
Ian	Hired services.
Bernard	You hire your services. What as? What services?
Ian	Trained . . . soldier.
Bernard	How do you feel?
Ian	Very weak?
Bernard	Why do you feel weak?
Ian	Feverish, very very hot. Very . . . resigned to it.
Bernard	You're resigned to it? What?
Ian	The end of it. It's easy . . . I suppose.
Bernard	The end of your life? Would you say you've had a good life?
Ian	That's not for me to, to judge.
Bernard	Who's it for, to judge?
Ian	God.
Bernard	All right, I want you to go to the day, forward, to the day you die. Relax, because no harm can come to you. Don't worry. Describe how you feel.
Ian	Hot.
Bernard	What?
Ian	Hot. Burning . . .
Bernard	What's going through your mind?
Ian	Back . . . and forward.
Bernard	What do you mean?
Ian	I'm . . . gonna meet God . . . I won't return to the . . . to the room. To die here . . . [inaudible] seems very final.

Bernard   Are you afraid?

Ian   No.

Bernard   I want you to go to the moment right after you died and tell me what you see . . . Or tell me what you feel.

Ian   [faintly] Just . . . emptiness . . . nothing . . .

Bernard   You don't see anything?

Ian   [faintly] No.

Bernard   Do you feel anything?

Ian   [murmur]

Bernard   Yet you still exist . . .? Do you exist . . .?

Ian   [murmur]

Bernard   Never mind, just relax . . . Relax. And go further back in time. Further back through time. To another set of memories. Further back. Don't worry, no harm can come to you. Further back through time to another set of memories. Tell me what you see.

Ian   A church.

Bernard   A church? What year is it?

Ian   Nine hundred . . . and four years after the death of Christ.

Bernard   What are you doing at the church?

Ian   Erm . . . priest . . . of . . . some kind.

Bernard   What is your name?

Ian   C—can't see that. Seems very . . . can't explain . . . er . . .

Bernard   Just relax and wait for things to clear . . . Just wait to get a vision. Just tell me what you can see.

Ian   Er, can just see a church.

Bernard   Nothing else?

Ian   Surrounded by countryside, grass, stands on its own, quite large . . . golden . . . stained windows, walls around, very large building.

Bernard   What are you wearing?

Ian   I c—can't, can just the outside . . . of the church.

Bernard Do you know who you are?

Ian No . . . just a building, abbey.

Bernard You're a priest there?

Ian I'm not sure. I know I, I live there.

Bernard Never mind. Go deeper, right? Deeper into a sleep. Relax your mind. Relax your body. Don't worry about anything. Relax your mind, relax your body, don't worry about anything. Now going back further in time, further back in time, to another set of memories. Tell me what you see. Concentrate. Concentrate.

Ian Erm . . . erm . . . can just see . . . unrelated . . .

Bernard Unrelated what?

Ian Just . . . images, pictures, I can't . . .

Bernard It doesn't matter, don't worry. Just try to explain how you feel in the images.

Ian There's a man walking over a hill. And there's a field with lots of people dead.

Bernard Dead?

Ian But they're not . . . doesn't seem to be the same part of the country, countryside.

Bernard What do you mean?

Ian [faintly] Can't . . .

Bernard How you feel? . . . Is it any time?

Ian I don't know?

Bernard You don't know what this memory, memory relates to?

Ian No.

Bernard Or why it's there. No?

Ian No.

Bernard So there's just the fields . . . describe them again, just once more.

Ian Someone walking over a hill, sunshine, and there's a field with lots of people dead.

Bernard And they're covered in blood?

Ian Flows red . . . flowed . . .

Bernard Has the man done . . . done it?

Ian No.

Bernard Do you know who the man is?

Ian No.

Bernard Can you see yourself?

Ian No.

Bernard Can't you even see your feet if you look down?

Ian No.

Bernard Can you touch yourself?

Ian No.

Bernard Does the field look real?

Ian Yeah.

Bernard Can you feel the grass? [pause] You can just see. OK then, just relax and listen to my voice, right? You understand? Can you hear my voice?

Ian [murmur]

Bernard I want you to come back forward, through time, to 1980, here in this room. Yeah? Do you know who you are now?

Ian Yeah.

Bernard What's your name?

Ian Ian.

Bernard Now can you remember all I've been saying to you? All we've just talked about?

Ian Erm . . . bits.

Bernard About the different people? Memories that you had? The visions?

Ian Can remember . . .

Bernard What can you remember?

Ian We talked about when I was little.

Bernard But not before that?

Ian   Can remember seeing some pictures.

Bernard   What of?

Ian   Of a man on a hill . . . and . . . some kind of massacre . . .
           fight or something.

Bernard   Just recognize my voice. Now, I want you to consciously
           remember that when I wake you up, right?

Ian   Yeah.

Bernard   Well, I want you to remember that, right, always
           remember that.

Ian   Yeah.

Bernard   Remember all the memories you've had as you open your
           eyes and sit up.

Ian   Yeah.

Bernard   Right? So, now I want you to open your eyes and sit up.
           And . . . just remember everything. Right? But you're
           perfectly OK. Perfectly relaxed. You're going to wake up,
           totally wake up, right? You're going to be totally awake.
           You're not going to be in this sleep any more, you're going
           to come out of this sleep. Can you hear me?

Ian   [faintly] Yeah.

Bernard   Sit up. How you feeling?

Ian   F— fine. [exhales]

Bernard   Can you remember anything?

Ian   I feel . . . I feel as if I've been dreaming . . . [inaudible] . . .
           you know like you remember a nightmare in the
           morning, when you've been dreaming . . . I remember
           being in a room . . . Can't remember why I was there.

Bernard   Do you remember any feeling from being in that room?

Ian   Yeah . . . not a very nice smell . . . I shouldn't have been there.

Bernard   You feel totally awake now?

Ian   Yeah . . . erm . . . I can remember this figure walking over
           a hill.

Bernard What else about the hill?

Ian Dunno, he was . . . just walking down.

Bernard See a massacre? Bodies? [pause] You just feel like you've been dreaming?

Ian Yeah, I feel like, you know when you wake up in the morning, and . . . there's just bits, and the feeling of . . . bits . . . [inaudible]

Bernard How long do you reckon you've been out for?

Ian Ten minutes? [Bernard snorts] Twenty minutes? . . . Half an hour?

Bernard You've been out for about . . . about an hour.

Ian *An hour?*

Bernard Perhaps an hour and a quarter.

Ian [inaudible]

Bernard It got really interesting. It's all down on there.

Ian Well, let's have a listen to it then.

Bernard Eh?

[End of recording]

Appendix Two:
A Conversation with Alan Wise

If you've been to our gigs in the UK or seen us at a festival, you may well have seen Alan Wise introducing us on stage. Alan is a promoter and impresario and has in the past managed acts like The Fall and Nico. People like Tony and Rob have always received most of the credit for their work on the Manchester scene — and rightly so — but Alan deserves to be spoken of in the same breath, as he's also been hugely influential.

I've known Alan for many years now and he's a good friend of mine. He's a delightfully eccentric, larger-than-life figure who has been a fixture on the Manchester scene since the earliest days of Joy Division.

When I wanted to confirm a few things about the very early days of the Factory Club I went to Alan and soon realized that the best thing to do would be to let him tell his version of the story in his own words. So, one night towards the end of May 2014, he came to my house and we had a chat, which is reproduced here.

Having characteristically nearly taken out my front wall while driving in, Alan lowered himself into a chair, sat almost supine with his trilby hat resting on his stomach like a bluebottle on a beach ball, and this conversation transpired.

Bernard Alan, because you're a special person, we're going to let you have your voice in the book too.

Alan Oh, lovely.

Bernard I was finding it difficult to find the words to sum you up, so how would you sum yourself up in the context of the Manchester story?

Alan Well. I wandered along, a lonely character who'd been ditched by a girlfriend, and I had a van which I used to do deliveries with. For the sake of finding some company I wandered down to Rafters, which was putting on punk groups, and allowed you to be a little bit eccentric. The owner of the place and still my flatmate and friend, Douglas Thomas James, said, 'That's a nice van, I could do with a van like that for my band.' So he turned me into his roadie, though I was still a theology student at university. He had this club and we would go down to the club and get in for free, as we were with him. We could meet girls there and other boys. I did meet down there all the friends who are still my friends in later years. A lot of the people who were musicians were more sensitive and intelligent kinds of people.

Bernard Mark E. Smith, for example?

Alan Well, I didn't know Mark at that time, but I met a lot of people there who were interesting, even though I may not have been a lover of that kind of music. I preferred blues, jazz and r 'n' b and our DJ, Rob Gretton, was also a soul DJ, but we liked the movement of the crowd. There was a certain anarchy and freedom there that record companies and promoters didn't control.

Bernard   What years would this be?

Alan   Seventy-six. I quickly fell in with a group called Slaughter and the Dogs and did their first tour, Slaughter Bite Back. Then, after that, I made friends with the Buzzcocks and then with yourselves.

Bernard   Was that a two-way friendship?

Alan   Yeah, I was very close to Shelley [Pete Shelley; lead singer], and all that. They were very nice people. Working with and going out on the road with groups, getting out, cured my depression, because I was very depressed about this girl leaving me. She was a lovely German girl, a dentist from the university. We got engaged and her parents came over to meet me. Her dad was an old SS officer – he'd still click his boots like Prussian nobility when he stood – who joked about how the Russians had had him against the wall ready for shooting but were so incompetent he had waltzed off and escaped. While he was laughing about this, my dad was searching the basement for his old army revolver to finish the job. Her father's advice to his daughter on meeting me, was 'Flee! Flee! He is a bohemian!' Which I am, and I took it as a compliment. He thought it meant the lowest dog on earth. He took her back to Germany with him. Anyway, I wandered down into this world and, while at Manchester University, I went for something to eat each day at a café run by a South American bloke. I'd seen people there slightly older than us called Music Force. Music Force had a young girl working the phone each day, doing nothing very much, and I had a crush on her. I used to go and see her and while there, I thought, I can do this, I can do this job as well, and then the two things tied up: what Music Force were doing and then . . .

Bernard   Wasn't Music Force something to do with Martin Hannett?

Alan   Yes. There were three people: Martin Hannett, Tosh Ryan and Bruce Mitchell. I became friends with Martin, and later Bruce Mitchell, and later Tosh Ryan.

Bernard   The bit we're interested in is not prehistory, so to speak, we're interested in starting at the Russell Club, say . . .

Alan   OK, well, it pre-dated the Russell Club because my first memories of you are at Rafters. You were an amusing chap, far from the dour image of the band. Songwriters normally have some creativity and sensitivity; you were as rude as me and for those reasons we bonded. You had a good sense of humour but always seemed to be broke, even when your band could sell twenty thousand tickets. I could never figure it out. When they all went bust you did get a sum, with which you bought a little refuge for the sick and needy, and I used to go round there every week with this week's girlfriend. Anyway, back then you used to come and play as Warsaw, and . . .

Bernard   I don't think we played many gigs as Warsaw.

Alan   Well, you did a couple and maybe did a couple as Joy Division — whatever it was, I've forgotten. But we all thought it was very good, and Rob Gretton in particular thought it was very good. Joy Division did it differently for a bit: you had a style and a philosophy, you weren't boring businessmen. You were for a time the real thing and that's why a critical young audience liked you. The groups were all known by Rob Gretton and Nigel Bagley; they knew the scene more than we did. Although we knew about

other kinds of music, we were not really *au fait* at that
time with the up-and-coming punk and new-wave groups.
My favourite thing we put on was Elvis Costello, but we
didn't really know the others, and Rob knew the scene,
Bagley knew the scene and there was …

Bernard   What would you describe yourself as in those days?

Alan   I was the beginnings of an impresario, but really I was
running the Factory Club. My actual position was roadie
for Dougie James.

Bernard   So, you were a roadie but you saw yourself as an
impresario.

Alan   Well, I was more than his roadie; I was the manager,
effectively. Then I started putting on the other groups we
saw when we were running the club. I didn't take a wage
for two years, but we started to get to know the groups.
Dougie was hopeless, because he used to go down to the
casino and gamble away all the money. Our office was …

Bernard   That's what you do now, isn't it?

Alan   Er, yeah. But we had nice offices, you'll remember them,
above Rafters and the club upstairs, Fagan's. Often Mr
Hook and yourselves used to turn up. Peter was actually
very active in pushing for gigs and he wanted to play there
as often as possible. We kept the club going for a couple of
years, and then Tony …

Bernard   This was Rafters?

Alan   Yeah. Tony came down to Rafters. He didn't have much
idea about music, he liked 10CC and that other
Manchester group, Sad Café, all long hair and saddlebags,
but he noticed there was a new type of group playing.

Bernard   That's not true, because Tony had a programme where he
wasn't putting on bands like 10CC …

Alan   Yeah, but he came to the indie pop thing afterwards,
          when he saw it was coming into fashion. He had a good
          sense of what would become fashionable, but he didn't
          start the fashion. The fashion was started by earlier people
          like yourselves and Shelley, and the other people who
          started it, who copied it from whoever you copied it from.

Bernard   Jumping forward to the Factory Club in Hulme, Don
          Tonay was a shadowy figure.

Alan   Don was actually quite an erudite gangster who'd been
          involved in political activities all over Africa. He went off
          to be a paratrooper and had been involved with certain
          members of the African National Congress. He'd gone to
          Africa and dealt in iron pyrites, fool's gold. Don was a
          fascinating character, and I really took to him. My uncle was
          the Attorney General, so Don thought it was very funny
          to have someone whose uncle was the Attorney General
          working for him. He got me to be the licensee of the club
          because he needed a licensee, that's the first time . . .

Bernard   So Don Tonay was involved in this political intrigue
          and . . .

Alan   He was a pirate.

Bernard   Didn't he have something to do with a shebeen in Moss
          Side?

Alan   Yeah, he ran two shebeens, the Nile and the Reno.

Bernard   So Don Tonay . . .

Alan   'Shebeen' is the Irish word for an illegal drinking club.

Bernard   A blues.

Alan   A blues.

Bernard   So Don Tonay had retired from all these piratical activities
          by this time.

Alan   No, he hadn't retired, he was still up to his old ways. He was a fence. The police used to come round to his house and he'd say, 'How's things, guys?' and they'd say, 'We're broke, Don': they used to openly come round to take money, so he was still involved. But the club was making no money at all. He had two clubs: the Russell Club, which was built by the council, and the Mayflower. He had a partner called Rudi, a Jamaican guy, and Rudi and Don had these two clubs, the Mayflower and the Russell, and decided they could put music on, people like Dillinger, reggae . . .

Bernard So was Don a licensee of the club or the owner?

Alan He was the owner.

Bernard He was the owner of the Russell Club.

Alan Yes.

Bernard So Tony and Alan Erasmus used to put Friday night . . .

Alan Tony and Alan hired the club one night a week.

Bernard I remember going there, yeah. It started off one night a week, didn't it, and then went on all through the week.

Alan I came in and started doing Thursdays, and then we'd do a Wednesday, and then we got together. Tony came down, and Don said, 'Look, I don't really want to run this club any more, you're doing better with your new wave groups than I'm doing with the Jamaican groups. I'll give you the keys to the safe'—

Bernard He gave *you* the keys to the safe!

Alan He gave me the keys to the club and said, 'You know, you run the beer, the club, run everything, just pay me so much a week.'

Bernard How did that go?

Alan To start with, we were very successful, we got a lot of people through the door.

Bernard   Why did it close in the end? I remember going in . . .

Alan   It closed in the end because there was a lot of sound leaking through its roof and there were objections from people living nearby. It was also losing on the bar. Although it was incredibly busy, the bars were run by amateurs — ourselves. A lot of the drinks were being stolen and taken out to the Nile and the Reno during the day, the booze was being ferreted away to the shebeens, which *were* making money.

Bernard   But what was your connection with Tony? You said you had—

Alan   'Well,' Don said, 'you'd better get together and run it, because he's a bloody idiot' — pointing at me — 'but I like him the most, so he's in charge.' I got together with Tony and Tony was very keen on the club and wanted to run more than one night a week. I already knew Tony from when I was running Rafters, and his wife was my friend. Because of that he suggested we become partners. Me, him, Alan Erasmus. Tony and I started a company, which was the original company running the Factory Club, Shop Floor Entertainments Ltd, trading as The Factory — not Factory Records, The Factory — pre-dating the record company. The club ran seven days a week, although Tony would only come on a Friday because, to be fair, he had a full-time job at Granada. We all liked him, because he had a lot of charisma and charm, but it was Alan Erasmus and me running the club and drawing a wage, a small wage, each.

Bernard   What was Alan Erasmus's background? He was always this quiet man of Factory.

Alan   I wouldn't say quiet man. Alan and Tony had a very close friendship.

Bernard He was an actor, wasn't he?

Alan An actor, yes. He was quite a nice guy, I liked him, and I liked Tony very much as well. The thing is, Tony was surrounded by people who weren't very erudite or knowledgeable and used to worship him — sycophants, 'yes' people. He wasn't sure whether they liked him or not. I had a similar education to Tony, but I got on with the groups better because I had the common touch. I quite admired the fact that they could play, and make instruments and stuff. I'd be very poor at — where's my glass of wine?

Bernard Oh, here, sorry. But, Alan, if we were summing you up in a couple of paragraphs . . .

Alan I was a scholarly bloke who drifted due to ill health into entirely the wrong occupation. I think I was built for the film industry. Because I had a neurotic illness I drifted into a place I was allowed to be . . .

Bernard Your neurotic illness, I remember you telling me, was caused by being struck by lightning.

Alan Perhaps it was because I was struck by lightning, it struck very close to me and seemed to fuck up my nerves forever afterwards.

Bernard You were at university . . .

Alan Yeah.

Bernard . . . which university did you go to?

Alan I went to Oxford and Manchester.

Bernard And you were studying . . .

Alan Theology. I was planning to become a priest.

Bernard Er, right!

Alan But I dropped out.

Bernard And you moved back to Manchester and moved into the music industry.

Alan	Well, it wasn't an industry, I didn't think of it as a job. There was a scene, there was a scene happening.
Bernard	And you were a kind of mover and a shaker.
Alan	I became a central figure who knew lots of people and they could come to me and talk to me.
Bernard	I think we were all movers and shakers, but we didn't realize it at the time.
Alan	Because I could communicate with people, I could put on shows. We weren't just putting on shows in our clubs; we were doing it at the university as well.
Bernard	You eventually became a promoter and, to me, you were one of the kind of unseen people everyone on the music scene in Manchester would know . . .
Alan	People would know me.
Bernard	So you'd describe yourself as an impresario of . . .
Alan	Well, I'm an impresario of Manchester people, but that came later. At this stage, I was a local promoter and eventually became a tour promoter and became involved with managing various groups.
Bernard	So you managed The Fall . . .
Alan	I wasn't the manager of The Fall, because Mark manages himself, but I've managed several people. But, at that stage, the early days, '76 to '80, we were putting on concerts and then after that I was a club runner. I ran clubs. You know me from that. I've known you . . .
Bernard	But, as a promoter, you promoted lots of concerts.
Alan	A lot of your concerts, a lot of concerts in general, in and out of the club.
Bernard	And compered a lot of concerts as well — you're quite famous for getting up and saying a few words before we've stepped on stage.

Alan	Well, the Factory Club meant I could perform myself, and I often used to get up and sing along . . .
Bernard	Do you think you might be a frustrated performer?
Alan	Definitely.
Bernard	You told me once that you'd love to run away to the circus.
Alan	Oh, I'd love to, I love the circus.
Bernard	I can see you as a ringmaster.
Alan	Well, I went for the job.
Bernard	You went for the job?
Alan	Hoffman's Circus — they offered it me.
Bernard	You'd be really good at that.
Alan	Here's something really sad: I went to Hoffman's Circus and a guy had just joined them to play the organ. I didn't take the job because the elephant stank. Thirty years later, Hoffman's Circus came back. I went to see them to see if anyone would remember me, and the guy on the organ was still there and he remembered me. He said, 'What's your life been like?' I said, 'What's yours been like?' He said, 'I married the girl on the high wire.'
Bernard	Why didn't you take the job?
Alan	It would have been lonely, and the elephant really stank. The circus life would have been the truer one. It was also more ambitious, because you had to leave home and everything, whereas the club was cosy and nestling, and I had an office. I liked having a club.
Bernard	You managed Nico, didn't you?
Alan	She was the most famous one. I loved Nico.
Bernard	What was it about Nico that you liked?
Alan	She was a genuine bohemian. She didn't give a damn about making money, or distinguish between people as to

whether they were famous or whether they were not. All she cared about was whether they were interesting or not. Nico was the real McCoy, so that's why I liked her. And then, later, I loved her.

Bernard   And John Cale, did you . . .

Alan   He was very nice; I thought he was very friendly. But when he sobered up and became proper, I think he thought we were like Hal in Shakespeare; he thought we were foolish, Falstaffian figures. We had to be dispensed with because we didn't take things seriously.

Bernard   Perhaps he wasn't a bohemian any more.

Alan   He wanted to make money, and when people want to make money and do it properly, they have to do it a different way.

Bernard   But you need money to live, don't you? We have to conform to a role where you have to earn money to live.

Alan   I wish I was like that, it's true. But as a gentleman . . .

Bernard   I wish you were like that too, because maybe then you wouldn't owe me six hundred quid.

Alan   [coughing fit]

Picture Acknowledgements

Section 1
Pages 1–3: author's own
Page 4: *top* Herman Vaske, *bottom* Kevin Cummins
Page 5: Mark Reeder
Page 6: *top left* Kevin Cummins, *top right* Andrew Catlin, *bottom* Anton Corbijn
Page 7: *top left and bottom right* Kevin Cummins, *top right* Andrew Catlin, *bottom left* author's own
Page 8: *all* Kevin Cummins

Section 2
Page 1: *both* Kevin Cummins
Page 2: *top* Kevin Cummins, *bottom left* Eileen Feighny, *bottom right* Andrew Catlin
Page 3: *top left and bottom left* Kevin Cummins, *others* author's own
Page 4: *right centre* Donald Christie, *others* author's own
Page 5: *top* author's own, *bottom* Mark Reeder

Page 6: *top left* Kevin Cummins, *top right and centre* Anton Corbijn, *bottom left* author's own

Page 7: *top left* Sue Dean, *bottom* Joel c. Fildes, *others* author's own

Page 8: *top and centre* Kevin Cummins, *bottom* Neilson Barnard

Index